marxism
in our time

marxism
in our time

Isaac Deutscher
edited by Tamara Deutscher

The *Ramparts* Press
Berkeley, California

contents

Introduction	7
Marxism in Our Time	15
Trotsky in Our Time	31
Marxism and the New Left	63
Marxism and Nonviolence	79
On Internationals and Internationalism	93
The Tragedy of the Polish Communist Party	113
An Open Letter to Wladyslaw Gomulka and the Central Committee of the Polish Workers Party	161
Germany and Marxism	167
The Roots of Bureaucracy	181
Ideological Trends in the USSR	209
On Socialist Man	227
Discovering *Das Kapital*	255
Was the Revolution Betrayed?	265
The February Regime	273
Georg Lukács and "Critical Realism"	283
The Poet and the Revolution	295

introduction

The essays collected and published posthumously in this volume have various origins. Some—"Marxism in Our Time," "Roots of Bureaucracy" and "On Internationals and Internationalism"—were lectures, or rather talks, given to young student audiences engaged in an eager search for theoretical and historical argumentation which would lend support to their socialist yearnings. These were informal talks insofar as Isaac Deutscher avoided the procedure of reading a "prepared paper": although subject and framework were clearly defined in his own mind, he modulated the approach and manner of presentation according to the public he faced—and while he faced it. He liked to "feel his audience" and to carry it with him; he was anxious not to sound condescending when his listeners disappointed him by a level of knowledge that was perhaps lower than he expected, nor did he want to sound didactic. But he was just as anxious not to overwhelm by the display of his erudition; when he resorted to a metaphor or a historical parallel, it was not in order to impress or dazzle, but to clarify the issue and explain it in terms which he thought might be more familiar to his listeners. He wished, above all, that his arguments should be understood, not that he should be admired. Whenever he felt that the link of understanding between him and his audience had snapped, he returned—from a different angle—to the same problem until he sensed that the cooperation between the speaker and the listener had again been established.

The three lectures referred to above were left among Isaac's papers in very rough and incomplete transcripts put together from poor quality recordings. Some gaps had to be filled, some stylistically sharp edges rounded off; but everywhere I have tried as far as possible to preserve the "spoken" tone and the spontaneity of the delivery that was so characteristic of Isaac as a speaker. The lecture "Marxism in Our Time," given at the London School of Economics, was recorded without Isaac's knowledge by an anonymous American student. I am grateful to him for letting me have the tape, which reached me only at the end of 1968. This recording, made at the back of the hall, is all the more valuable because it conveys the general atmosphere of the meeting and the lively reaction of the public.*

The essay on bureaucracy (which appears here in a condensed form and which Isaac had planned to expand and elaborate further) consisted originally of a series of lectures. It was an attempt to lay bare the initial causes of this "evil of human civilization" which grew to such terrifying proportions and which no revolution—no matter what the character of the *ancien régime*—has so far been able to eradicate. Current clichés about the "managerial society" and semantic exercises in defining bureaucracy, a phenomenon as old as civilization, as a new class were explaining nothing. The lecturer, steeped in the tradition of classical Marxism, saw the "withering away of the State" as the only guarantee of the

---

* The British Broadcasting Corporation, having improved considerably on the level of voice and the quality of the recording, transmitted the lecture in its Third Programme on 29 July 1969 and 16 May 1970.

"withering away of bureaucracy." To this theme Isaac returned in his *Unfinished Revolution*,* where he analyzed the social structure of Russia half a century after the revolution.

To the more controversial pieces in this volume belongs without doubt the essay dealing with the irrelevance of the Internationals and the relevance of internationalism. Although no Marxist (indeed no socialist) will quarrel with the historical survey of the role, the achievements, and the fortunes (or the misfortunes) of the first three Internationals, voices of protest are likely to be raised against the summary treatment of the Fourth International. The author's critical views will not, however, come as a surprise, because right from the beginning he was opposed to the whole venture, considering it untimely and futile. At the founding conference of the organization, in 1938, the two delegates representing the Polish section of the Trotskyist movement expressed their *votum separatum* and advanced arguments formulated by Isaac against the proclamation of the International.† An internationalist by instinct and temperament as well as by deep conviction, Isaac attached far greater importance to the spirit animating the workers' movement than to the organizational forms which the movement was to adopt. To him the very hallmark of socialism and one of its most vital elements was internationalism; and he saw that a new International, conceived among the rising waves of nationalism, would remain stillborn, largely, as he said, "because no international revolutionary movement was there to breathe life into it."

---

* *The Unfinished Revolution—Russia 1917–1967*, G. M. Trevelyan Lectures delivered in the University of Cambridge (Oxford University Press, London, 1967).

† The older of the two delegates was "Karl" (Hersch Mendel), a heroic fighter of boundless courage who knew tsarist prisons as well as Pilsudskist jails. He was sentenced to death but escaped the guards leading him to the place of execution and died in 1968 in Israel, an embittered and tired man, half-reconciled to Zionism. See *The Prophet Outcast* (Oxford University Press, London, 1963).

The hostility of some (but by no means all) adherents of the Fourth International toward Isaac had its source not only in this initial divergence of views. Over the years there have been added differences in the assessment of most major contemporary events, from the appearance of "Titoism" to the Chinese Revolution and down to the evaluation of the role of Malcolm X.* There might have been other reasons for the coolness of many of Trotsky's former collaborators towards a critical outsider who, single-handedly and without the support or blessing of the organization, produced in his outstanding biography a worthy *monumentum aere perennius* to the memory of their great teacher, leader, and idol.

Polemics of quite a different kind followed the speech "On Socialist Man." This was the address given by Isaac to the second annual Socialist Scholars Conference held in New York in 1966. To quote George Novack: "Deutscher had come from London as the principal invited guest.... His speech, which opened the proceedings ... elicited a thunderous ovation from the overflow audience. It likewise provoked lively controversy during the meeting and since." Isaac's main antagonist was Professor Herbert Marcuse, who was unable to attend in person but submitted some theses relevant to the theme of the conference. Unfortunately, he did not allow his theses to be published and so we have on record only Isaac's rather vehement reaction to them.†

"The Tragedy of the Polish Communist Party," reproduced here for the first time in English, dates from 1957, when a young French journalist of Polish origin asked Isaac for a brief outline of the history of communism in Poland. It might be worth recalling that shortly after the dramatic

---

* Isaac was not a little amused at seeing the detailed information which the *Militant*, the organ of the American Socialist Workers Party, provided for the benefit of its readers on the progress of Malcolm X's widow's pilgrimage to Mecca.

† See George Novack's introduction to Isaac Deutscher, *On Socialist Man* (pamphlet; Merit Publishers, New York, 1967).

Twentieth Congress of the Communist Party of the Soviet Union, in February 1956 (at which Khrushchev in his famous "secret speech" revealed for the first time to a Russian audience some of Stalin's crimes and misdeeds), a communiqué from Moscow announced the "rehabilitation of the Polish Party and its leaders," who, it was stated, had fallen victims to "provocations and slanders" during the period of the "cult of personality." This short announcement, hardly noticed in the West, was in fact a strange epilogue to one of the greatest tragedies of communism, in which a whole party had been annihilated. In 1938 the Comintern announced the dissolution of the Polish Party under the pretext that it was corroded by "Trotskyist and Pilsudskist influences" and had become merely an agency of fascism and the Polish political police. Yet all the members of the Central Committee, threatened by the very same police, escaped from Poland to seek refuge in Moscow. On Stalin's orders they were imprisoned and executed as traitors. Among them were Adolf Warski (Warszawski), the founder of the party and friend of Rosa Luxemburg; Lenski (Leszczynski), a veteran of the October Revolution and a former member of the Executive of the Comintern; Wera Kostrzewa (Koszutska), a most militant woman revolutionary. At the time not much was known about the fate of the victims: Stalin did not bother to stage even a mock trial and at the height of the terror his dealings with the "fraternal party" were enveloped in murky silence. In Poland the remnants of the illegal party, persecuted by the police, led a precarious existence.

Isaac, himself a former member of the party—he was expelled in 1932 for "exaggerating the danger of Nazism" and "sowing panic" in Communist ranks—traced the circumstances of its wholesale destruction. He was fully aware that "the views expressed here must . . . provoke opposition." "I do not pretend," he wrote, "that what I have to say is a revelation of infallible truth. I would be quite satisfied if my work were to bring new elements into a discussion about the history of the Polish Party and if it helped to a more thorough understanding of its tragic fate." This wish was fulfilled in a rather unusual manner. The interview, which was recorded, was translated from Polish into French and appeared in *Les Temps Modernes* in March 1958.* Soon afterwards the editors of the Warsaw *Polityka*, the official organ of Gomulka's party, planned to reproduce it, but had to abandon the idea after protracted negotiations with the censors. Then the more esoteric theoretical quarterly *Zeszyty Teoretyczno-polityczne* intended to publish it, but did not succeed either. The problem "to publish or not to publish" came before the Polish Politburo. There was no clear majority either for or against, so a compromise was reached: it was decided not to publish the text, but to duplicate it and distribute it among party cells. Nicknamed "Isaac Deutscher's secret speech," it soon became the subject of passionate debate.

I hesitate to describe the last section of the book as "literary" essays, because intrinsically they are as Marxist and as "literary" as all the other writings. They all express the same philosophical *Weltanschauung*, make consistently the same approach to social, political and aesthetic problems, and show the same concern with language and form—all of which are inseparable from genuine Marxist analysis. In the essay "Georg Lukács and 'Critical Realism' " the author subjects one of the foremost exponents of Marxist aesthetics to realistic criticism and exposes the degree to which the erudite philosopher became dependent ideologically on Stalinism and on the counterfeit Marxism that was holding sway over Russia's cultural life by Zhdanovist decree.

Finally, the last essay—"The Poet and the Revolution"—was one of the first pieces of literary criticism which Isaac wrote in English. He still struggled with the tongue that was foreign to him, but then he always struggled to achieve a lucidity of style to match the lucidity of his thought. Maya-

---

* I have translated the interview into English for this volume, using both the Polish version and the French one, which had been checked by the author himself.

kovsky, *le poète maudit* of the revolution, committed suicide because he could not by reasoning resolve the dilemmas which were to face him at the end of the heroic phase of the revolution; nor could he bear the vision of the new orthodoxy. Not so the historian. The historian took it upon himself to fight that orthodoxy. And indeed right through his life, from early adolescence, Isaac Deutscher remained the most militant of heretics fighting against all canons, old and new; all dogmas; and all orthodoxies.

TAMARA DEUTSCHER

London, August 1970

marxism
in our time

What is our time, for a Marxist and for Marxism? Is it a time of the ascendancy of Marxism? Or is it an epoch of the decline of Marxism? In those countries where Marxism is supposed to be the ruling doctrine, the official answer is, of course, that this is a time of an unseen, unheard of, unprece- dented flourishing of Marxism in theory and practice. Here in the West, especially in our Anglo-Saxon countries, we are told day in and day out, goodness knows from how many academic and other platforms, that Marxism has not only declined, but that it is irrelevant—that it bears no relation to the problems of our epoch. From my native country, Poland, comes the voice of a brilliant young philosopher, but a very poor political analyst, who tells us that it is no use discussing Marxism any longer because Marxism has already gained and won and conquered the human mind to such an extent that it has become an organic part of contemporary thinking, and

---

This is an edited transcript of a lecture given in February 1965 at the London School of Economics.

this marks the end of every great doctrine—when it becomes the organic part of human thought. This young philosopher lived in Warsaw after an epoch of Stalinism during which he and people of his generation identified Stalinism and Marxism. They knew Marxism only in the Stalinist form; they were served, and they accepted, the official Marxism as Stalinism and Stalinism as Marxism. Now they want to get away from Stalinism, and this—as they equated Stalinism and Marxism—means for them getting away from Marxism. It seems to me—such is the bitter dialectic of our epoch—that Marxism is in ascendancy and decline simultaneously.

Since the beginning of my adult life (that is, over forty years ago), I have been a Marxist, and I have never for a moment hesitated in my—I wouldn't say allegiance because it is not a matter of "allegiance"—I have never hesitated in my Marxist *Weltanschauung*. I cannot think otherwise than in Marxist terms. Kill me, I cannot do it. I may try; I just cannot. Marxism has become part of my existence. As someone who owes this kind of "allegiance" to Marxism, I would not like to give any of you, who perhaps only recently made an acquaintance with Marxism, the idea that this is one of the golden ages of the Marxist doctrine. Far from it. This is a time of triumph for Marxism only insofar as this is an age of revolution which develops an anticapitalist, a postcapitalist kind of society. But it is also an age of degeneration of Marxist thought and of intellectual decline for the labor movement at large. Precisely because the modern labor movement cannot find another creative and fertile doctrine except Marxism, all its intellectual standards decline catastrophically whenever and wherever Marxism becomes ossified. We have an expansion in Marxist practice and a shrinkage and degeneration in Marxist thinking. There is a deep divorce between the practical experience of revolution and the whole Marxist theoretical framework within which that revolution has been anticipated, within which that revolution has been justified on philosophical, historical, economic, political, cultural, and, if you like, even moral grounds.

For a student of philosophical or historical schools of thought and doctrines this is not an extraordinary statement. Almost every really great school of thought that dominated the thinking of generations has known its periods of great expansion, awakening and development, and its periods of decadence and decline. In this respect the only other school of thought that comes to mind is the Aristotelian school, which dominated human intellect for nearly two thousand years. In the course of this series of epochs it went through various phases of great creative interpretation and creative influence, and also epochs in which it found its triumph in a parody of itself, in the medieval Catholic scholasticism which, although based on Aristotelian philosophy, yet bore to it the same relationship which caricature bears to the real picture of an original object. This did not deprive the Aristotelian philosophy even in the Middle Ages of its *raison d'être*, of its creative phases, of its stimuli which still existed and later helped medieval Europe to overcome the scholastical degeneration. In this respect Marxism stands comparison with the Aristotelian philosophy as a way of thinking that epitomizes and generalizes the entire social, economic, and, to some extent, the political experience of the world under capitalism and exposes the inner dynamism of the historical development which is bound to lead from capitalism to some other postcapitalist order, which we have agreed to describe as a socialist order.

Marxism is not an intellectual, aesthetic, or philosophical fashion, no matter what the fashion-mongers imagine. After having been infatuated with it for a season or two they may come and declare it to be obsolete. Marxism is a way of thinking, a generalization growing out of an immense historical development; and as long as this historic phase in which we live has not been left far behind us, the doctrine may prove to be mistaken on points of detail or secondary points, but in its essence nothing has deprived it, and nothing looks like depriving it, of its relevance, validity, and importance for the future. But at the same time we face the problem of degeneration in Marxist thinking. We have the divorce between theory and practice, and we have a striking, and to a Marxist often humiliating, contrast between what I call classical Marxism—that is, the body of thought developed by Marx, Engels, their contemporaries, and after them by Kautsky, Plekhanov, Lenin, Trotsky, Rosa Luxemburg—and the vulgar Marxism, the pseudo-Marxism of the different varieties of European social-democrats, reformists, Stalinists, Khrushchevites, and their like. I am speaking here of a contrast between classical and vulgar Marxism by analogy with the way in which Marx spoke of classical and vulgar economy. You know that for Marx the term "classical economy" has a different meaning from the one it has in your textbooks at the London School of Economics. According to your textbooks, if I am not mistaken, classical economy lasts till the very end of the nineteenth and even the beginning of the twentieth century, and Marshall still forms part of it. To Karl Marx classical economy ends practically with Ricardo. All that follows is for him the vulgar economy of the bourgeoisie, and for a very good reason. In the classical economy, in Ricardo and Smith, Marx saw the main elements out of which he developed his own theory, especially the labor theory of value—of value based on human labor. This was the revolutionary element in the classical bourgeois political economy. For this revolutionary element the bourgeoisie had no use later on and, moreover, was afraid of it. Post-Ricardian economy wants to deduce value from anything *but* human labor. Later schools of vulgar economy deduce value from circulation; still later they "dismiss" value altogether and build a political economy without it because in this concept of value created by human labor was the seed of revolution. And bourgeois thinking instinctively shied away from it and, frightened, turned in other directions. Classical economy, the economic thinking of Smith and Ricardo, Marx argued, had given an insight into the working of capitalism that far exceeded the practical needs of the bourgeois class.

Ricardo, who understood capitalism so well, knew that the bourgeoisie neither wished nor could afford to understand the workings of its own system, and therefore it had to get away from the labor theory of value in the first instance. This phenomenon of a doctrine and a theory that offers insights into the working of a social system far greater than are the practical requirements of the social class for which it is meant—this phenomenon occurs sometimes in history. And it has occurred with Marxism. The body of classical Marxist thought gave such profound, immense, and till this day unexhausted and unexplored riches of insight that the working class for its practical purposes seemed not to need it. This idea was once expressed by Rosa Luxemburg on the occasion of the publication of the second and third volumes of *Das Kapital.* She said that the social-democratic movement in Europe had conducted its propaganda and agitation in the course of thirty or forty years on the basis of the first volume of *Das Kapital*—that is, on the basis of a fragment of Marx's economic theory; then came the second and the third volume and the huge structure was rising before our eyes—yet the labor movement did not at all feel that it conducted its practical and theoretical activities on an inadequate foundation: the intellectual content even of the fragment of *Das Kapital* was quite sufficient to keep, so to speak, the labor movement intellectually alive for decades.

Marx created a body of thought far in excess of the narrow practical needs of the movement for which he intended his work to serve. Then came the vulgarization, which was in sharp contrast with the original doctrine but which reflected the requirements of the labor movements and of the revolutions that were coming under the banner of Marxism. I hope I have explained in what sense I am using these terms—classical Marxism and vulgar Marxism. I shall perhaps sum up my argument: classical Marxism offers deep historical insight into the working of capitalism, into the prospects of the dissolution of capitalism, and, broader still, into man's relation under this system with other men, with his own class and other classes, his relationship and attitude towards the technology of his age. Vulgar Marxism does not need all that insight; it is fully satisfied with a small fraction of all that understanding, which it places in the severely limited orbit of practical needs, practical strivings, and practical tasks. We have here a historic hypertrophy of practice and an atrophy of thought. Practice is sometimes the enemy of thought; thought sometimes suffers from contact with practice. Here is the dialectic in its crystalline form: basically thought can exist *only* through contact with practice; practice cannot in the long run ignore theory. Nevertheless there are these temporary, transitional periods of unresolved tensions between theory and practice, and it is in such a period that we have been living these last decades. These unresolved tensions affect the whole structure of Marxist thinking.

The intellectual structure of classical Marxism was entirely based on the assumption of a socialist revolution taking place within a mature capitalist bourgeois society. The vulgar Marxism of our decade, by which I mean the Marxism that comes from the postcapitalist third of the world, is all based on the fact of revolutions occurring within underdeveloped societies. Now, how does this affect the structure of Marxist thinking?

If a revolution takes place in a mature bourgeois society, then what you assume, and what would in fact follow, would be first of all a material abundance, an abundance of goods, an abundance of means of production and a relative or even an absolute abundance of means of consumption, an abundance of human skills, of tools, of abilities, of experience, of resources, an abundance of culture. If the revolution takes place in underdeveloped societies, then the basic, decisive, and determining factor with which we have to reckon is the all-round scarcity: scarcity of means of production, of means of consumption, of skills, of abilities, of schools, scarcity of civilization and of culture—scarcity all round—only an abundance or super-abundance of revolutionary elements. If abundance is the basis of the whole structure of the revolution and of Marxist thinking within the revolution, political freedom is the element which you take for granted. Even if a revolution entails civil war and the dictatorship of the proletariat, this is viewed as a transitory phase during which the dictatorship is to serve only one immediate purpose: the breaking down of the armed resistance of the former possessing classes, but not the disciplining or forcing into obedience of the working classes or even the middle classes of one's own society. Marx rarely, if ever, spoke about "political freedom." Precisely because he assumed a revolution amid the abundance of a mature bourgeois society, he took political freedom so much for granted that he discussed only, so to say, the higher mathematics of freedom, those refinements of genuine freedom of which only a socialist society would be capable. On the basis of material scarcity there is no freedom. On the basis of abundance there would be no need for those sharply differentiated wage scales, the Stakhanovism,* and other systems and tricks which result in the re-creation of revolting inequality. This inequality was inevitable in a society like the Russian one where—as I used to argue in the old days—fifty million pairs of shoes were produced for a nation of one hundred and sixty million. This was my old argument and old simile; but it is still valid, in one way or another, if applied to nearly all the underdeveloped countries.

In a revolution which takes its course amid abundance and growing equality, there is no question of constraint in cultural matters. This coercion and constraint is presented to you as proletarian culture, as socialist culture. The constraint in the cultural field comes from nothing else but political fear. Censors confiscate poems because they are afraid that these poems may become political manifestoes. When the censors call for novels of "social realism," they wage a preventive battle against political manifestoes of opposition or revolution that might come not even from the poets, but from very prosaic young men somewhere in factories or

* Soviet worker-incentive system named for the miner Alexei Stakhanov, who devised it in 1935.

universities. Intellectual constraint goes together with political constraint, with scarcity, with inequality.

Classical Marxism never envisaged "socialism in a single country"—in Germany, or in France, or in England. Its ground was always Europe, at the very least Western Europe. It was always international in its outlook; yet in the actual historical development it became national in scale. It became national in the sense in which Stalin viewed socialism within the framework of a single state on the basis of economic and even cultural self-sufficiency. This was a profoundly anti-Marxist view. It was the reflection of the false consciousness of the isolated Russian Revolution. Till this day in the East—in Russia, in China, among the foremost Stalinists in Eastern Europe—the whole way of thinking is still shaped by the tradition, the implications, and the tacit assumptions of "socialism in a single country," that is, of autarkic socialism, closed within itself. And of course, while you have scarcity, lack of freedom, inequality, cultural and intellectual coercion, and socialism on a national scale, and consequently the renewed struggle of nationalisms, you have a new form of what it is now fashionable to call, after the youthful Marx, *alienation.* This is a new form of alienation; man feels estranged from society; he is the plaything of what looks to him like blind social forces. He himself forms part of these forces, which are of his own making, and yet he is their victim. To Marx this estrangement from society was unthinkable in a socialist society, a society which was to grow out of the rich soil of mature capitalist civilization. However, contrary to Marx's expectations the revolution did not develop in Europe, in countries which we like to describe as the cradles of Western civilization, but in the East. And there, in the East, Marx's socialism could not be built. How could it if no material basis for it existed? People there could only engage in the primitive accumulation of the preconditions of socialism; and this they are achieving. Let us not be supercilious, and let us not belittle their immense task and their immense achievement. They are learning with long delays what the Western European nations had learned generations earlier, but they also know what the nations of the West never learned. The development is combined. There is backwardness and there is tremendous progress—it would be unrealistic ever to leave out of sight any one of these contradictory aspects of history.

"Why then did the West not respond to the appeal of Marxism?" I will be asked. The revolution first won in a country which was underdeveloped and backward in 1917; underdeveloped and backward in its whole social structure despite its brilliant and fantastic artistic-literary achievement. The whole edifice was going up on unstable, unhealthy foundations and in the process became as if adjusted to these existing conditions of backwardness. Full of *Galgenhumor*, old communists used to sigh: "Couldn't God help us to start the upheaval in a more suitable country than this Russia of the muzhiks?" No, God did not help. Hence, the incongruity of a modern revolution against the background of murky age-old traditions. This had its negative impact on the possibilities of revolutionary development in the West. The revolution in a precapitalist society, which nevertheless aspired to achieve socialism, produced a hybrid which in many respects looked like a parody of socialism. The western worker, however seemingly non-political, followed events very carefully and was quite aware of the famines, the hunger, and the deprivation that the people of Russia suffered after the revolution; he was aware of the terror and persecution they were subjected to. And, unsophisticated as he was, the British worker, the German worker, and even the French one, often wondered: Is this socialism? Have we perhaps in our century-old allegiance to socialism followed a dangerous will-o'-the-wisp? Workers have been asking themselves these questions. Uncertain, hesitant, the Western European worker has preferred to wait and see. The Russian Revolution has acted as a deterrent to revolution in the West.

By and large we must look at the developments in the West and the relation of Marxism to the course of the class struggle in the West as upon a war which has lasted for generations—for a century and a half. And this class war has had its ups and downs, its intervals, its pitched battles, its long lulls between battles and campaigns. Anyone may say during a lull between two pitched battles: "Ah, your Marx said history is the history of class struggle and there is no class struggle!" Of course, when Marx wrote in the *Communist Manifesto* that the history of mankind is the history of class wars, he knew perfectly well that there were times during which the war of the classes was at a very low ebb, almost stagnant. Churchill once wrote that the history of mankind is the history of wars—perhaps an unconscious plagiarism from Marx? The difference, of course, is that for Marx it is the history of class war, and for Churchill it is the history of war *tout court*. But Churchill also knew that wars are not fought ceaselessly; and Marx also knew that class wars have their time of truce, of open struggle, latent struggle, doldrums and intervals.

We have had a war against capitalism lasting many generations. There was 1848, 1870, 1905, 1917–18, 1945–46: all great battles, concluded partly with a victory of revolution in the East, and with heavy defeats of the revolution in the West. Marx never promised victories for the revolutions at any definite date of the calendar. All that he forecast was that there was going to be a struggle, a heavy, at times a bloody struggle, between classes and peoples, a struggle that would go on for generations and which should—if civilization did not in the meantime collapse into barbarity—lead to the dissolution of capitalism and the emergence of socialism. And, of course, parallel with this there has also been a mobilization of all the forces of the counterrevolution. Those who like to speak now about the unfulfilled prophecies of Marx— do they imagine (how shall I put it?), do they imagine that Marx was as shallow as his critics and saw the road towards socialism without the barricades of counterrevolution? We have had the mobilization of counterrevolution all over the world, in all its various forms, from fascism to the most refined social democratic reformism, all mobilized in the defense of the existing social order. Those forces have benefited from every difficulty, from every wound in the body of socialism. Never yet, except in extraordinary moments like the Commune of Paris, has the working class mobilized itself even to a fraction of that intensity and strength at which the possessing and ruling classes have maintained their mobilization on an almost permanent footing. Even during the Commune the insurgents never really mobilized for a life-and-death struggle—we have all the descriptions showing their light-mindedness, their good-humored and good-tempered optimism.

When I speak of classical Marxism and of its validity, I have in mind what is essential in Marx. Marx was politically active in 1847–48, in 1868, and 1878; he wrote letters to his friends and to Engels in which he expressed his hope that perhaps the labor movement would take a revolutionary impetus in a year's time, in two or three years. And then Engels, after his friend's death, was writing to his disciples—and there were many of them in Western Europe—communicating to them his hope still to live and see the coming together of the workers of Britain and France and Germany. It was only natural that they had all these sanguine expectations but they were also thinkers who could step back from their immediate and tactical involvements and look at the historical perspective. There was Marx who laid the foundations of the First International and hoped that soon, very soon, that International would be able to produce some great upheaval. But there was also Marx who was writing *Das Kapital*, and he did not commit himself in this severely scientific and historical work to any forecast or any prophecy except to a conclusion which followed from his profound, detailed and meticulous analysis of capitalism—the conclusion that this system must collapse because its inner contradictions would not allow it to function in the long run. When it will dissolve and collapse—into this he never entered, not because (as so many of his clever critics suggest) he was so clever, but because he had a sense of responsibility. A politician may have to bank on certain events occurring within a certain time; he can rally for the coming struggle his own strength and that of his friends and followers. The historical thinker cannot do this; nor can he foresee the complications of history or map out its exact route.

I said that I shall concentrate on what is essential in Marx and I have slipped into what is inessential, so allow me just to touch on another problem which is marginal, namely the problem whether the working class under capitalism is condemned to absolute impoverishment. This has long been passionately discussed in the European, and especially in the French, Communist Parties. Well, you can find in Marx some support for such a theory and you can find some refutation of it. Marx's mind was too rich and complex to play with narrow formulae. In Marx's time, in Western Europe, there certainly were empirical facts which pointed to progressive and absolute impoverishment.

But let us return to the very essentials in the Marxist critique of capitalism. When people say that Marxism was a doctrine, highly elaborate and realistic for the nineteenth century but now obsolete, may we ask: obsolete in what? In its essentials? There is one, only one, essential element in the Marxist critique of capitalism. It is very simple and very plain, but in it are focused all the many-faceted analyses of the capitalist order. It is this: there is a striking contradiction between the increasingly social character of the process of production and the antisocial character of capitalist property. Our mode of existence, the whole manner of production, is becoming more and more social in the sense that the old free-lance producers can no longer go on producing in independence from each other, from generation to generation, as they did in the precapitalist system. Every element, every fraction, every little tiny organ of our society is dependent on all the rest. The whole process of production becomes one social process of production—and not only one national process of production but one international process of production. At the same time you have an antisocial kind of property, private property. This contradiction between the antisocial character of property and the social character of our production is the source of all anarchy and irrationality in capitalism.

This contradiction cannot be reconciled *à la longue.* The collision must come. That was all that Marx said. Now, has this essential critique of capitalism become obsolete? We are told that it has, that since Keynes capitalism knows how to plan the economy. For eighty years planning was supposed to be a bee in Marx's bonnet. Now that bee has been elevated almost to a divine insect, and we are told that capitalism can also plan. Has it ever planned except for war purposes? If it has, I have not yet heard of such a case. But suppose that it can. Is planning congenial to capitalism? Some capitalist enterprises were, after all, conducted on a feudal basis; one can also, I suppose, create a simulacrum of socialism on a capitalist basis. But is this congenial to capitalism? And can capitalism, even when it plans, achieve the rate of growth that planning in a really publicly owned economy has achieved? Of course not, because if there is national or international planning, then national or international ownership and organization are the congenial and natural conditions for planning. You can, of course, put planning into capitalism, but it is almost like putting a motor engine into a horse-drawn *drozhka.* And can capitalism create international societies? You will say: What about the Russians and the Chinese? Have they created an international society? Of course not. The way in which the Russians and the Chinese conduct their affairs is still a reflection of a capitalist way of thinking. But there it is a reflection of capitalism, a projection of capitalism into a postcapitalist structure of society, while here it is historically inherent in the whole working of the capitalist order. Wherever capitalism tries to break out of its national crust, it always does so in a catastrophic way, by staging world wars, by swallowing smaller and weaker nations or competitors.

If you look at the nearly two decades of postwar capitalist prosperity, what do you see? A refutation of Marxism? This is not the first time in history that we have seen twenty years running their course without the old-type slump and boom that have been characteristic of capitalism from at least 1825 to the Second World War. After the Franco-Prussian War of 1870–71 there were twenty-five years of Germany's tremendous industrialization, of capitalist development without a real crisis. At the end of these twenty-five years came the revisionists, the friends and disciples of Marx and Engels, who said: "The masters must have been mistaken. They said there would be a collapse, there would be crises, there would be slumps. There are no slumps. From now on capitalism will develop smoothly in an evolutionary manner." And after only a few years, in 1907, came the tremendous collapse. Then the next tremendous slump led into the First World War.

I don't want to be a Cassandra, but I cannot say that I have confidence in the further smooth, evolutionary development of Western capitalism, or in the perpetuation of its so-called prosperity. After these twenty years of prosperity, what do we see in Western society? We see an intensification of all those trends which Karl Marx diagnosed as the trends leading to the further development of capitalism and its doom. We see all over the West the disappearance of those middle classes that were supposed to constitute the conservative foundation of capitalism; of the small-owning, small-holding peasantry. The peasantry that was the mainstay of French conservatism is vanishing, and France has ceased to be a peasant country. So have most Western European countries. America has no peasants, and only a small percentage of its population is engaged in farming. That was what Marx prophesied: that what will be left will be the bourgeoisie and the propertyless working class. For decades it seemed that this particular prognostication was not coming true. Karl Kautsky wrote a very learned and voluminous work on the agrarian problem, in which he explained why in agriculture there was no such concentration of capital as there was in industry. Nevertheless, he maintained, the Marxist prognosis was correct. Lenin accepted Kautsky's argument and pointed out that the peasantry remained in existence although it was getting progressively impoverished. Now this peasantry is vanishing! The proletariat is growing in numbers. Proletarianization, that horror of the bourgeoisie, is progressing with every year of our prosperity, with every year of our welfare state. The processes of production are becoming larger and larger in scale, centralized, social in character, calling more and more for social control, for social ownership. The productive forces of our countries cry out against the national self-sufficiency in which tradition and the ruling classes have kept them. That is the Marxist inferno coming through, almost invisibly, almost unnoticed, in the midst of this welfare state paradise.

In the meantime, one feels as if the whole development of class struggle here in the West has become arrested for a while, waiting for some great chapters to come to a close. There is one great trend in the historic development which promises—but this is only a promise—to turn the whole tide of Marxism and socialism: the growth of the productive forces of the Soviet Union, and with it that of the other postcapitalist countries. The process of primitive socialist accumulation, which has caused such tremendous distortion in the intellectual and moral structure of Marxism, does not have long to run. I do not know whether this is a matter of another decade or two, but the development will come full circle when Russia, this underdeveloped and backward country, and with it the other countries, will at last turn fully into modern, industrial nations—when the educated countries (with a socialist tradition surviving in them in spite of everything) realize in their midst those preconditions for socialism of which Marx and Engels and generations of socialists had dreamed: the material and cultural abundance, the lack of constraint in politics and in culture, the growing equality, the growing internationalism.

I have no doubt that despite the very ugly scenes

between Moscow and Peking, the social systems of those countries are more intelligent and more progressive than their leaders. The social systems will force the leaders into internationalism even if they are the most chauvinistic idiots under the sun; they will push and drive them aside and bring out new people who will be capable of following the call of internationalism that comes today from the whole of mankind. And when this happens the development of those countries will not only catch up with classicial Marxism, but it will probably surpass it. So, I think, we can confidently look forward to the prospect, even if it is not an imminent one, that theory and practice in Marxism will come together again. You and people of your generation should look wholeheartedly to this perspective, when Marxism will no longer be the Marxism with which we had to live—the Marxism projected through the distorting prism of backwardness, of backward civilization and backward societies. Your generation, I hope, will see this new upsurge, this new ascendancy of Marxism undimmed by any intellectual decline.

Marxism and socialism have been the products of Western Europe. They have gone out of Western Europe to conquer the world and they have lost ground in Western Europe. When will they come back? The country in medieval Europe from which the rest of Europe learned the arts of capitalism was Italy. The Italian cities, the Italian economists, the Italian bankers were the foremost in Europe. And then, in the nineteenth century, when nearly the whole of Europe had already gone bourgeois, Italy had not yet achieved its own capitalism. Capitalism came back to Italy belatedly, after the whole of Europe had accepted it. Is Western Europe going to be the Italy of socialism? Are we going to wait until Marxism and socialism have conquered the world, and then stand there, last in the queue, waiting for its return to us? Or shall we save ourselves from our own increasing and terrifying backwardness?

trotsky
in our time

In what does Trotsky's greatness consist? And how relevant
are his ideas and struggles to the problems of our time? Trotsky's chief characteristic is that he is a "forethinker" in the
sense that the Greek myth tells us Prometheus was a forethinker, in contrast to his brother Epimetheus, the "afterthinker." His mind, his will, his energy are directed towards
the future. He stakes everything on the change and upheaval
that Time, the great subversive, must bring about. He never
doubts that the change and upheaval are worth working and
waiting for. The established order, the powers that be, the
status quo are merely evanescent "moments" in the flux of
history. His whole being is permeated by an almost in-
exhaustible and indestructible revolutionary optimism. His
life is one fierce controversy with Epimetheus—a fratricidal
struggle between himself and the afterthinker.

This essay was originally published as part of the introduction to The
Age of Permanent Revolution: A Trotsky Anthology, *edited by Isaac
Deutscher with the assistance of George Novack (Dell; New York,
1966).*

"Dum spiro spero," he cries out as a boy of twenty. At the very threshold of the twentieth century he takes this vow: "As long as I breathe I shall fight for the future, that radiant future, in which man, strong and beautiful, will become master of the drifting stream of his history and will direct it towards the boundless horizons of beauty, joy and happiness!" And at the spectacle of blood and oppression with which the century had ominously opened he exclaims: "You—you are only the *present.*"

Here, with boyish fervor and naiveté, Trotsky had in fact struck the keynote of his life. Through all its phases he was to remain true to himself; at every change of fortune, in triumph and disaster alike, his leitmotif is the same. At the pinnacle of power nothing is further from him than acceptance of the status quo; he still works for change, upheaval, permanent revolution. At the bottom of defeat, when persecution drives him around the globe, while his children are perishing, his friends and followers are being exterminated, he still utters, in a voice almost stifled with pain, his *dum spiro spero.*

> The experience of my life [he said at the end of the "Counter-Trial" before the Dewey Commission in Mexico in 1937], in which there has been no lack either of success or failure, has not only not destroyed my faith in the clear, bright future of mankind, but, on the contrary, has given it an indestructible temper. This faith in reason, in truth, in human solidarity, which at the age of eighteen I took with me into the workers' quarters of the provincial Russian town of Nikolayev—this faith I have preserved fully and completely. It has become more mature, but not less ardent.

The arm of the assassin was already raised over his head when he repeated this pledge; and the only hope he expresses in his testament is that it may be given to him to bequeath his hope to posterity:

> But whatever may be the circumstances of my death, I

shall die with unshaken faith in the Communist future. This faith in man and in his future gives me even now such power of resistance as cannot be given by any religion. . . . I can see the bright green strip of grass beneath the wall and the clear blue sky above the wall, and sunlight everywhere. Life is beautiful. Let the future generations cleanse it of all evil, oppression, and violence, and enjoy it to the full.

During a spell of disillusionment and cynicism nothing is easier than to dismiss such an attitude as old-fashioned "Victorian" optimism or rationalism, if not as "metaphysics of progress." Trotsky, however, does not invoke the innate goodness or rationality of man, nor does he believe in any automatic perfectibility of the human society. He sees the graph of history as a line terribly broken and twisted, not as one rising uninterruptedly. He is all too well aware of the somber impasses into which men had driven themselves so many times, of the vicious circles within which rising and declining civilizations had moved, of the countless generations, faceless and nameless to us, that have lived in unredeemable slavery and of the huge, immeasurable mass of cruelty and suffering man has inflicted on man.

History is not to him the manifestation of any mastermind or masterwill; nor is it a story with an underlying purposeful design. Yet, amid all of history's savage chaos and sanguinary waste, he sees the unique record of man's achievement: his biological rise above "the dark animal realm," his social organization, and his stupendous productive and creative capacity, which has grown with particular intensity in these last few generations. This capacity enables modern man to perpetuate the basis for the further growth and enrichment of his civilization. It enables him to make his culture as immune from decay as no earlier culture could be. All the vanished civilizations of the past had been dependent for their existence on too small and feeble productive forces, which, in slave societies, degenerated all too easily, until a single blow—natural calamity, social disaster, or foreign invasion—wiped them out. Thus, the lack of continuity in man's cultural growth was due, in the main, to the underdevelopment of his productive power. Modern technology has at last created the preconditions of continuity; it has given man all the means for recording, fixing, and consolidating his achievements. Time and time again it has enabled him to rebuild his social existence from ruins, and to reproduce his material and spiritual wealth on an expanding scale. This was to Trotsky the major source of his historical optimism.

But Trotsky, the pessimist will say, did not foresee the advent of the atomic age—he did not reckon with the ultimate weapon invented by our scientists and technologists. We are now capable not merely of destroying civilization but even of shattering the biological foundations of our existence. The growth of our productive power has given us the power of self-annihilation. Trotsky's optimism about man's productive capacity as the mainspring of history is, at best, a pathetic relic of the pre-atomic age.

The pessimist is mistaken. For one thing, Trotsky did foresee the advent of the atomic age; he forecast it nearly two decades before the first nuclear weapon was exploded, when the idea did not even occur to any statesman or political leader and while eminent scientists still viewed it skeptically. Even in this field he was the forethinker; he stated explicitly that the great social and political revolution of our age will coincide with a gigantic revolution in science and technology. As a Marxist, he was well aware that throughout history every advance in man's productive and creative power has increased his capacity for oppression and destruction and that in any social system torn by its internal contradictions every act of progress is internally contradictory. In class society our power to control the forces of nature is monopolized by the dominant social class, or by ruling groups, who use that power also to control, subjugate, or destroy the social forces hostile to them (as well as foreign enemies). Marx and Engels had realized this; and this realization set apart their social optimism from the liberal belief in the automatic progress of bourgeois society. They formulated a dual historical prognosis: mankind, they said, will either advance to socialism or relapse into barbarism.* Trotsky constantly elaborates this dual prognosis. Fifty or thirty years ago the bourgeois liberal considered it to be unduly dogmatic and unduly pessimistic; now he is inclined to dismiss it as "starry-eyed optimism."

Granted that the danger of society's relapse into barbarism now looks more menacing than ever, and that even Trotsky could not foresee just how desperately acute the alternative—socialism or the collapse of civilization—would become in the atomic age. But then the Marxist school of thought and Trotsky in particular can be reproached only for not being fully aware of how profoundly they were right. Yet Trotsky's optimism was no profession of passive faith; nor were his forecasts the horoscopes of a soothsayer. His confidence in man's future is predicated on man's capacity and willingness to act and fight for his future. His *dum spiro spero* was a battle cry; each of his prognostications was a summons to action. So understood, his optimism in the

---

* In her famous "Junius Brochure" written in a German prison during the first World War, Rosa Luxemburg said: "Friedrich Engels stated once that bourgeois society is confronted with this dilemma: either transition to socialism or relapse into barbarism. What does 'relapse into barbarism' signify at the present level of European civilization? We have certainly all read these words more than once, and repeated them thoughtlessly, without even a premonition of their terrible gravity. . . . The present world war is a relapse into barbarism. The triumph of imperialism leads to the decay of culture—temporary decay during any modern war, or complete decay, if the era of world wars that has begun were to last and go on to its final conclusion. Now therefore . . . we stand again before this choice; either the triumph of imperialism and the devastation of all culture, as in ancient Rome—devastation, depopulation, degeneration, a huge cemetery; or the victory of socialism. . . ." (Rosa Luxemburg was a Polish-born revolutionist, propagandist, and theoretician of Marxism. She opposed the First World War, founded the Spartacus Bund with Karl Leibknecht, was imprisoned by the Kaiser's government and released by the German Revolution in 1918. In January, 1919 she was assassinated in Berlin by right-wing thugs.)

atomic age is more valid than ever. The closer man may be to self-annihilation the more firmly must he believe that he can avoid it, the more intense and fanatical must be his determination to avoid it. His optimism is essential to his survival, while supercilious disillusionment and resigned pessimism are sterile and can only prepare us for suicide.

Trotsky is a classical Marxist in more than one sense. He represents the Marxist school of thought in its purity, as it existed before its debasement by the social-democratic and Stalinist orthodoxies. His writings convey the original inspiration, the intellectual splendor, and the moral élan of the idea and the movement. The generations of socialists and communists who, in Tsarist and Stalinist Russia, went underground to struggle against exploitation and oppression, who filled the prisons and places of deportation, who braved penal servitude, gallows, and execution squads, and who hoped for no reward except moral satisfaction, were animated by the mood and the vision of society to which Trotsky gives consummate expression. His writings are therefore a grand document of the time. American readers will find in them deep insights into the ethos of a society very different from their own, a society in the throes of revolution, a society electrified by peculiarly powerful currents of political thought, passion, and action.

Like every major school of thought and every great movement, Marxism has gone through various metamorphoses and transmutations; different aspects of it have come to the fore in different phases of its development. Trotsky is deeply committed to one element in classical Marxism, its quintessential element: permanent revolution. Marx had formulated the idea by the middle of the nineteenth century, in the era of the 1848 revolutions; Trotsky reformulated it at the beginning of this century, during the first Russian Revolution of 1905–1906. The idea has since been the subject of ferocious controversy; for over forty years it has been banished from the communist world and banned as the heresy of all heresies.

What has been its meaning and what bearing has it on the events of our time? The Stalinists (including the Khrushchevites and even the Maoists) have done all they could to discredit permanent revolution as the phantasmagoria of the obsessive ultra-radical. Before Stalin came to denounce Trotsky as "the leader of the vanguard of world counter-revolution" (and as the ally of Hitler and the Mikado), he described him as a "firebrand" and "wild man" bent on staging communist coups all over the world, as the dogmatist of a "purely proletarian" revolution, and as the enemy of the peasantry and of the "small men" of other "intermediate" classes. What finally repudiates all these charges is the fact that in the long list of errors and crimes that Stalin attributed to Trotsky there is hardly one that he himself did not commit; and so his distorting portrait of Trotsky can now be seen as his own self-projection.

Trotsky's theory is in truth a profound and comprehensive conception in which all the overturns that the world has been undergoing (in this late capitalist era) are represented as interconnected and interdependent parts of a single revolutionary process. To put it in the broadest terms, the social upheaval of our century is seen by Trotsky as global in scope and character, even though it proceeds on various levels of civilization and in the most diverse social structures, and even though its various phases are separated from one another in time and space.

It should be remembered that when Trotsky first expounded his view, nearly sixty years ago, the stability of the old order seemed unshakeable; nearly all continents were still dominated by Europe, whose great empires and dynasties seemed indestructible. Only in Russia had the first breach just been torn in tsardom—a breach soon to be plastered over; and through it Trotsky glimpsed the horizon of the century that lay ahead. He was, in this respect, unique among contemporary Marxist leaders and theorists, for none, not even Lenin, had the audacity to maintain that Russia would be the first country in the world to establish a proletarian dictatorship and attempt socialist revolution. What Marxists generally believed then was that Western Europe was "ripe" for socialism, although with most European socialists the belief was rather Platonic. As for Russia, no one saw her as standing at the threshold of socialist revolution. It was commonly held that she was heading towards a bourgeois revolution that would enable her to free herself from the heavy legacy of her feudalism and transform herself into a modern capitalist nation; in a word, that she was about to produce her own version of the Great French Revolution.

One section of the socialists, the Mensheviks, deduced that the leadership in the coming revolution should belong to the liberal bourgeoisie. Lenin and his followers realized that the liberal bourgeoisie was unable and unwilling to cope with such a task, and that Russia's young working class, supported by a rebellious peasantry, was the only force capable of waging the revolutionary struggle to a conclusion. But Lenin remained convinced, and emphatically asserted, that Russia, acting alone, could not go beyond a bourgeois revolution; and that only *after* capitalism had been overthrown in Western Europe would she too be able to embark on socialist revolution. For a decade and a half, from 1903 till 1917, Lenin wrestled with this problem: how could a revolution led, against bourgeois opposition, by a socialist working class result in the establishment of a capitalist order? Trotsky cut through this dogmatic tangle with the conclusion that the dynamic of the revolution could not be contained within any particular stage, and that once released it would overflow all barriers and sweep away not only tsardom but also Russia's weak capitalism, so that what had begun as a bourgeois revolution would end as a socialist one.

Here a fateful question posed itself. Socialism, as understood by Marxists, presupposed a highly developed modern economy and civilization, an abundance of material and cultural wealth, that alone could enable society to satisfy the needs of all its members and abolish class divisions. This was obviously beyond the reach of an underdeveloped and backward Russia. Trotsky therefore argued that Russia could only *begin* the socialist revolution, but would find it extremely difficult to *continue* it, and impossible to *complete* it. The revolution would run into a dead end, unless it burst Russia's national boundaries and brought into motion the forces of revolution in the West. Trotsky assumed that just as the Russian Revolution could not be contained within the bourgeois stage, so it would not be brought to rest within its national boundaries: it would be the prelude, or the first act, of a global upheaval. Internationally as well as nationally, this would be permanent revolution.

Curiously, the international aspect of the theory was, when Trotsky first formulated it, less controversial than it became later. It was less disputed by Marxists than was Trotsky's insistence on the thesis that Russia would initiate the socialist upheaval.

Classical Marxism had been acutely aware of the international scope and character of modern capitalism and emphasized in particular international division of labor as one of its most progressive features. Marx and Engels had argued, in the *Communist Manifesto*, that socialism would begin where capitalism had ended: it would evolve, broaden, intensify, and rationalize the international division of labor inherited from capitalism. This idea was part and parcel of the intellectual tradition of Marxism. But at the turn of the century it was already falling into neglect or oblivion, and it had little impact on the practical policies of the labor movement.

Trotsky revived the idea and threw it into fresh relief. He saw socialism and the nation-state as being incompatible. Thus implicitly he repudiated Stalin's "socialism in a single country" about twenty years before Stalin began to preach it.

This is not to say, as the Stalinists maintained, that when the Russian Revolution became isolated, in the nineteen twenties, Trotsky saw no hope for it—no possibility of survival and development. He had always held that the revolution must *start* on a national basis and had made allowance for the possibility of its temporary isolation in a single country. So when the Bolshevik regime had in fact become isolated, he fought for its survival vigorously and successfully—first as commissar of defense, and then as chief advocate of the rapid industrialization of the USSR. But it is true that he went on viewing the confinement of the revolution to a single state as an interlude and an interim. He refused to see the Russian Revolution as a self-sufficient development capable of finding its consummation within its national boundaries. He persisted in treating it as the first act of a global drama, even after the "pause" before the next act had turned out to be unexpectedly long. Of course, even Stalin never renounced quite explicitly the "link" between the USSR and world communism—the Bolshevik commitment to Marxist internationalism had been far too strong to be flouted openly. But the idea, to which Stalin merely paid lip service, permeated all of Trotsky's thought and activity.

Here an analogy drawn from American history may be pertinent. The dichotomy of isolationism and internationalism, which runs through so much of United States history, runs also through Soviet history, where it appears in a far more confused but also far more violent and tragic form. Stalinism was the Bolshevik isolationism—positive isolationism between two world wars, and disintegrating isolationism afterwards; Trotskyism was Bolshevik internationalism, unadulterated and undiluted. (The confused and ambiguous character of Soviet isolationism stems from the fact that, unlike its American counterpart, it had inherited an internationalist ideology with which it was in continuous conflict. Soviet isolationism was not anchored in geography: the USSR was not separated from hostile or potentially hostile powers by two oceans.)

In the course of twenty or twenty-five years, from the early nineteen twenties to the late nineteen forties, all appearances of the world situation spoke against Trotsky's doctrine. Revolution made no progress outside the USSR and seemed contained within the Soviet boundaries for good. It may be moot to what extent this was due to "objective" circumstances and how much Stalinism contributed to prolonging the "pause" in revolutionary development. In any case, Stalinism not only made peace with the national containment of the revolution, but proclaimed its self-containment and national self-sufficiency. Many anti-communists (who preferred Stalin, the "realistic statesman," to Trotsky, the "dreamer" or "incendiary") applauded him for this. So did all Communist parties. "Is not Stalin right," they argued, "to bank on socialism in one country? Only the spirit of capitulation or counterrevolutionary malice can prompt Trotsky to maintain that socialism cannot be achieved within a single country."

Stalin's triumph, long-lasting though it was, turns out to have been as transitory as the situation that had produced it. "Socialism in a single country" can now be seen as the ideological reflex of temporary circumstances, as a piece of "false consciousness" rather than a realistic program. The next act of permanent revolution began long before the USSR came anywhere near socialism. (It is a travesty of the truth to claim that the Soviet Union is—or was in Stalin's days—a socialist society; even after all its recent progress, it still finds itself somewhere halfway between capitalism and socialism.) Stalin's famous "statesmanship" is now repudiated and ridiculed by his former acolytes, who describe his rule as a long witches' sabbath of senseless violence inflicted upon the Russian people. These denunciations must be taken with a grain of salt, for they tend to obscure the deeper underlying realities of the Stalin epoch. The isolated Russian Revolution could not cope satisfactorily with the tasks it had set itself, because these could not be resolved within a single state. Much of Stalin's work consisted of squaring the circle by means of mass terror; and his single-country socialism was indeed, as Trotsky maintained, a pragmatist's utopia. The Soviet Union abandoned it to all intents and purposes towards the end of World War II, when its troops, in pursuit of Hitler's armies, marched into a dozen foreign lands, and carried revolution on their bayonets and in the turrets of their tanks.

Then, in 1948–49, came the triumph of the Chinese Revolution, which Stalin had not expected and which he had done his best to obstruct. The "pause" definitely had come to an end. The curtain had risen over another act of international revolution. And ever since, Asia, Africa, and even Latin America have been seething. In appearance each of their upheavals has been national in scope and character. Yet each falls into an international pattern. The revolutionary dynamic cannot be brought to a rest. Permanent revolution has come back into its own, and whatever its further intervals and disarray, it forms the socio-political content of our century.

History hardly ever gives a hundred percent confirmation to any great anticipatory idea. It does not accord such a confirmation even to Trotsky, for no thinker or political leader is infallible. Trotsky's great forecast is coming true, but not in the way he forecast it. The difference may not seem to posterity as great as it appears to us. A historian looking back on our time from the vantage point of another age will almost certanly see this century not as the American or Russian century, but as the century of permanent revolution. In retrospect he may see the continuity of the whole process and attach little importance to the breaks and intervals. But to contemporaries, to Trotsky's generation and our own, the breaks and intervals are just as full of tension and conflict as are the main acts; they fill large parts of our lives and absorb our energies and efforts. Trotsky spent the first half of his militant life on a rising tide of revolution and the second on the shoals. Hence the frustrations and defeats that followed upon his triumphs, and the relative fruitlessness of so much of his struggle against Stalin. In the USSR his large and important following was physically exterminated so that the Soviet Trotskyists, like the Decembrists over a hundred years earlier, now appear as a generation of revolutionaries "without sons," i.e., without *direct* political descendants. Outside the USSR, Trotskyism has not been a vital political movement: the Fourth International has never been able to make a real start. Even Trotsky's political genius could not turn ebb into flow.

Moreover, permanent revolution has taken a course very different from that which Trotsky had predicted. In accordance with the tradition of classical Marxism, he expected its next acts to be played out in the "advanced and civilized" countries of the West. Readers of this anthology will see for themselves how large Germany, France, Britain (and the United States) loomed in his revolutionary expectations and how urgent was the immediacy of the hopes he placed on them.* Instead, the underdeveloped and backward East has become the main theater of revolution. It is not that Trotsky overlooked the East's potentialities—far from it—but he saw these as being secondary to the potentialities of the West, which, in his eyes, were to the end decisive.

This fault of perspective (if this is the right term here) is closely connected with the Marxist assessment of the role of the industrial working class in modern society, an assessment summed up in the famous epigram that "the revolution will either be the work of the workers or it will not be at all." Yet not one of the social upheavals of the last two decades has been strictly "the work of the workers." All have been carried out by closely knit military organizations and/or small bureaucratic parties; and the peasantry has been far more active in them than the industrial proletariat. This has been so especially in the greatest of these upheavals, the Chinese. Mao's partisans carried the revolution from country to

* Compare this with the message which F. Engels addressed to the National Council of the Parti Ouvrier Francais in 1890, on the occasion of his 70th birthday: "It was your great countryman Saint-Simon who first saw that the alliance of the three great Western nations—France, England, Germany—is the primary international condition of the political and social emancipation of the whole of Europe. I hope to see this alliance, the nucleus of the European alliance which will once and for all put an end to the wars of cabinets and races, realized by the proletarians of these three nations. Long live international social revolution!"

town; whereas with Trotsky it was an absolute axiom that the revolution must come from town to country and cannot succeed without urban initiative and leadership.

Yet it is rash to jump to the conclusion, drawn by some writers, notably the late C. Wright Mills, that all this disproves the Marxist conception that considers the industrial working class as the chief "historic agency" of socialism. We must not forget that for over a century the working classes of Europe were indeed the chief agents of socialism and that generation after generation they struggled for it with an intelligence, passion, and heroism that amazed the world. Nothing can delete from history the deeds of the English Chartists and of the French Communards, the fight of the German workers against Bismarck and the Hohenzollerns, the epic underground struggle, lasting over half a century, of Polish socialist and communist workers, and the Russian proletarian insurrections of 1905 and 1917. This is a record unparalleled in the annals of mankind, for none of the exploited and oppressed classes of earlier societies—slaves, serfs, "free" peasants, or urban plebeians—had ever shown any even remotely comparable capacity for political thought, self-discipline, organization, and action. It was the "factory hands" of St. Petersburg, not any Bolshevik or Menshevik intellectuals, who "invented" the institution of the council of workers' delegates, the soviet. Even the debased soviets of today, like the bureaucratized trade unions of the West, remain monuments—malignantly disfigured monuments—to the political creativeness of the working class. All the defeats suffered by the workers, all their failures to secure the fruits of their victories, and even their failure to act any decisive part in the upheavals of the last two decades—are not enough to deprive them of the title of the "chief agents of socialism," a title gained in the course of a century. A sense of proportion and perspective is needed to avoid generalizing about a long-term historic process from one particular phase of it.

Having said this, we must admit that the complexities of the historic development put to a severe test the Marxist conception of proletarian socialism and the beliefs and hopes of everyone involved in the labor movement. The world is in the throes of permanent revolution, but is this the revolution of proletarian socialism? In order that Trotsky's idea should retain its full validity, its main premise must yet be fulfilled: the workers of the industrially advanced nations—and these include now the USSR as well as the West—must recover from the apathy, confusion, and resignation into which Western reformism and Stalinism have driven them; they must reassert themselves as the chief agents of socialism. The question as to who will ultimately be in control of the revolution of our century is still open: will it be irresponsible and tyrannical bureaucracies or the working class as the representative of the general interest of society? On the answer hangs much more, infinitely more, than the validity of any doctrine—all the material and spiritual values that man has created and accumulated are at stake.

The idea that the working class is, or should be, the chief actor in social revolution determines the whole of Trotsky's political thinking, his conception of the Soviet regime and of the Bolshevik party, and his entire struggle against the social-democratic and Stalinist orthodoxies. "Proletarian democracy" is the key notion of all his reasonings and arguments.

Like all revolutionary Marxists, Trotsky considers proletarian dictatorship to be the necessary political condition of the world's transition from capitalism to socialism. No one among his comrades and rivals, not even Lenin, was "harder" and "tougher" in upholding this principle in theory and practice. To portray Trotsky as a soft humanitarian, an intellectual dreamer, a preacher of nonviolence, a Gandhi-like figure in Bolshevism would be to falsify history. This great martyr did not live on goat's milk, nor did he trade in the milk of human kindness. He knew how many of the momentous turns in history have been stained by human blood—he often evoked the American Civil War as a major example. He did not shrink from ruthlessness when he was convinced that this was necessary for the progress of society. And it would be cant and hypocrisy to condemn him, because of this, in the name of Western civilization and its values, a civilization that has on its conscience the mass slaughters of two world wars and has exposed mankind to the perils of nuclear war. Where Trotsky differs from all the glorified butchers of history is that he never, not even for a single moment, relished his own ruthlessness and the taste of blood. He staged the greatest of all armed insurrections, the rising of November 7, 1917, in such a way that, according to most hostile eyewitnesses, the number of all its casualties did not exceed ten; and as captain in the civil war he treated bloodshed in the surgeon's manner, as an indispensable but strictly limited part of a necessary and salutary operation.

He stood for the proletarian dictatorship because he took it for granted that landlords, capitalists, and slave-owners do not, as a rule, yield up their possessions and power without a savage fight. (They did not so yield it up in Russia, and they were armed and supported by all the great Western democracies.) Only a dictatorship could make Russia safe for the revolution. But what was to be its nature?

It is necessary here to restore to his ideas the meaning they had to him (and indeed to Lenin and the early Bolsheviks), because in the meantime, with the experience of totalitarian regimes, these ideas have become overgrown with heavy and repulsive accretions alien to them. In Trotsky's mind the proletarian dictatorship was, or should have been, a proletarian democracy. This was no paradox. It should not be forgotten that, like other Marxists, Trotsky was accustomed to describe all bourgeois democracies (the British constitutional monarchy, the German Weimar Republic, the French Third Republic, and the political system of the USA) as "bourgeois dictatorships." He knew, of course, that, in strictly political and constitutional terms, these were not dictatorial or even semi-dictatorial regimes, and he was very well aware of the freedoms people enjoy under parliamentary democracies. (What importance he attached to these can be seen from his controversy with the Stalinist Comintern over fascism and democracy in Germany).

But Trotsky insisted on describing the Western parliamentary system as a bourgeois dictatorship in a broader sense, as a regime that, being based on capitalist property, assures the propertied classes of their economic and social supremacy, and consequently of cultural and political predominance. The term "bourgeois dictatorship" describes precisely that supremacy and dominance, and not necessarily any particular constitutional system or method of government. Similarly, when he (or Lenin or Marx) speaks of proletarian dictatorship, he uses the term in its broadest sense to denote a regime that should assure the working class of social supremacy; he does not prejudge constitutional form or method of government. Like the bourgeois "dictatorship," the proletarian may be politically either dictatorial or democratic; it may take on various constitutional forms. In the period immediately after revolution, and during civil war, it must tend to be strictly dictatorial; in more normal circumstances it should tend to be democratic. But even in its strictly dictatorial phase it should still be, as the Soviet regime was at the outset, a proletarian democracy, assuring genuine freedom of expression and association, at least to the workers, and enabling them to exercise effective control over the government. This conception of the dictatorship had nothing to do with—indeed it was the very negation of—any self-perpetuating rule of a "socialist" oligarchy or of an autocrat, or with any "monolithic," totalitarian system of government. No wonder that under Stalinism this conception came to be denounced as a Menshevik heresy and was eradicated from communist thinking. From minds formed in its school Stalinism has indeed eradicated the belief that the working class is, or ought to be, *the* agency of socialism.

Like so much else, Trotsky's conception of the party also stemmed from that belief. It is impossible within the compass of this anthology to illustrate adequately the complex evolution of Trotsky's views on this subject—readers interested in it must be referred to the three volumes of my biography of Trotsky.* Here it will be enough to recall that on this point Trotsky was in disagreement with Lenin for nearly fifteen years and in bitter opposition to Stalin for about twenty—he marched in step with the Bolsheviks only for six years, the "world-shaking" years from 1917 to 1923. The whys and wherefores of his polemics against Lenin differ widely from the grounds for his antagonism to Stalin. Nevertheless one motif runs through both controversies: Trotsky's abhorrence of any form of party tutelage over the workers. It was of the ambition to exercise such a tutelage that he had suspected Lenin before 1917, and he saw that ambition incarnate and fulfilled in Stalin. He himself recognized that he had been grievously mistaken about Lenin, who had trained the Bolshevik Party to *lead* the workers, not to *tame* or subjugate them. In drawing a distinction between legitimate leadership on the one hand and tutelage and usurpation on the other, the mature Trotsky corrected a certain one-sidedness in himself: he had relied too strongly on the spontaneous class-consciousness of the workers, on their inherent revolutionary intelligence and will, which by themselves would secure the victory of socialism. He had tended to see the working class as a homogeneous social body, all animated by the same socialist awareness and all possessed by high capacity for political action. Such a working class needed no special guide— the party had merely to identify itself with it and express its aspirations.

Lenin, for whom also belief in the "historic mission" of workers as chief agents of socialism was basic, saw the working class more realistically and critically. He saw it as a complex and heterogeneous body consisting of different layers, each with its own origin and background, each related differently to the peasantry, the petty bourgeoisie, and the rest of the working class, each with its level of education and

---

* Isaac Deutscher: *The Prophet Armed* (1954); *The Prophet Unarmed*, (1959); and *The Prophet Outcast* (1963); Oxford University Press, London.

social awareness, and each with its own degree of capacity (or incapacity) for revolutionary action. This highly differentiated mass was united only by its proletarian status in society and by its antagonism to capitalist exploitation; it was disunited by centrifugal forces in its midst and the varying degrees of receptiveness to socialism. The *real* class consisted of progressive and backward elements, of the clearsighted and the dull, the courageous and the meek; it needed the party's guidance in order to rise to its revolutionary "mission." Consequently, the party could not merely identify itself with the workers and content itself with absorbing and expressing their moods. It had to shape their moods. It had to identify itself primarily with the advanced workers in order to be able with them and through them to educate politically the backward ones. The party must therefore be a "proletarian vanguard," a Marxist elite, lucid, self-disciplined, indomitable, and capable of providing the "general staff" of revolution.

The mature Trotsky accepted this Leninist idea and never abandoned it. It would be idle to deny the dangers inherent in any elite party, the dangers to which the young Trotsky had been so sensitive that his early philippics against Lenin's scheme of the party read now like uncannily prophetic previews of the Stalinist regime.* The elite could (and would) turn into an oligarchy all too easily; and the oligarchy would bring forth the irremovable and infallible dictator. Trotsky nevertheless accepted Lenin's scheme because of Lenin's overwhelmingly realistic analysis of the relationship between party and class, but mainly because of the manner in which Lenin's party (as distinct from Stalin's or Khrushchev's) exercised its leadership. Highly disciplined though the party was, it was a free association of revolutionaries, taking for granted, and making full use of, their democratic rights within the organization, criticizing their leaders without fear or favor, and debating, most often in public, every

---

* See *The Prophet Armed*, pp. 88-97.

major issue of policy. The large prerogatives of the Leninist Central Committee, the strong concentration of power in its hands, and the obligation of party members to act in unison on its orders were effectively counterbalanced by uninhibited criticism and control from below.

Lenin's "democratic centralism" must be distinguished from the bureaucratic ultra-centralization characteristic of Stalinism. The elite party was not, in Lenin's intention, to have been a self-sufficient body replacing the working class as agent of socialism. It was to remain part of the working class, just as in any army the vanguard remains part of the fighting force even while it acts as a special detachment to perform a special function. In the Leninist party the rank and file were free to change the composition of the Central Committee, just as in the Soviet republic the working class was in precept entitled to depose and replace the party in office. Proletarian democracy included inner party democracy as its particular aspect.

We know that however irreproachable this scheme may have been ideally, the realities of the revolution have ridden roughshod over it. This was no "historic accident" or the result merely of Stalin's ill will. The backwardness of the old Russia found its most cruel expression in the advent of Stalinism. The Soviet working class had been exhausted by revolution and civil war, catastrophically reduced in size, disorganized, and demoralized through the collapse of the entire economy. It proved unable to safeguard proletarian democracy and control the party in power. Within the party, too, the rank and file failed to preserve their rights and to control the leaders. The Bolshevik regime took on the bureaucratic and monolithic character it was to maintain for decades.

Stalin's struggle against Trotsky constituted a crucial phase in this transformation. The extraordinary cruelty and fury of that struggle came from the fact that "Trotskyism" represented the conscience of the revolution, that it insistently recalled to the Bolshevik Party its commitment to proletarian democracy, and that it kindled in the working class the never quite extinct aspiration to become once again *the* agent of socialism. For a whole epoch Trotskyism was the sole revolutionary alternative to Stalinism.

Trotsky's ideas on the "construction of socialism" were also diametrically opposed to Stalinist theory and practice. A brief recapitulation may help to put the contrast into focus. Trotsky was the original prompter and promoter of the rapid industrialization of the USSR—he has therefore his share in the present economic ascendancy of the USSR. Also he regarded the collectivization of farms as a necessary accompaniment of industrialization and as the way to a mode of agricultural production superior to that based on the old rural smallholding worked with archaic tools. In a sense Stalin stole Trotsky's clothes after he had defeated him—he took over the program of industrialization and collectivization from the Left Opposition.*

This has led some "Sovietologists" to argue that there was not much difference between Stalin and Trotsky, that there is indeed "not much to choose between them." The argument misses a point of importance, namely that Stalin, as he was putting on Trotsky's "clothes," soaked them in the blood of Soviet peasants and workers. There, in a nutshell, lay the difference between the two men's "methods of socialist construction."

In Trotsky's scheme of things, rapid industrialization was to be promoted with the workers' consent, not against their will and interests. This presupposed a balanced and simultaneous expansion of producer and consumer industries, a more or less continuous improvement in the population's standard of living, and an increasing, conscious, and willing participation of the workers in the processes of planning— "planning from below as well as from above." Stalin, however, promoted a one-sided development of the producer

---

* The Left Opposition was formed in 1923 by a large group of prominent Bolsheviks under Trotsky's leadership around the question of workers' democracy and state-planned industrialization. After a five-year struggle for its program within the party, it was outlawed by the Fifteenth Party Congress in 1927.

ever, promoted a one-sided development of the producer industries, neglecting consumer industries. Consequently the standard of living of the masses was depressed or remained stagnant, and the workers, resentful at being denied the benefits of industrialization, were deprived of any share in determining economic policy; they were robbed of any right to protest, strike, or otherwise express an opinion. In the course of two decades the workers paid for most trivial offenses against "labor discipline" with years of slavery and torture in the inferno of Stalin's concentration camps. Throughout the nineteen thirties Trotsky was their only vocal defender; his voice resounded in the world against the deafening din of a mendacious Stalinist propaganda. Similarly, collectivization of farming, as Trotsky advocated it, was to be carried out gradually, by persuasion, with the peasantry's consent, and not "wholesale" as Stalin enforced it in the years 1929-32.

It is sometimes said that if persuasion rather than coercion had regulated the tempo of industrialization and collectivization, the USSR would not have been able to build up its economic and military power as rapidly as it did—not rapidly enough to enable it to emerge victorious from the Second World War and break the American monopoly of atomic energy soon thereafter. A reasoning of this kind cannot either be accepted or refuted on purely empirical grounds. Great weight, however, must be given to Trotsky's counterargument that under an economic leadership more rational and civilized than Stalin's, and more sensitive to the people's needs, the economic and military power of the USSR would have been placed on firmer foundations and would have been even more effective. Much of what Stalin gained on the swings through an excessive tempo of development he lost on the roundabouts through bureaucratic mismanagement and waste, a terrible waste of men as well as materials. (Nor should one forget the "waste" that Stalin's conduct of foreign affairs caused the USSR, when, *inter alia*, it enabled Hitler's armies to occupy and devastate the wealthiest Soviet lands during the Second World War.) In any case, the criticisms Trotsky once made of Stalin's Five Year Plans are now voiced by Stalin's successors, who themselves were closely associated with their master's practice. If the Stalinist "method" was historically inevitable, then it was so in one sense only—because the Soviet ruling group, or, more broadly, the Soviet bureaucracy itself was too backward, too crude, and too brutal to attempt a more civilized and more socialist way of building up Soviet power. In the last instance, the vices of the bureaucracy stemmed from that old Russian barbarism that survived the October Revolution and overpowered it. It was Trotsky's and Russia's tragedy that even in struggling to rid herself of that barbarism Russia was unable to rise above it.

Many Western readers may find it difficult to visualize the awe-inspiring immensity of the conflict that raged through two decades of Soviet history. But I hope that the following pages may convey to them something of the intellectual and moral élan, and of the dramatic pathos and warm humanity that Trotsky brought to the struggle. The freedom of his spirit and the astonishing range of his interests and activities are reflected in his writings. He himself once said of Lenin that Lenin thought in "terms of continents and epochs." This is also true of himself. Even though his thought, like his epoch, was still European-centered, it constantly transcended this limitation. And it reached out to the other, then still "silent" continents and peoples, and to our epoch in which they were all to acquire their own voices and at last to impart a truly global character to current politics. In the years of Trotsky's last exile, from wherever persecution—Western "democratic" as well as Stalinist persecution—had driven him (from a remote Turkish island, from a hiding place in the French Alps, from a Norwegian village, and, finally, from a suburb of Mexico City), his mind and heart never ceased embracing the world. His internationalism was not merely an intellectual conviction; it was instinct-like in its spontaneity; it showed itself in an ever alive and active solidarity with every segment of oppressed and struggling humanity. He was as intensely preoccupied with the prospects of the Chinese Revolution in the period of its eclipse as he was with the fate that awaited the German workers in the event of Hitler's rise to power, or with the baneful illusions of the French and Spanish Popular Fronts. He followed the struggles for independence of India, Indonesia, and Indochina (as Vietnam was then called) and delved into their class relations. His ear caught every social tremor that passed through Latin America. And even in his last days his thoughts were with the North American Negroes who, he knew, would one day rise en masse against their oppressors. He felt at home with every nation and every people on earth, for every one of them had to contribute its share to the Permanent Revolution.

In another sense also the range of his ideas and work is exceptional. Political leader, sociologist, economist, war captain, military theorist, outstanding "specialist" on armed insurrection, historian, biographer, literary critic, master of Russian prose, and one of the greatest orators of all times, Trotsky brings his searching and original mind and his extraordinary power of expression to every field of his activity. He treats every subject he tackles in his own way, as no one has treated it before or after. Even when sometimes he repeats the commonplaces of Marxism, he rediscovers, as it were, the truth they contain and invests them with fresh life, so that with him they are never clichés; he restates them in order to deduce from them novel and creative conclusions. He is, in many ways, the most orthodox of Marxists, but his personality dispels the odor of orthodoxy. He speaks with authority, not as one of the scribes; and in spirit, temperament, and style he is closer to Marx himself than any of Marx's disciples and followers.

"The style is the man," but it is also the epoch. Trotsky's style mirrors superbly the heroic period in the history of revolution and Marxism, its ethos and color. That period has since been overlaid, at least to the eye of the present generation, by the blood and mud of Stalinism, and by the drab ambiguities of the post-Stalinist regimes in the USSR and other Eastern countries. It is all the more important for the student of contemporary history to try to penetrate through the crust of these accretions to the original, half-forgotten inspiration of the October Revolution. The mental effort required for this may be compared to the effort of cleansing and restoration that is nowadays being spent on old works of art in our museums and galleries. These works were for so long covered by dirt and patina that often their original color and even shape were forgotten; and art historians came to regard the dim incrustations as part of the old master's own palette and of his vision of the world. Learned dissertations have been written about the "color schemes" of a Goya or an El Greco on this erroneous assumption, until one day inquisitive and courageous students began to scratch cautiously and cleanse the surface of a famous masterpiece. As they went on quite a different "color scheme" of the master revealed itself to their astonished eyes—it was bright and brilliant, and had little in common with the "color scheme" construed by the learned experts. The images of Marxism, of Leninism, and of the Russian Revolution purveyed by Western Sovietologists and Soviet ideologists alike have this in common with the theories of these unfortunate art experts: they too assume that all the muck and soot and blood on the surface somehow belong to the originals. In the meantime history has just set to work slowly and hesitantly to scratch off the distorting accretions from Marxism and the revolution. Trotsky's writings are already, and will increasingly be, a most important and active element in this work of restoration.

What is involved here, however, is not merely the recovery of the authentic historical image of a great epoch. Trotsky's ideas belong not only to the past. In curiously tangled ways they are closely intertwined with the critical controversies of the present. True enough, Trotsky himself failed in his attempts to create an independent and politically effective communist movement. Yet, as he liked to stress, ideas deeply rooted in social reality are not destroyed even when their advocates are assassinated or exterminated en masse. The ideas crop up again and take possession of the minds of other people, who may not even know or suspect who had first formulated and expounded them. Sometimes a stream runs its course a long distance in the open; then suddenly it vanishes from sight, sinks underground, and remains submerged for a lengthy stretch of its road; until eventually, in an unfamiliar landscape, it re-emerges either as a single stream or as several divergent currents. Something like this is happening with "Trotskyism" now. A quarter of a century after its "final" suppression, it has been surging up in the communist world, not in its old recognizable form, not even under its own name, but as if it were split into its elements and broken up into diverse currents.

In the controversy between Khrushchev and Mao Tse-tung, which is tearing asunder the communist world, the disputants accuse each other of Trotskyism. Of course, Mao and Khrushchev attach the label each to the other in order to discredit each other all the more easily, for in each, and in the followers of each, the Stalinist horror of the Trotskyist heresy is still trepidatingly alive. Yet there is more than mere polemical trick in the mutual accusation. Khrushchev does in fact appear to Mao as a disguised Trotskyist; and so does Mao appear to Khrushchev. Moreover, each has some grounds for thinking of the other as he does, for both carry out, unwittingly and perhaps even unknowingly, Trotsky's political testament—but each carries out a different part of it. The Khrushchevite de-Stalinization is Trotsky's posthumous triumph: every progressive domestic reform carried out in the USSR since 1953 has been but a faint echo of the desiderata and demands Trotsky once put forward, whereas Soviet foreign policy is still largely dominated by the spirit of Stalinist self-sufficiency and opportunism. Conversely, Mao's domestic regime, reflecting China's poverty and backwardness, is still closer to the Stalinist model, whereas in his criticism of Khrushchev's foreign policies and in his approach to international communism, Mao expounds, crudely yet unmistakably, some of the basic tenets of permanent revolution.

What an ironical illustration this is of the "law of uneven development"! Trotskyism is, in a sense, having its comeback, but its elements appear disparately in strange combinations with elements of Stalinism. The communist movement, which is still suffering from political amnesia, is not even conscious of the way in which the continuity of its own submerged traditions is asserting itself—as continuity in discontinuity. But the re-emergence of Trotsky's ideas has only begun. It remains to be seen how it is going to proceed—whether, how, and when his ideas may coalesce again, not in order to reproduce the old Trotskyism, but in order to absorb it and transcend it in a new phase of Marxism, and in a new socialist consciousness enriched by the experiences of our epoch. This much, however, is certain: a knowledge of Trotsky's work is absolutely essential to an understanding of the ferments the communist world is undergoing and of the changes it will undergo in the coming years.

"But Trotsky has hardly anything to tell us," an American critic will say, "about our own society. Marxism has none of the relevance to our own problems that he claimed for it. Was he not patently mistaken in the belief he held in the late thirties that the USA (as well as Western Europe) was entering an era of proletarian revolution, that Marxism was about to conquer the American mind, and that we Americans were going to create the truly modern, up-to-date version of Marxism? Not only have none of these prophecies come true, but the whole development of our society has gone in the opposite direction!"

Trotsky's American prognostications were indeed farfetched. In the last quarter-century, American capitalism, far from collapsing, has displayed immense vitality, achieved quite unparalleled expansion, and drawn abundant assurance from its wealth and power. Consequently Trotsky's prediction of "a great epoch of American Marxism" remains unfulfilled. Not only has the United States "refused" to create any up-to-date version of proletarian socialism, but its working class seems to be further than ever from accepting any brand of socialism at all. And what was once the leftish, and even Marxist, American intelligentsia is now a legion of Panglosses believing that the American "way of life," slightly refurbished according to the Keynesian prescription, is the best of all possible ways of life.

Yes, Trotsky's confidence in "American Marxism" was sadly misplaced, but does this speak against him or against his critics? He, at any rate, remains true to character: great revolutionaries always hope for much more and aim at much more than they can achieve, for otherwise they would never attain what they do attain. They must, as a rule, overreach themselves in order to grasp the things that are within reach. The Panglosses (even the "radicals" among them) never commit such mistakes; and now they are able to point exultantly to prolonged postwar prosperity in order to dismiss the Marxist analysis as obsolete and inapplicable to American society. The question that is left still open, however, is whether Trotsky, the forethinker, was thinking too far ahead in his American prognostications, or whether his thought was moving in the wrong direction.

His American critics would have more solid grounds for their confidence *if* the great postwar prosperity of American (and Western European) capitalism did not contain an ingredient as poisonous as an armament fever lasting a quarter-century, including the madness of the nuclear arms race of two decades; *if* the postwar booms were not ever more frequently and sharply interrupted by recurrent depressions; *if* American governments, so enlightened by Keynesian theory, proved able to cope with the unemployment of millions, which reappeared amid booms even before automation had its full impact on the industrial manpower; and *if* recurrent dollar crises and furious competition in world markets did not signal the end of America's exceptional postwar supremacy, and the approach of overproduction throughout the

West. The critics have perhaps "buried" Marxism somewhat prematurely. After the two decades of prosperity the basic flaws of the system, as diagnosed by Marxists—its irrationality and anarchy—persist. The social character of the productive process is still in conflict with the antisocial property relations, and the international needs and demands of the modern economy are in conflict with the nation-state. It was on the persistence of these "flaws," and on the conviction that they cannot be remedied within capitalism, that Trotsky had based his American prognostications; and as long as his premise remains valid, the element of error in his forecasts concerns the tempo rather than the direction of the course of events. For all its outward signs of flourishing health, the American (bourgeois) "way of life" carries within itself its incurable disease. In years to come this may well show in the way the United States reacts to the challenge from the rising communist powers.

This is not to deny the importance of Trotsky's misjudgment of the tempo of the development, for the mistake about the tempo inevitably turns into an error about the circumstances. When, in the late thirties, Trotsky spoke of the approaching crisis of American capitalism, he did not imagine that in such a crisis the United States would have to confront communist governments established over a third of the globe, and that it would find itself under the direct pressure of modern Soviet economic and military power. The victory of the Chinese Revolution was then still about ten years off, and the USSR was in an early phase of its industrial "takeoff." The shifts in the world's balance of power have come about not in the way Trotsky visualized them—they have come about through revolution (and revolutionary growth of industrial power) in the East, not in the West. And in the next decade or so, this trend almost certainly will continue and change the balance even more radically. Eventually the American "way of life" is likely to be subjected to a far graver and far more severe test than the one Trotsky predicted; the test is likely to be so much graver and more severe precisely because it has been "delayed" by decades. If the Panglosses were not Panglosses, they would not rejoice over the fact that Trotsky's American predictions have not come true; they would be deeply perturbed. Because of its social conservatism and political complacency the United States may have missed, or may be missing, its greatest historical chance.

Long ago, even before the First World War, Trotsky himself provided a clue to this situation. In a characteristic generalization, he wrote about the remarkable fact that by the turn of the century Western Europe had "exported" its most advanced idea—Marxism—to Russia, which was, industrially and technologically, the most backward of European nations; and it had "exported" its most advanced technology to the United States, which was the most backward politically and ideologically. Such has been the fateful one-sidedness of the historical evolution! How much easier this age of transition might have been, how much bloodshed and suffering might have been avoided, if advanced technology had gone hand in hand with advanced ideology; and if the United States, instead of Russia (and/or China), had led the world from capitalism to socialism!

This was not to be. In the meantime, however, in the USSR "advanced ideology" has, despite all the cruel Stalinist distortions, helped to produce advanced technology as well, whereas the USA, for all its technological and industrial triumphs, has made no decisive advance in political ideas. Yet without such an advance, American technology may well be defeated even in its own field. Of the two great European "exports," the export of modern "ideology" may well turn out to have been far more fruitful than the export of technology and, historically, far more profitable to the "importing" nation.

One would like to believe that the Americans can as a nation still make good their lag in the field of ideas, but they have not much time to lose. In recent years the Russian Sputniks and Luniks have greatly shaken the social and political complacency of the USA. But the effect of the shock, as far as the outsider can judge it, appears limited. American energy has been intensely geared to competition with the Russians in the new fields of science and industry, in astrophysics, in construction of space vehicles, etc. This is all to the good insofar as it contributes not merely to military power but to the progress of knowledge and to man's control over nature. Even so, the creative American reaction to Soviet successes remains one-sidedly technological. In sociopolitical ideas American conservatism seems unshaken. Yet it is in the field of ideas, Marxist ideas, that Americans have most to learn, if they are not to land themselves in a grim historical impasse.

And in the field of ideas, Trotsky, I am sure, is still a superb teacher.

marxism
and the new left

In the spring of 1967 Isaac Deutscher spent six weeks at Harpur College (now the State University of New York at Binghamton) as Distinguished Visiting Professor of Political Science. The following is part of a tape-recorded discussion with Harpur students which was published in the first number of New Left Forum, *a student magazine which Isaac Deutscher helped launch. The other participants were Eric Davis, Allan Whiteman, Gary Wurtzel and Professor Melvin Leiman.*

The first point Deutscher tried to make clear was how the so-called New Left considers itself different from other radical groupings of the past, and the content of its claim that it adheres to a pragmatic, non-ideological orientation.

Isaac Deutscher: The term "ideology" has different meanings in different languages and in different contexts. Even in English the terminological confusion reflects the mental confusion. A few years ago some writers proclaimed "the end of ideology." What did they mean? When one looked closely at their proclamation, one realized that what they wanted to announce was "the end of communism and Marxism," but as this would sound trivial, trite and reactionary, they used a more respectable formula: the end of ideology. The great aspirations and ideas about the way to change society were old-fashioned and should be discarded, they maintained. When they proclaimed the end of ideology, they actually proclaimed the end of *their* ideology, their own quietism and reconciliation with society as it was. Among those "prophets" were various ex-leftists, ex-communists, ex-socialists and ex-Trotskyists.

We also have to consider the other sense of the term "ideology." One might say that Marx also tried to get away from ideology, but his was quite a different conception: it was the false consciousness, the false ideas, the fetishes which various classes of society make for themselves in order to veil, unconsciously, their own situation, in order to idealize their own position in society. In this Marxist sense the watchwords *Liberté, Egalité, Fraternité* of the French Revolution were an expression of ideology. The reality of the French Revolution was the crystallization of a bourgeois order of society. The ideological veil which covered that reality was "Liberty, Equality, Brotherhood."

When your ex-leftwingers proclaim the end of ideology, they say in fact: "I am going back to respectable society. I am no longer storming the fortress of the existing order." Some of you, on the so-called New Left, want to leave behind *all* ideology in favor of pragmatism. This means, in fact, that you are endeavoring to get away from great ideas about society and its transformation, and embrace pragmatism. But pragmatism is also an idea. I suggest that you are deluding yourselves if you think that by exchanging ideology for pragmatism you are "getting away from ideology"; no, you are only exchanging one ideology for another. Pragmatism says: "Practical success, practical benefit—that is my supreme test of the rightness or wrongness of what *I think*." But this is an ideological appraisal, and hence an ideology like any other. By the way, have you anything to get away from? Have you had an ideology until now which you want to jettison? If you really are exchanging ideology for pragmatism, why do you call yourselves New Left—what then is "new" in your program? Pragmatism is almost as old as American philosophical thinking.

It is obvious even to the most casual observer that you call yourselves New Left not because you have a new philosophy, but because you want to be distinguished from the previous generation of Marxists, or Leninists, or Trotskyists; you think, quite rightly, that your elders have done badly and you want to make a new start. This sounds very tidy: new people make a new beginning and call themselves New Left. But in what sense are you the "new people"? You are young? Young people can be very old if they start with very old ideas, and surely this is a more important consideration than the age group to which you belong. I suggest that you have, first of all, to define what is the new idea you stand for. In what way are you opposed to your elders, and to which of their ideas are you opposed? If you just announce "this is the end of ideology," you start from their own bankruptcy, and bankruptcy cannot be a starting point.

It is also obvious that what unites you, the New Left, is really an emotional alienation from, and opposition to, this self-satisfied, complacent, well-fed and yet stupid bourgeois society.

Whiteman: This dissatisfaction is part of a common denominator; so is pragmatism. But the main element is, I think, humanism.

Deutscher: Humanism has been for generations seen as the common denominator of all political movements, ideologies, religions, and parties, and this fact alone shows that it cannot be a common denominator. If you ask President Johnson whether he is a humanist, he will surely answer, "Yes, I am."

Even Hitler would have considered himself a humanist; he treated only *some* segments of humanity as subhuman. How do you interpret humanism?

Whiteman: Humanism holds the individual human being as infinitely precious.

Deutscher: This definition is too vague and much too broad to have any meaning at all. "The individual human being is infinitely precious"—this is not a very new idea. It dates back to old Christianity or to old Judaism, if you like, but surely it cannot be the idea of the *New* Left. Why don't you call yourselves old Christians or old Jews?

Whiteman: The name was granted us.

Deutscher: Excuse me, a political appellation is not a name given at a baptism which, as a baby, you have to accept, and which, incidentally, as an adult you are free to change. "New Left" indicates a political attitude.

Wurtzel: By the term "New Left" we mean that group of our generation which corresponds to the radical groups of the thirties.

Deutscher: Here you are establishing a link and a break with the "old" left. You are its equivalent and yet you are different. In what sense is the New Left a counterpart of the radical groups of the thirties? They represented an opposition to the existing social order and an inspiration to overthrow or change that order. Do you want to change your society, and by what kind of society do you want to replace it? Do you see in social control and social ownership of the means of production a principle vital for your and other societies? In a word, are you socialists? I am aware that the New Left comprises those who consider themselves socialists and those who might be described as nonsocialist radicals. It is politically very important, especially at this time in the United States, that they all should cooperate for certain limited objectives—in their opposition to the war in Vietnam, in their struggle for civil rights. But nevertheless this difference between socialists and nonsocialists cannot be viewed only as a slight dissent. It is a major division because behind it are two different ideals of the organization of society. It is quite plain that a socialist will see the question of war and peace in a different context from the nonsocialist. The latter will assume that the racial problems can be solved within the existing economic and social order. The socialist, on the other hand, will say, "We should try even within this social structure to improve as much as we can the lot of the Negro. But ultimately only a different type of society will bring about the disappearance of race discrimination." The radical will say, "Perhaps another president will adopt a more sensible foreign policy and we shall not be plunged periodically into repulsive, unjust wars at one or another end of the globe." The socialist will say, "As long as you have this social system, no matter what president you choose, you will still have imperialist wars waged by your country." The difference in approach and conclusions of the socialist and the nonsocialist is quite fundamental: it reflects a divergent perspective and aspiration. You are shying away from these questions, and this only weakens you. You will have to thrash them out sooner or later.

Wurtzel: The New Left of today tends, perhaps reluctantly, to draw the battle lines at the oppressed minorities—oppressed racially and economically.

Deutscher: What is the meaning of "oppressed minorities"? Does this imply that the majority of this society is not oppressed? Do you consider the majority of the white workers in this country as not being oppressed?

Wurtzel: Yes, but there are different degrees of oppression.

Deutscher: In other words you appeal only to those minorities that suffer a kind of double or triple oppression. Obviously, these minorities respond more readily to any call for opposition to the powers that be. But no society has ever been changed when the movement for change could count only on minorities.

Davis: I see that the whole society feels oppressed, alienated, frustrated and dissatisfied with our distasteful and superficial culture.

Deutscher: You may not suspect it, but yours is in a way a very Marxist conception. Marx himself says that it is not only the worker's but also the capitalist's thinking and identity that gets distorted by the function he performs in society. There are passages in Marx in which he speaks, almost with compassion, about the capitalists who are also the victims of the system of which they themselves are agents. It is the system which makes both the oppressor and the oppressed a caricature of human beings. It is the basic material and political interest which causes the possessing classes to defend this system. The working classes may condone it, but they have no interest in maintaining it. They may help in this by a lack of comprehension and a false consciousness. However, by not making a distinction between the possessing and the non-possessing classes, between the worker and the shareholder, we are running away from realities.

Professor Leiman: We should perhaps keep in mind that there is an extremely high level of class consciousness in America—not, unfortunately, among the working classes but among the bourgeoisie. Let us assume for a moment that the New Left's aim is to change the present order in the socialist direction—and in this consists its link with the mainstream of radical thought of the thirties. There still remains a fundamental difference in the way of thought between the two movements. The radicals of the 1930s believed that the working class, aided of course by the intellectuals, perhaps even led by them, would be the decisive element of change. As I understand it, the New Left, which received most of its early impetus from C. Wright Mills, abandoned this notion. And they abandoned it on the "pragmatic" ground that the working class did not seem radically oriented. The whole militancy of the trade unions was directed towards securing higher wages and better conditions: it was a bread-and-butter struggle, not a class struggle. From this the New Left concluded—and here I am speaking about the position some ten years ago—that since reliance cannot be placed on the working class as the main agent of change, we have to rely on other groups. On which ones? On the intelligentsia? Perhaps on the Negroes?

Deutscher: I knew Wright Mills very well and my last discussions with him shortly before his death did center precisely on this issue: which force in society is to give effect to socialism? He did not believe the working class would bring about a socialist society. But Mills's concept of the elite as the main agent of change begged the question. An elite of what? Of whom? An elite does not exist in a vacuum. It is part of the society, it is part of a class. But Wright Mills had moved very close to a Marxist position in many respects. And one should not go back, so to speak, to an early Wright Mills instead of benefiting from his intellectual experience and development. One should start at least from where he ended, not from where he began. The concept of the elite as the main agent of socialism appeals to you because you think it frees you from the need to analyze the economic and class structure of society. It envelops the whole big mountain in a fog, with the peak—the elite—sticking out clearly for you to see. You maintain that your New Left corresponds in some respects to the left groups of the thirties, but you want to improve on their performance—and there is certainly room for improvement—but this does not mean that you have to reject their analysis of society, which is valid now just as it was valid in their time.

Davis: This economic and class analysis brings with itself a rigidity which the New Left wants to avoid. In the thirties there was a genuine opportunity for a real social revolution, but the left disintegrated as a result of ideological squabbles.

Deutscher: Here you are mistaken. The whole of history is full of "ideological squabbles." Over thousands of years people "squabbled" over matters of ideology. There is no end to the ideological divisions in Christianity, in the Reformation, in the Catholic church, in the Moslem religion, in the Jewish religion, and in the political parties. All human thinking and all human organization is subject to differentiation. Whether you like it or not, "squabbling" is the stuff of life; do not be contemptuous of it. What to you is squabbling is nothing else but differentiation in thinking. You saw that some groups differed in their views and ended in an impasse, and now you want to avoid their fate. First of all, you have to consider whether they reached a dead end because they differentiated in thinking or for some other reason. In my view, the left reached an impasse precisely because *it did not want* to debate the divergencies in aims openly and frankly. The Communist Party did not want to "squabble" with Roosevelt, and it supported fully and uncritically the New Deal. From Stalin's viewpoint—though not from the viewpoint of the American left—there were good reasons for that "peaceful coexistence." The members of the CP from Marxists became Rooseveltians. Then the Communists did not want to "squabble" with Stalin, to criticize his policy, and therefore they allowed themselves to be turned into mere stooges of Stalin's policy. In this way they committed moral and political suicide. They did not want to "squabble" with Stalin, nor with Roosevelt—and you will not be much wiser if you too shun ideological debate.

Davis: Why do you think there has to be a strict ideological foundation before the New Left can start being active? Can't ideology develop out of action?

Deutscher: I am not saying that you should not be active right now. I started from the assumption that socialist and nonsocialist radicals should cooperate in the New Left for definite purposes. You need not necessarily agree on all the issues with the fellow who marches next to you in demonstrations against the war in Vietnam. This we took for granted right at the beginning of our discussion. But before the Vietnam war we had the Korean war, and before that the Suez war. Is it not likely that we shall have another war after Vietnam? After all, we are students, so-called intellectuals; we are not interested only in our next anti-war demonstration. We are also interested in principles and prospects. Whither are we going? In what direction? Korea, Suez, Vietnam, civil rights, racial problems, dissatisfaction with our complacent consumer society: are all these not only part of a much bigger issue with which we ought to be concerned?

I am not a little uneasy about another aspect of the New Left. The New Left is confined mostly to students and intellectuals. I derive great satisfaction from our meetings. Only a few years ago, during my previous visits to the USA, I had no common language with university youth. They were either indifferent to political and social affairs or highly reactionary and chauvinistic. Today I have much sympathy for students of your age group, but I am worried about the confusion in your minds and about your conceit, and about your shirking the really great issues, and also about your isolation from your society. You sow your wild oats within the campus, but you have no missionary zeal to carry your message to people outside the campus.

What in fact is the campus? It is only a bus in which you spend three, four or five years; then you take your final exams, you get off, and look round for a job. New people get on the bus. One can, in the company of fellow travelers on the bus, be very radical. But after all, you are not going to solve the problems of your society on the journey between two bus stops. Any political movement which bases itself only on students is characterized by a basic political and moral instability. The students now play a very big role in various countries all over the world. Don't forget that behind the slaughter of several hundred thousand unarmed and defenseless communists, men, women, and children, in Indonesia, the driving force was the students. In this country the students are, from my point of view, on the right side of the barricades. But I remember also a time when the students were in the vanguard of fascist movements in Europe. I remember the students in my native country who vented all their political energy on forcing through the segregation of the Jews in the University of Warsaw. The role of students is transient. They are not a stable element in society; they are, if you allow me to use this despised term, ideologically unstable. Students can be very good vanguards of fascism or very good vanguards of the New Left, or even very good vanguards of communism in some circumstances. I am uneasy because I knew your predecessors—those who either favored McCarthyism or viewed it indifferently. And I do not know those who will come after you onto the same campuses. I am concerned with moral and political continuity in the development of any given society.

Your present broadly based cooperation on the campus gives you the illusion of being self-sufficient. How much continuity and stability is there in your opposition to the treatment of the Negroes, to imperialist wars abroad, to the violation of civil rights? As long as this opposition is not based on a stable class in society (I shall explain what I mean by a stable class in society), it is largely ineffective, no matter how important it is at the present moment. Have you asked yourselves why you are so ineffective? Precisely because you are active within the confines of the campus and during the short spell of your university "bus ride." You will soon disperse and, so to speak, dissolve in your bourgeois milieu: you will have your families, your jobs, your careers, to look after. Now you are unattached—you are like kites that fly into the sky without any ropes tying them to the earth. Very soon you will feel the rope. You do not express just your own particular moods; you express the mood of your class in opposition to your class. Unlike your parents, who are tied down by moral commitments and conventionalities, you are unattached and express strongly, volubly and loudly all the disgruntlement and frustration which at heart your own parents feel (even if they will not admit it to you). When you say that you do not believe in the workers being capable of bringing about the change in the present unsatisfactory order of society, you really vent nothing but your parents' lower -middle- class (or middle-middle-class) attitude towards the workers.

Davis: But the trade unions in America today are just interested in a ten-cent-an-hour wage increase. The only radical group the New Left appeals to is the lumpenproletariat.

Deutscher: Lumpenproletarians don't change society. If the basic classes change society, then the lumpenproletarians may follow them. But when I speak of the working class, I do not have in mind the trade unions, which are only a bureaucratic outgrowth of the working class. I do not even have in mind the older workers, who have been corrupted and demoralized by this society and are the victims of this society. They remember how desperately badly off they were in the thirties. Now they are a little better off, so they gaze at their televisions and ride in their cars. But these crumbs from the table of the affluent society do not satisfy you and they do not satisfy the young workers. Have you tried to talk to them? How do you know that they are not as disgruntled as you are? As disappointed and frustrated as you are, only with far deeper wounds hidden in them? You start from the premise that because you are on the campus you are intelligent, sensitive, the *Schöngeist* who really sees how bad this society is:

and you think the boy who spends his life at the most monotonous dehumanizing job at the conveyor belt does not see this?

You are frustrated by the ineffectual character of your opposition to the things you loathe. Why is your opposition ineffectual? You are intellectuals, and your main weapon is the word. Your protest cannot be anything else but verbal, and verbal protest wears itself out by repetition and does not lead you anywhere. In order that a protest should be effective, it must be anchored in the realities of social life, in the productive process of a nation. Forty-odd years ago the dockers of London went on strike against the British government and refused to load munitions for the White Armies fighting against the Russian Revolution. You cannot strike and refuse to load munitions sent to Vietnam. Here the Marxist concept may be useful in explaining your own position. You are outside the productive process. You are confined to verbal protest—and this is important. "In the beginning was the word." You should go on with your protest, but it will be effective only if it can pass from the word to the deed. You are not capable of the deed, but the young worker is— provided you move him—because he *is* right in the middle of the productive process that sustains the existence of society. You are effervescently active on the margin of social life, and the workers are passive right at the core of it. That is the tragedy of our society. If you do not deal with this contrast, you will be defeated.

The other group of people with whom you work, and should continue to work, the Negroes, are also a minority on the margin of the process of production. Their possibilities are also marginal and verbal; and I am not sure that they don't talk often in racial terms instead of class terms. Just as the contrast between your activity and the passivity of the white worker is one of the incongruities of your social life, so there is another incongruity between the isolated activity of the Negro and the indifference of the white worker.

Davis: We are all too aware that the campus is not society. But we still need techniques more than we need general over-all ideological pronouncements.

Deutscher: No one can prescribe "techniques" for you. Try to establish a spiritual and intellectual contact with those young workers who are inclined to think, who can read popular books about social affairs and want to understand what is going on around them. We shall then reopen the discussion on the "agents of change" in your society. In the Russian Revolution the students played an important part: they were the messengers who carried the idea of socialism out of the university halls to all classes of society and especially to the working class; and in this they proved both valuable and effective.

My criticism of the New Left is caused precisely by the anxiety that so much idealism, fervor and good intentions may be wasted if the New Left fails to find its correct way and direction. You have a link and you want to break with the left of the thirties; but you still have a great deal to learn from them. And, first of all, you cannot run away from the fundamental problems of society. Those very rudimentary Marxists of the thirties learned no more than the ABC of Marxism. Then came Stalin and turned the ABC into hiero-glyphs. But Marxism still is a great store of knowledge, which you will be ill-advised to ignore. In the last two or three hundred years of world history was not Karl Marx the most influential thinker? Whose work has had a greater impact than his? All your mass media, which work full steam to dull your wits and stultify your mind (and which are so distaste-ful to you), drum into your head that Marxism is obsolete; and ninety-nine percent of the New Left takes on a super-cilious attitude and echoes: "Marxism is obsolete." And yet, if I may paraphrase a popular English saying: never have so many talked so much about a thing they knew so little. You do not have to accept Marx, but before you reject his ideas you should read him, acquire the knowledge, and then think independently. And there is no need to be too utilitarian and "apply" Marx to the United States, or to Europe, or to Russia.

Davis: The New Left has the feeling that Marxism was corrupted, and this revulsion is caused not only by the Russian experience.

Deutscher: It is precisely the Marxist method that will help you in analyzing your revulsion against Marxism as it has been "applied" hitherto. Stalinism was not "contained" in Russia; it had its unfortunate impact on the labor movement in your country, and it distorted the beginnings of growth of Marxism here as elsewhere. Your earlier American Marxists were not perhaps as creative and inspiring as those that Russia, Poland or Germany produced. But if you read their old writings, you will still find a great deal of ideas which illuminate the present-day American scene. America has its own tradition of socialist thought; nothing in history begins *ex nihilo*, and the world does not begin with the New Left. Half a century ago there were also young people in revolt, and you have no lack of revolutionary tradition to link up with. But every reaction against tradition is also linking up with it.

Your predecessors of half a century ago had to contend with a society in full dynamic capitalist expansion, while you are witnessing a degenerate capitalism which can expand as imperialism only. You are also aware of another paradox of your society: the more it expands economically, the more, in a sense, it seems to shrink culturally. And you are just as impatient and disgusted with the poverty amidst plenty as you are with the complacency and self-satisfaction of the gadget-minded, acquisitive bourgeoisie. But do not delude yourselves that your aim—"participatory democracy," or, as you yourselves put it, "that each individual should have a say in the decision-making process"—is anything more than a vague and meaningless slogan. It implies that you want to participate in the management of society as it is; but the society as it is excludes you from participation by definition. For this, a new form of society is needed. And when you proclaim the end of ideology you also implicitly accept the dominant ideology of the very society which excludes you from participation, the very society against which you are in revolt.

marxism and
nonviolence

*In 1966, shortly after he spoke at the second Vietnam Day
rally in Berkeley, Isaac Deutscher participated in a discussion
on Marxism and nonviolence organized by Dave Dellinger.
The following is taken from a transcription of the discussion
originally published in the July 1969 issue of* Liberation. *The
other participants were Dellinger, the late A. J. Muste, and
Hans Konigsberger.*

Dave Dellinger: I operate on the theory that nonviolence is
not sufficiently developed yet, that it can't be fully appraised
or understood in its present form as revealing of the true
potential of nonviolence. I think the same thing can be said
of socialism at a certain stage; there was the pre-Marxian
stage of Christian Socialism and various forms of what is
called romantic socialism. Socialism has been going through a
gradual sophistication and process of maturation. I think the
same thing has to happen in relation to nonviolence, but that
unfortunately revolutionary Marxists have had a tendency to

discard nonviolence as a revolutionary weapon, based on its earliest and most primitive formulations.

There has been a transition from nonviolence as either a symbolic witness or as the special vocation of a small group of people somewhat set apart from the rest of society by their religious training, to the kind of nonviolence which has the determination to change history, to actually change events, a determination which is as strong and as dominating as the revolutionary impulses of non-pacifist revolutionaries of the past. . . .

In this respect I like to think in terms of the dialectic, at least in my limited understanding of it. The old-fashioned nonviolence of nonresistance, perhaps inadequate preoccupation with institutional violence, I think of that as the thesis. The anti-Nazi resistance movement during World War II, the guerrilla movement in Cuba of the Fidelistas, the heroic resistance in Vietnam today, I think of that as the antithesis. What I would like to have us consider is the possibility that there is a synthesis that will be something new that we've had hints of but has really not been developed. Guerrilla warfare rests on an identification with the population of the country that is conducting the resistance, and that identification is not a facile or a facetious thing; it's something that stems from an identification with the aspirations for liberation, dignity, justice of the country. This is an example of one of the things that has come out of the synthesis. On the other hand, nonviolence has a deep and universal humanism which is also characteristic of historical, not-nonviolent revolution at its best, but which tends to be betrayed and squeezed out in the course of the actual conflict. I think we've learned that anything that looks on the class enemy or the institutional enemy as also the human enemy tends to lead to internal corruption and a cumulative deterioration within the movement of its original idealism and its original methodology.

I have one other example. Isaac Deutscher, when he spoke at Berkeley recently of the negative effects of the present conflict in Vietnam within the Communist world, indicated that although the de-Stalinization process has not been totally lost, it has nonetheless been halted or possibly even set in reverse a little bit. He spoke of the fact that in fighting supposedly for freedom in Vietnam, one of the indirect effects has been to encourage the throttling of freedom within the Communist world. I think this stems from the fear and from the reaction of like producing like, violence and hatred and distrust producing violence and hatred and distrust, and I wonder why it isn't equally true that even the most idealistic revolutionary movements who rely on hatred and violence provoke a similar misunderstanding, a similar fear, a similar hysteria in the opposition so that there is again this cumulative effect and we actually antagonize the people it is our job to win over. . . .

Isaac Deutscher: I must admit that talk about the challenge of nonviolence tends at the beginning to stare at all my deep-seated Marxist bias against this kind of argument. I am at once aroused to suspect some wishy-washy idealistic generalizations that lead us politically, analytically and morally nowhere. But as I listen to your argument I become increasingly aware that my bias is directed against an opponent who doesn't stand in front of me at all; my bias is directed against the escapism of absolute pacifism. Even against the high principles of absolute pacifism it is difficult to argue without feeling a certain moral embarrassment, because one would like the absolute pacifist who denies absolutely any positive role of violence in history to be right. And yet one knows that he isn't right and that this is a very dangerous escapism. Therefore, one tends to react, if one is a Marxist, with a certain venom. But you are not romantic creatures of nonviolence. To my mind, and I hesitate to use strong words, you have taken a heroic stand over the war in Vietnam. When you started your protest you could not have foreseen that you would be backed by such wide popular response: you have taken great risks in order to express not only your opposition to the violence used by American power, by

American imperialism, but also to defend to some extent, morally, the violence to which the Vietnamese have to resort in order to save their own dignity, their own interests, their own present and their own future.

One might say that there is an inconsistency in your attitude, a contradiction in your preaching nonviolence and yet accepting morally to some extent the violence applied by the Viet Cong in Vietnam and probably by the FLN in Algeria. But I think that this is a creative inconsistency, a creative contradiction in your attitude. Although you start from an idealistic and to my mind somewhat metaphysical principle, nevertheless your inconsistency opens for you an important horizon into the realities of our age. I think that you are carrying out something like truthful self-criticism. It is the self-criticism of a variety of pacifism which is not afraid of bringing its own apparent formal inconsistency into the open in order to achieve a greater moral and political consistency in action. And may I say that arguing philosophically from places partly opposed, I admit a similar, but a much larger, perhaps a more tragic inconsistency in the history of revolution, in the history of communism and Marxism.

The fact is that there is a whole dialectic of violence and nonviolence implied in the Marxist doctrine from its beginnings and throughout all its historic metamorphosis from 1848 to 1966. As Marxists we have always preached proletarian dictatorship, and the need to overthrow capitalism by force. We have always tried to impress on the working classes of all countries that they would have to be prepared to struggle, even in civil wars, against their oppressing and ruling classes. We were quite devastating in our rejoinders to all those who doubted the right or questioned the need for all those preachings. But here is the dialectical contradiction; after all, what has been the idea of Marxism? That of the classless society in which man is no longer exploited and dominated by man, a stateless society. So many people of the left consider this the utopian element in Marxism, the aspiration to transform societies in such a way that violence should cease forever as the necessary and permanent element in the regulation of the relationship between society and individuals, between individuals and individuals.

In embracing the vision of a nonviolent society, Marxism, I maintain, has gone further and deeper than any pacifist preachers of nonviolence have ever done. Why? Because Marxism laid bare the roots of violence in our society, which the others have not done. Marxism has set out to attack those roots; to uproot violence not just from human thoughts, not just from human emotions, but to uproot it from the very bases of the material existence of society. Marxism has seen violence fed by class antagonism in society—and here Marxism should be assessed against the two-thousand-year record of futile Christian preaching of nonviolence. I say futile in the sense that it has led to no real consequences, to no real diminution of violence. After two millenia of "love thy brother" we are in this situation: that those who go to church throw the napalm bombs and the others who were also brought up in a Christian tradition, the Nazis, have sent six million descendants of Christ's countrymen to the gas chambers. After two millenia the preaching of nonviolence has led to this! One of the reasons for this is that the roots of violence have never been attacked, never been dug up. Class society has persisted and therefore these preachings, even when most sincere, even when the Christian teacher put both his heart and soul in them, were bound to be futile, because they attacked only the surface of the nonviolence. But then the dialectic of Marxism has also been at fault—Marxism itself, thoughout its history of deep and tragic contradictions. How strong the dream of nonviolence lay at the root of the Russian Revolution one can find out if one studies Lenin's statement on revolution, which is written in outwardly a very dogmatic form, almost like an ecclesiastical text interpreting Biblical verses. Behind these somewhat ecclesiastical formulas there is the dream of the stateless society constantly welling up. The October insurrection was carried out in such a way that, according to all the hostile eyewitnesses (such as the

Western ambassadors who were then in Petrograd), the total number of victims on all sides was ten. That is the total number of victims of that great revolutionary October insurrection. The men who directed this insurrection—Lenin, Trotsky, the members of the military revolutionary committee—gave some thought to the question of violence and nonviolence and organized this tremendous upheaval with a very profound although unspoken concern for human lives, for the lives of their enemies as well as for their own people. The Russian Revolution, in the name of which so much violence has been committed, was the most nonviolent act of this scale in the whole history of the human race!

The revolution was won not with guns, but with words, with argument, persuasion. The words were very violent, the words were terribly forceful, but this is the violence of emotion in the revolt against the actuality of violence, of a world war which cost millions of human beings. All those people nowadays who take it upon themselves to preach morality to the makers of the Russian Revolution assume, of course, that there was a kind of good and angelic status quo, an angelic nonviolence which was upset by those Dostoevskian possessed fiends the revolutionaries, who appropriated to themselves the right to dispose of human lives. Nearly ten million people had perished in the trenches of the First World War when the Bolsheviks carried out that great revolution which cost ten victims.

The deep universal humanism inherent in what you call the challenge of nonviolence has been there in Marxism as its most essential element. We were a little more shy about talking about humanism; we are more shy about this because what scoundrel in history hasn't spoken about humanism—hasn't Stalin, hasn't Hitler, hasn't Goebbels? I always get more than a little shocked when I hear leftwingers and ex-Marxists suggest that Marxism needs to be supplemented by humanism. Marxism only needs to be true to itself.

But what happened really after this very promising beginning of the Russian Revolution, after Lenin had written

The State and Revolution, which is the great revolutionary dream about nonviolence expressed in Marxist terms, what happened? The others who preached nonviolence, for instance Kerensky, preached nonviolence to the oppressed by reintroducing the death penalty for soldiers who were refusing to fight on the front. Perhaps in the nature of people who really detest violence there is a greater shyness about speaking about nonviolence. I distrust those who have so many noble words on their lips. I very often trust more those who speak frankly and even brutally about the necessities of the political struggle as long as they don't get carried away by their own righteousness.

Then came the intervention, the civil war. Violence had to be used on an increasing scale, just as the Viet Cong today have to use violence on an increasing scale. They can't help it; either they go under or they use the violence. But even in the civil war what did the Bolsheviks do? Again they tried to keep a balance between argument, persuasion and violence; a balance in which they still attached far greater importance to persuasion and argument than to the gun. In sheer arms they were infinitely inferior to the British, the French, and the Americans (who sent both troops and munitions for the White armies in Russia). The Red army, led by Trotsky, at that time was far inferior. What happened? They agitated, they appealed to the consciousness of the soldiers, of the workers in uniform in those interventionist armies. The French navy, sent to suppress the revolution, rose in mutiny in Odessa and refused to fight against the Bolsheviks: another triumph of nonviolence in the civil war. This revolt of the sailors was the result of what was called Bolshevik propaganda, but this "subversion" prevented violence. (In Britain in 1920 during the intervention, during the Russo-Polish war, the dockers of London struck and refused to send arms against Russia and the docks of London were immobilized—this was nonviolence.)

Then comes the great tragedy of the isolation of the Russian Revolution; of its succumbing to incredible, unimaginable destruction, poverty, hunger, and disease as a result of the wars of intervention, the civil wars, and of course the long and exhausting world war which was not of Bolshevik making. As a result of all this, terror was let loose in Russia. Men lost their balance. They lost, even the leaders, the clarity of their thinking and of their minds. They acted under overwhelming and inhuman pressures. I don't undertake to judge them, to blame them or to justify them. I can only see the deep tragedy of this historic process, the result of which was the glorification of violence.

But what was to have been but a glassful of violence became buckets and buckets full, and then rivers of violence. That is the tragedy of the Russian Revolution. The dialectics of violence and nonviolence in Marxism were so upset that in the end the nonviolent meaning of Marxism was suppressed under the massive, crushing weight of Stalinism. It wasn't a matter of chance that Stalin implicitly denounced the Leninist and Marxist idea of the withering away of the state. It was in that idea that the whole Marxist nonviolence was epitomized. The Stalinist regime couldn't tolerate, couldn't bear the survival of that dream. It had to crush it out of human minds in order to justify its own violence. I'm not saying this to blame the whole thing on single individuals. It was more than that. It was the tragedy of an isolated and poverty-ridden revolution incapable of fulfilling its promise in isolation and poverty: a revolution caught in this tragic situation—of the irreconcilable contradiction between promise and fulfillment, between dream and reality, sunk into irrationality.

To what extent is Marxism, as such, responsible for this? It would be wrong to identify Stalinism with Marxism, and to blame Marxism for the things that have been done under Stalinism. On the other hand, it would show a lack of moral courage in Marxism to draw the formal line of dissociation and say that we are not responsible for Stalinism, that that wasn't what we aimed at. You see, in a way Marxism is as responsible for Stalin as Christianity was responsible for the Borgias. The Borgias are not Christianity, but Christianity cannot bleach the Borgias from its records. We cannot delete Stalinism from our records although we are not responsible for Stalinist crimes. To some extent we (and when I say we I mean that generation of Marxists with which I as an individual identify morally, I mean Lenin, Trotsky, Bukharin, Zinoviev, the early Communist leaders in Europe) participated in this glorification of violence as a self-defense mechanism. Rosa Luxemburg understood this when she criticized the first faint signs of this attitude.

But the issue is larger and deeper than just human intentions. The violence isn't rooted in human intentions. The human intentions are, shall we say, the mechanism, the psychological, the ideal mechanism through which material factors and material necessities transmit their pressures. Marxism had not made any allowances for the possibility of such tremendous outgrowth of violence, of such tremendous abuse of violence that would be done in the name of Marxism, for a simple reason. Marxism assumed that revolution would always be an act of change in society carried out violently, but with the support of immense popular majorities. It assumed revolution in an industrialized West carried out by working classes committed to socialism, supporting the revolution with all their heart and confronting as their enemies a really small minority consisting of the exploiters. In such a confrontation of revolutionary majorities with counter-revolutionary minorities, the need to use violence would indeed have been very limited and the dream of nonviolence would have had all this hope for fulfillment.

It is said that Marxism suits the underdeveloped countries but not the advanced and industrial West. I still maintain that the original dream of Marxism and the real original inspiration and hope of Marxism still suits the industrial West much better than it can suit the underdeveloped countries, even if revolution in certain phases is the job of great majorities as it was in Russia in 1917, as it was in China in 1949, as it is in Vietnam today. In underdeveloped countries there comes a moment after the revolution when again there is a breach between promise and fulfillment. Therefore there come frustrations, explosive dissonances and the desire of the postrevolutionary rulers to secure the revolution as they understand it and are able to secure it. The more underdeveloped the country, the more bound to come, after the revolution, a moment of bitter truth and violence.

However, I think that the violence in China already is much smaller than it was in Russia. The irrationality of the Chinese Revolution, though goodness knows there is a lot of irrationality, so far is much less, I think, than what came to the top in the Russian Revolution. But then the Chinese Revolution wasn't the first pioneer, wasn't the *isolated* revolution: it was already assisted by Stalinist Russia, and this reduced the amount of irrationality. I think that with the spread of revolution, with the advance of the industrial and technological aspects of revolutionary societies, with the growth of their wealth, with the rising in their standards of living, with a relative contentment in the popular masses, the irrational element will decrease. The final vindication of the dream of nonviolence in Marxism will come with socialism gaining the advanced countries. That is my belief, and it is not a belief of wishful thinking; it is the whole theoretical structure of Marxism that leads me to this conclusion. I think that the de-Stalinization carried out in Russia, partial, self-contradictory, inadequate, hypocritical as it has been, has already somewhat re-established the balance between the contradictory elements in the Russian Revolution by reducing the violence and giving more scope to the nonviolent element in Marxism.

You have asked me what I meant when I spoke about the negative effect on the Communist World of the war in Vietnam. The war in Vietnam may or may not be a prelude to new confrontations of violence surging back from the Western world and flooding the world again. The fear of the ultimate violence promotes a recrudescence of the authoritarian and violent trend within Russia and in China. I made an analogy between the effects of the Vietnamese War in the

Communist part of the world and the repercussions of the Korean War in the last years of Stalin's era. The fears and panics let loose by the Korean War expressed themselves in Russia in the insanity of Stalin's rule in the last years, in the repetition of the witches' sabbath of the thirties. I don't foresee and I'm not afraid of something as terrible as that in Russia in response to the American aggression in Vietnam, but we have already seen some recrudescence of the authoritarian trend. The Twenty-third Congress of the Communist Party testifies to this. The trials of Daniel and Sinyavsky were symptomatic of the partial return of the authoritarian trend.

On the other hand I don't think that one can say that the Korean War had only one effect, i.e., the encouragement of domestic violence in the Soviet Union and China. It also had a positive effect parallel to the effect that it had in our part of the world. It gave one a sense of human solidarity with a small nation so ruthlessly attacked, so ruthlessly crushed by the most powerful, the greatest, the richest nations in the world. The Korean War disposed of certain illusions which Khrushchevism spread; namely, the illusion about the possibility of the peaceful transition from capitalism to socialism in such countries as France or Italy. Try to go now to French and Italian workers and tell them that they can accomplish this miracle when in such small nations as Korea and Vietnam it is so resisted by the great capitalist powers.

A. J. Muste: . . . A question that gives me problems and which you have left in an overview is the tragedy of the Marxist movement in its orgies of terror and violence in the Soviet Union and Eastern Europe, under Stalin. It seems to me that the great tragedies of which we must be aware should actually be the Soviet Union and the United States. But there is something that needs further analysis in order that, given the example of the communism in the Soviet Union, those of us who are revolutionaries may guard ourselves against going further in that kind of evolution of violence. In the second place we must ask whether in the concept of nonviolence there are other forms of force than military forms. This means guarding against accommodation with a system whose very essence is violence, even in so-called peacetime. Now on my part, I am constantly frustrated in trying to know what we should think when we think about nonviolent revolution. What do we do if concretely we are in Vietnam? Are there concrete ways of struggle other than those used by the Vietnamese? I think we have only an elementary concept of nonviolent force as a constant in struggle with the arms of imperialism, which is a very reactionary force. I think there is no room for compromise but I think we do have suggestions on how perhaps to avoid what happened in the Soviet Union in this country. . . .

Deutscher: We have to make known the long, terrible road leading us to classless society. You speak as if we stood already on the threshold of a classless society. You see it's so easy to make the slogan of nonviolence an escapism; so easy to overlook the realities of this long road, and on this road we shall live with violence, and if we are socialists we shall use violence.

My point is this. As Marxists, whenever we are driven to use violence what we must know and tell those people whom we shall call to act, is that violence is a necessary evil. And the emphasis will be on both the adjective and the noun, on the necessary and on evil. To preach nonviolence to those always the object of violence may even be false. I say the lesson we should learn from Soviet history is that we can't overemphasize the evil of violence. But if I were a Vietnamese and also in the ranks of the Viet Cong I would try to tell my comrades in arms we should not make a virtue of the bitter and terrible necessity of violence. But we are acting in the West—where this argument has much more chance of being understood and accepted.

On the Left in the West we must foster a way of thinking which would not shirk realities. We have in front of us— and this is where Marxism parts from anarchism and pure pacifism—we share with anarchists the dream of a stateless society, but we ask: how do you arrive at it? You accept the view that the Vietnamese war is not an accident of history; that it expresses the structure of your society, expresses the imperialist character in your relationship to the outside world. If you accept this, you imply that the social order has to be changed. How is it to be changed? How is it going to be changed by nonviolent methods when those who refuse to move an inch in Vietnam to their class enemies—will they yield the territory of the United States to socialism without defending the status quo? Can you imagine this? I can, but only under one condition. That is when you have the overwhelming number of Americans ready to use violence in order to bring about socialism, only then may socialism conquer the United States without the use of violence. The capital of the revolution was its moral supremacy. You see, if you achieve for socialism a moral supremacy in American society comparable to that of the Russian Revolution, then you might have to use only an infinitesimal amount of violence. But—here again is the dialectic—only if you're ready to use violence without making a virtue of it.

on internationals and internationalism

More than a century has passed since the foundation of the First International; over sixty years ago the Second International, which collapsed so ignominiously, was founded; and it is nearly half a century since the Third International constituted itself. I should like to consider here the role of these three Internationals and the relevance and vitality of the basic idea which, in their best periods, inspired them all—the idea of internationalism. My theme therefore is the fortunes (or misfortunes) of the Internationals and the relevance of internationalism. I want to concentrate especially on one crucial problem: the interplay and the conflict between nationalism and internationalism throughout the whole history of the modern labor movement.

The First International was founded here in London on the initiative of British and French socialists. Their great concern was to establish some cooperation and solidarity

This is the transcript of a lecture given in October 1964 at University College, London.

between working men in France and Britain in order that they should be able to defend themselves against the import of cheap Belgian, Italian and German labor. They had to protect themselves too against strike-breaking action organized by international capital. Such was the prosaic origin of the Working Men's Association, that great legendary, almost poetic International, which established the tradition of an internationally organized working-class movement.

The origins of the International were, one might say, almost trade unionist in the narrow meaning of the word. But among the small group of men sitting on the platform at that memorable meeting in St. Martin's Hall here in London, in the last week of September 1864, was one man whose genius put its stamp on the whole enterprise and raised it to a much higher level than, judging by its origin, it would have ever attained. That man was Karl Marx. He wrote the inaugural address to the International Association of Working Men and also the rules of that new organization.

There was also another curious circumstance: the organization was founded in order to proclaim the idea of internationalism and the need for international solidarity among the workers. But the immediate reason for the gathering of delegates at St. Martin's Hall, the immediate issue which was eloquently debated there, was the support of, and solidarity with, one nation fighting not for socialism, not even for any progressive political reform, but for its very independence. The meeting was called to express the solidarity of Western working classes with the armed rising of the Poles against tsarist Russia. Here lies the apparent paradox of the whole situation: the issue that excites the passions and the enthusiasm of the First International is a national issue, a struggle of a very remote people of Eastern Europe for its national existence. Right at the birth of the new international organization we are confronted with the interplay of internationalism and nationalism in the labor movement.

The First International was not, in reality, the first attempt to create an international organization. One should not forget that already the *Communist Manifesto*, written jointly by Marx and Engels in 1848, had ended with the memorable call: workers of the world, unite! Various working class circles, associations, and propagandist groups had for decades tried to establish some sort of international link between each other. Not much came out of these strivings. And after the collapse of the 1848 revolution fifteen years had passed during which the labor movement was in the doldrums, or rather in that state of deep depression and demoralization which usually follows upon the wake of defeat. The idea of internationalism had, nevertheless, been deeply rooted already in the socialist consciousness. I shall come back to this later. For the moment let us look a little longer at the background to the formation of the First International.

Since the defeat of the revolution in Europe, capitalism, which meant almost exclusively Western European capitalism, had gone through a period of extraordinary development and progress. In the year when the First International was founded, the British chancellor of the exchequer, Gladstone, spoke about this "intoxicating growth and augmentation of all our wealth and power." Reading that speech one almost has the impression that these are the words of a Tory or a right-wing Labour politician proclaiming in 1962 or 1963, "We never had it so good! What tremendous progress our welfare state has made, how outdated are all the revolutionary ideas about class struggle!" And so on and so on.

Such was the mood in Western Europe around the year 1860. The labor movement had not recovered from its defeat of 1848–49; but then suddenly, in 1864, new stirrings made themselves felt in England, in France, and, to a lesser extent, in other countries of Western Europe. We find some echoes of this new mood in the correspondence of Marx and Engels and their friends, but if one were to judge the circumstances of the foundation of the International by the remarks and allusions contained in these letters, one would come to the conclusion that the whole enterprise looked like an interesting but relatively modest incident in the political life of certain European émigrés in London in contact with some representatives of various continental labor groupings.

Marx joined the movement with some reluctance; he did not want to get involved with the various small sects and circles of agitators active in London in those days. He still remembered his exasperation at the bickerings of his fellow émigrés, and Engels's words, valid when they were written in 1851, held good more than a decade later: "How do people like us, who flee official positions like the plague, fit into a party?" Marx preferred at that time to concentrate on his work, on *Das Kapital*, which he rightly considered as being much more important. But in September, 1864, when a group of French workers came to London to appeal to their British comrades for a common defense against their bourgeoisie, he was greatly impressed both by their élan and by their determination; he became drawn into the movement and gave to it a tremendous intellectual impulse. Marx's internationalism had a greater depth than the internationalism of the other participants.

Socialist internationalism sprang from two sources: one was the practical experience of the workers who felt that they had to cooperate with each other across frontiers and boundaries in order to defend their interests, their wages, and their working conditions. The day-to-day experience of a man standing at the factory bench next to a foreigner who, often through necessity, undersold his labor, brought an understanding of common interests, an instinctive kind of internationalism. On a different plane, however, the history of political ideas in Europe provides another source of socialist internationalism, one that links up, as it were, with the bourgeois cosmopolitanism of the French revolution and of the various bourgeois political movements that followed in its wake.

There is a historical affinity between bourgeois cosmopolitanism and what we call proletarian internationalism; paradoxically that affinity does not rule out, but in fact presupposes, also a conflict between the two. *Egalité, Fraternité, Liberté*, which were supposed to exist between individual Frenchmen, were projected, so to speak, onto the European scene and appeared there as the equality and fraternity of the nations. But in bourgeois society this equality between individuals turned out to be only formal and legal, not social and economic. The French bourgeois and the French worker were equal "before the law"—they were granted the same formal rights. Of this equality Anatole France once said: "In its majesty the law of the French Republic allows neither the millionaire Rothschild nor the Paris *clochard* [beggar] to sleep under the bridges of the Seine."

Cosmopolitan bourgeois equality between nations was similarly formal. The free trader, the importer and exporter, the seller and the buyer of any country had equal rights on the international market. That concept had some meaning for the bourgeoisie of highly developed industrial countries. But what sort of genuine equality was there between "the workshop of the world" and the primitive and colonial countries, between the strong and the weak—between the Rothschilds and the *clochards* of the world—where the trade works always to the profit of the strong and to the detriment of the weak?

Nevertheless, the call for equality and fraternity prompted people to look deeper and to advance from the demand for formal legal equality to the demand for economic and social equality. The proclamation of bourgeois cosmopolitanism of the early nineteenth century also led many thinkers—in the first instance, Marx and Engels—to stress all the implications of the idea and to carry it to its logical conclusion: from the cosmopolitanism of the free traders of bourgeois nations they moved on to the socialist internationalism of the proletariat.

Behind the cosmopolitanism of the bourgeoisie there always loomed the reality of competition between the traders of various nations. In the ranks of the proletariat there went on an incessant competition and scramble for jobs. The bourgeois trader was fighting for markets and underselling his commodities; the workers were jostling each other for a place at the factory bench and were underselling their labor. Marx and Engels were well aware of this very real and unedifying element in the existence of the working classes in a society where competition permeated every aspect of social life. This strife would end only with the abolition of private property in the means of production—that is, with the abolition of capitalism. The aim of the modern labor movement was to curb the competitiveness of the workers, to bring under control that individualism which made them an easy prey for capitalist exploitation. The aim of the labor movement was to instill in the workers the sense of solidarity which would benefit them all as a class. That was the origin of the trade unions, the origin of modern socialism, and also the origin of the International. "Workers of the world, unite!" was nothing else but a call to eliminate harmful competition between workers within each country and to eliminate it also on an international scale. From this point of view nationalism was, in the first instance, the workers' self-destructive competitiveness; internationalism was their solidarity transcending national boundaries.

In that sense, socialist internationalism developed from the cosmopolitanism of the trader; but it also surpassed that cosmopolitanism, overcame its limitations, and, finally, became its negation; socialist internationalism stood in opposition to the bourgeois cosmopolitanism.

I have said that Marxist internationalism had its roots in bourgeois cosmopolitanism, and these roots went quite deep. Already in the *Communist Manifesto*, in 1848, Marx described with unmistakable enthusiasm the progressive aspect of capitalism. By creating a world market, by breaking down or transcending regional, feudal, or national boundaries of separate economic units, by enlarging the horizon of the bourgeoisie, capitalism also enlarged the horizon of other classes of society. International trade, which expanded so startlingly with the development of nineteenth-century capitalism, here demonstrated its progressive features. From this Marx concluded that socialism would go much further beyond the national economies than capitalism ever could go; it would create an international economy and a society planning and rationalizing its own needs, its own production and consumption, on an international scale. Already at the end of the eighteenth century Adam Smith listed from how many various countries came the goods that an Englishman (or a Scotsman) found on his breakfast table; already then an international division of labor was required to lay one table for one hearty meal. How much greater, how much vaster, how much more grandiose would be the division of labor attending the development of socialism, a division of labor which would indeed encompass the globe and mankind. What Marx in fact proclaimed was the end of the nation-state. He did not envisage it in terms of a political reality of his century, but he had that broad vision of an emerging new international society that would, of necessity, break down the constricting barriers and national frontiers.

And here again we see this apparent paradox: the First International, in whose inaugural address Marx proclaimed the future advent of that international society, was nevertheless convened in order to express sympathy with the struggle of the Poles to recreate their own independent nation-state On the one hand the International proclaimed the anachronism—the decay and death—of the national state, on the other it demanded the creation and independence of a new state. And it was not only the fate of Poland which presented itself in these terms; Germany was fighting for its national unification, for the fusion of the dozens and dozens of its principalities, for the overcoming of the division between Hapsburg-ruled and Hohenzollern-ruled Germany; Italy was fighting for its national independence and unity; not to speak of the other small nations in eastern and southeastern Europe. In a vast part of the continent a struggle was indeed going on for the achievement of independent statehood and nationhood. This apparent paradox finds its explanation in the fact that Marx, Engels and the socialists of their generation took it for granted that an international socialist community could not be created otherwise than by the free will of the peoples constituting it; it was through their independence, through their freedom from oppression, through the fulfillment of their national aspirations that the road to an international society lay. Only those free to create their own state can freely—not forcibly—give up their nation-state.

Over half a century later, Lenin, with his extraordinary talent for didactic popularization, compared this attitude to the woman's right to divorce. Every woman, he said, should have the freedom to divorce her husband; socialists and even progressive liberals must help her to achieve that freedom. But this did not mean that we were out to persuade all women that they should divorce their husbands. In the same way, Lenin said, we are not going to urge every nation to create its own state, but we must recognize that every nation has a right to do so. Our task, as Marxists, is to work towards the international socialist community; but we must also support the struggle for national independence waged by any oppressed nation, and by those colonial and semi-colonial countries exploited by foreign capital. But to glory in the nation-state, to seek to perpetuate it, to make a fetish of it, is simply reactionary, archaic and anachronistic; to think within the narrow framework of a nation-state is to remain tied to the past and not to move towards the future.

* * *

Marx saw how nascent industrial capitalism was beginning to create the material conditions for a supranational organization of society. "In place of the old local and national seclusion and self-sufficiency, we now have the many-sided intercourse of nations and their mutual interdependence," Marx and Engels wrote in 1848. And it is only now, over 120 years later, that our politicians, realizing at last the "mutual interdependence of nations," try in their own awkward way to create that much-vaunted European

International. In terms of what is called "practical politics" it did not achieve great things. It was split by the controversy between the Marxists and the anarchists. The police of Paris accused the First International of having provoked and organized the Commune of Paris. But the First International, though its adherents took part in the Commune of Paris, was quite innocent of the charge laid against it. And yet the defeat of the Commune led to the final disintegration of the International. By our standards, and by the standards of its time, this was a very small movement; it did not possess such modest media of publicity which even small parties possessed then, and yet it was the first great proclamation of what became a vital principle, the principle of internationalism.

The International died young, but it left behind the powerful call which resounds in the ears of the working classes of Europe and the world to this day, the call: Workers of the world, unite! It bequeathed a testament which molded also the thinking of the left and of revolutionary intellectuals of the world. The principle it proclaimed was far greater and far more vital than the International itself, and this was its only real achievement.

*   *   *

After the dissolution of the First International came two decades during which the labor movement was growing in nearly all European countries. For the first time there was a great modern working class party in Germany. In France, in Italy, and in Spain the labor parties were gaining in strength. And yet, in spite of this fact—or perhaps as a result of it?—no international organization existed. The initiative to set up the Second International came from the French and Belgians in 1889. In the mythology of socialism, Frederick Engels figures as the originator of that International. He was warmly applauded and acclaimed as Marx's surviving friend and continuator of his work. It must have been very tempting to present the venerable prophet of socialism as the godfather of the new organization. Yet, when we read the private correspondence between Engels and Laura and Paul Lafargue we find that Engels viewed without great enthusiasm the prospects of the international socialist congress which was being rather feverishly prepared in Paris. In a letter to Laura (Marx's daughter), written less than three weeks before the event, he mentions in passing "that congress of yours" and opposes any plan (which was evidently mooted) of keeping "the administrative sittings in private." The Germans, he says, would certainly prefer public meetings throughout "unless there is in some quarters a hankering after a restoration of the International in some form or another." This the Germans, and the Austrians, "would and ought" to oppose with all their strength. They cannot afford, Engels further maintains, "to play at international organizations which are at present as impossible as they are useless." *

And yet the International grew and expanded; and for a quarter of a century, from 1889 until the outbreak of the First World War, it was an impressive and in a way an immensely influential organization. Writing in 1919, Lenin commented that if the First International covered the period of growth of socialism in depth, the Second International brought the expansion of socialism in breadth. Outwardly, the Second International looked like the inheritor of the First, propagating the same idea and program of the revolution; in this the roots of both were deep in the tradition of 1848. It flourished all the symbols and watchwords of proletarian unity, sang all the songs about the brotherhood of the toilers, and spoke in the name of workers of every country and of the world. This, however, proved to be only a thin veneer covering deeply ingrained nationalism.

*   *   *

In 1914, in the first days of the war, the International crumbled. All the official parties affiliated with it, with the exception of the Russian and Polish parties, became, as Rosa

* *Correspondence: Frederick Engels and Paul and Laura Lafargue* (Foreign Languages Publishing House, Moscow), vol. 2, p. 292.

Luxemburg called them, social-patriotic, social-chauvinistic; socialist in words only and jingoistic in fact. The leaders of European socialism threw to the winds the whole of their solemn, antimilitaristic international phraseology, and called upon the working classes to fight for "their" emperors, "their" government and "their" general staffs.*

What destroyed the Second International (although it still survives, but only as a necrotic bone), apart from the upsurge of nationalism, was the supremacy of one party, the German Social-Democratic Party, over the whole organization.† The German Social-Democratic Party was the master of the International, and in this lay the inherent contradiction of the situation which, like a charge of dynamite, exploded the whole edifice when, on 4 August 1914, the first shot was fired on the battlefield. Four years after the setting up of the Second International, Engels warned Lafargue, "The emancipation of the proletariat can be only an international event; you render it impossible if you try to make it simply a French event." Up to that "date of tragic significance" it looked as if the powerful German Social-Democratic Party took it upon itself to make of the emancipation of the proletariat "simply a German event."

The triumph of nationalism within the Second International was not fortuitous; it reflected the development and expansion of capitalism, which brought a spurious prosperity and relative improvement in the standard of living of the workers of the advanced countries. Parliamentary socialism, trade unionism, peaceful bargaining, the belief (so familiar to us) that "we have learned to manage our economic affairs,"

---

* "At one blow, the war scattered the revolutionary ideals in which the International had found its strength," writes Julius Braunthal, the secretary of the Second International, calling 4 August 1914 "a date of tragic significance" in the history of socialism. (*History of the International*, vol. 2)

† In September or October 1914, Trotsky wrote in Zurich: "It [the German Social Democratic Party] was for us not one of the parties of the International, but *the* party."

tied the labor movement more and more closely to the nation-state, as it ties it today to our so-called welfare state. But suddenly, with the outbreak of the war, this labor movement was subjected to a most severe test; and it failed. Lenin could not believe that the disciples of Marx and Engels, the German socialists with their impressive following and "perfect" organization, had betrayed all their internationalism, their pledges and oaths, and had come out on the side of the Kaiser's empire, calling upon their workers to wage a holy war against Russia. No, Lenin could not believe that. He was on the verge of a nervous breakdown. He was in such despair at the collapse of all his hopes that for a time he thought of abandoning all politics and emigrating to the United States, as some of the defeated revolutionaries emigrated from Europe after 1848. But with Lenin, idle despair never lasted for long. He fought with his pen, unmasking the opportunism and the cowardice of the leaders of the German party; he mercilessly flayed Kautsky, the renegade, and thundered: What was the Second International if not "a union for the international justification of national chauvinism?" Would the Kaiser have ordered the Social-Democrats to be imprisoned or even shot if they had voted against the war credits? So what would be wrong with that? What were the leaders of the workers for? It is precisely in times of great strain, when the fortunes of peoples are in balance, that their duty is to lead forward even at the risk of their lives.

A few months after the outbreak of the war, both Lenin and Trotsky were already contemplating the setting up of a new International. The old one had died an ignominious death. The "chauvinist falsifiers of Marxism" were beyond redemption; they had dragged the whole organization too deeply into the quagmire of national patriotism. The only constructive task ahead was to "gather the forces for the Third International."

But long before the "forces for the Third International" were gathered, the thunder of the Russian Revolution shook the world. Right through the war the socialists of allied countries went through the ritual of conferences and solemn declarations; and so did the socialists of the Central Powers. While those meeting in London spoke of "pursuing the war to the bitter end," those assembled in Vienna spoke of their determination to defend their Fatherland with all their might. Only in September 1915, at Zimmerwald, was a timid attempt made to reassert anew, independently of the old International, proletarian solidarity among the embattled nations.

And when the great storm of 1917 came, no International was in existence; what was relevant was internationalism. And once again, this time from the other end of Europe, from backward Russia, resounded the call: "Workers of the world, unite!"

*   *   *

In 1919 Lenin, Trotsky, Bukharin, Zinoviev and other Bolsheviks set themselves the task of rescuing the European labor movement from its social patriotic morass and of raising again the level of revolutionary internationalist consciousness. On Lenin's initiative they founded the Third International. Rosa Luxemburg was, till her martyr's death, opposed to that venture. According to her evaluation, the European labor movement was not yet ripe enough to absorb the idea and to act upon it. In these circumstances the new International was bound again to become dominated by one party, the party of the victorious socialist revolution. The preponderance of the German party in the Second International had been an element of weakness: the breakdown of the most powerful component resulted in the collapse of the whole structure. Nevertheless, Lenin and his comrades were convinced that the proclamation of the principle of internationalism once again was vital for the reawakening of the labor movement. But there was also another reason for which they were so anxious to form the Third International. They wanted to introduce another feature into the conception of the International; they saw it not only as a means to unite the workers of all countries, but also as a political general staff in the coming European revolution. They imagined that the Russian upheaval was only the prelude, which would soon, very soon, be followed by the next act in the struggle against capitalism at large, and that there was a need for a political headquarters from which all the fighting activities of the various revolutionary working masses would be planned and directed in a harmonious way, all watchwords and slogans coordinated, and a certain international discipline established, which would prevail over the centrifugal national interests, local or regional ambitions and aspirations. For some time it seemed that these hopes might indeed materialize. There was in the period following the Russian Revolution a tremendous upsurge of internationalist feelings. From our vantage point it may be difficult to visualize this, but if we recall that a man as moderate and right-wing as the late Ernest Bevin—the same Bevin who ended his life as one of the most energetic warriors of the cold war—was in 1920 leading the British dockers to strike against the dispatch of arms and munitions destined to be turned against the Bolsheviks, we can appreciate the full impact the first workers' state made on their western comrades.

The Third International helped perhaps to unite the various groups of revolutionary socialists, but it disappeared without achieving much more. What were the roots of its failure?

The basic factor was the one foreseen and feared by Rosa Luxemburg: the supremacy of one single party. The victorious Russian party began automatically to dominate the whole International and in the course of years to stifle the independent rhythm and development of the communist movement outside and also within the USSR.

A new nationalism—postcapitalist, postrevolutionary nationalism—showed itself in an ideology which stressed and emphasized the self-sufficiency of the Russian Revolution. Enclosed within the *cordon sanitaire*, isolated by the action of all the counterrevolutionary forces of the world, the first workers' state was forced into autarky; to make it easier to endure, the bitter necessity was then presented as a virtue. This found its utmost expression in Stalin's doctrine of socialism in one country and became the dogma of consolation for the unfulfilled hopes and expectations of revolution in the West. The new doctrine clothed itself in pseudo-Marxist, pseudo-dialectical pretexts and formulas, yet it was nothing else but the *cri de coeur* of a new and weak society. Stalin's promise of socialism in one country bred, in its turn, national egoism and it led Russia to treat foreign communism as expendable or as a bargaining counter in diplomatic dealings with the western bourgeois states.

The Third International, founded to the accompaniment of all the thunder and lightning of the Russian Revolution, was disbanded and buried by Stalin in the process of diplomatic bargaining with Churchill and Roosevelt in 1943. Such is the inescapable logic of the situation that, whenever in an International nationalism wins, it crushes and buries the International or tramples it underfoot. Such was the fate of the First and of the Second Internationals, and such was the fate of the Third.

*　　*　　*

In 1933, after Hitler came to power, Trotsky considered the Third International just as bankrupt as the Second was. The German workers were not, as the Comintern's specious argument ran, "on the eve of great battles"—they had already suffered a terrible defeat. Stalinism, Trotsky said, had had its "fourth of August." This analogy led Trotsky to the obvious conclusion that now, as in 1914, it was time to prepare for the building of a new international organization, because the old one lay in ruins. He was, however, full of hesitations. It was not easy for him to turn his back on the "general staff of the world revolution," of which he was one of the main architects; he himself pointed out that while in 1914 the Second International consciously betrayed all its high ideals, the Comintern, in 1933, had facilitated fascist

victory through sheer stupidity, complacency, and blindness.
The plan to set up the new International was ripening
slowly in Trotsky's mind. Four years of propaganda and
groundwork were to pass before he was ready to convene a
foundation congress. (It took exactly the same length of
time from the moment when in 1915 he and Lenin first
contemplated the idea of the Third International until the
organization was actually launched.) But the Fourth International proved to be a stillbirth, and this was largely because
no international revolutionary movement was there to
breathe life into it. Through no fault of his own, Trotsky's
International was cut off from the only area in which a victorious revolution had taken place and in which that revolution, though monopolized and distorted by an oppressive,
mendacious bureaucracy, was still in being. In a sense Trotsky himself had foreseen the main circumstance which would
condemn his organization to ineffectiveness when he pointed
out that no matter how irresponsible Stalin's policy in
Germany and elsewhere was, the revolutionary workers of all
countries still looked to Moscow for inspiration and
guidance.

* * *

And now we have to consider one of the most striking
paradoxes in the history of the Internationals. Just as the
Russian Revolution took place at the time when no International existed, so in our lifetime the Chinese Revolution
occurred, again at a time when after the Third International
had been buried, the Fourth International had turned out to
be a stillbirth, and there was no living revolutionary international organization. Our century saw two great social upheavals, embracing over eight hundred million people; both
occurred in the period when there was no "general staff" to
guide, advise and coordinate. They came into being within a
national framework; and within it the revolution grew, transcended the limitations of a national ideology, and again
became the object of a new struggle between the conflicting
elements of nationalism and internationalism.

We must leave outside our survey the new waves of nationalism in the western labor movement; they are in a sense only a continuation of the same nationalism that came to the top in 1914. Qualitatively there is not much difference between the nationalism of social-democratic parties today and their social-patriotism of 1914. The internationalism of the communist camp in the Stalinist and post-Stalinist, Khrushchevite and post-Khrushchevite period has been more or less spurious and has reflected only a certain *Konjunktur;* it was dictated by the state of diplomatic relations between Russia and the West.

In China, in Russia, and in Eastern Europe there is a rising tide of nationalism. Yet, side by side, we can sense a new upsurge of internationalism. The tug of war between nationalism and internationalism, the perennial conflict between national egoism and international solidarity, becomes more and more visible.

The wave of nationalism is, of course, one of the after-effects of Stalinism. Struggling with his last illness, Lenin denounced Stalinism as the *dzierzhymorda*, the great brute and bully reminiscent of the old tsarist times. Full of Great Russian pride and chauvinism, the *dzierzhymorda* came back to kick and insult the small nations; and to this the small nations replied with an intense, at times morbid, yet understandable nationalism. It is often said of the Jews that, having suffered so much persecution, they are oversensitive in their Jewish pride. In this sense all the nations of Eastern Europe are like the Jews; they have suffered, they have been humiliated, and they react with suspicion and mistrust against the Russians. And this reaction is as strong among the communists as among the noncommunists, whatever the outward show of solidarity may be. This explains the events of 1956, the Gomulka upheaval in Poland, and the civil war in Hungary. The *dzierzhymorda*, the Great Russian bully of whom Lenin spoke, still persisted in the much milder Khrushchev when he suddenly withdrew all economic aid from China, bringing the whole Chinese economy to the brink of collapse.

Lenin had a premonition even of this, when, on his deathbed, in the so-called remarks on nationalities, he wrote: "If we behave like the old Russian gendarme, the old Russian bully, we will pay for it in China, we will pay for it in India, we will harm ourselves because we shall become discredited in the eyes of all the nations of awakening Asia." But Lenin's warning went unheeded and still goes unheeded.

But even if the people who ruled from Moscow and Peking were all internationalists without blemish, a socialist revolution on such a huge part of the globe and embracing so great a segment of humanity would still present them with a tremendously difficult problem, vast in dimensions, and often tragic in its implications. In one camp there are the Czechs, the East Germans, the Russians, with their high standard of living; and there are also the Vietnamese and the Chinese who still carry the burden of millennia of poverty and illiteracy. The development and advance of these post-capitalist societies is taking place simultaneously on many different levels of civilization, amid dissimilar social structures, against a background of diverse and conflicting national traditions. In such circumstances, national conflicts and antagonisms are bound to erupt, even if at the head of these national entities stand paragons of all international virtues. There would still remain tensions and animosities, even if they had all agreed on an equalization of material resources—though obviously this would not be the right way to proceed, for socialism cannot be achieved by lowering the standard of living of a highly developed nation. Some sacrifices on the part of the richer nations must, in communism, be made, but even these would not at a stroke remove all sources of potential conflicts.

When Marx and his adherents proclaimed internationalism as the duty and ethics of socialists, they perceived, so to speak, first of all what should be the climate of the labor movement and, secondly, the ultimate outcome of the development towards a new society. Socialists must be internationalists even if their working classes are not;

socialists must also understand the nationalism of the masses, but only in the way in which a doctor understands the weakness or the illness of his patient. Socialists should be aware of that nationalism, but, like nurses, they should wash their hands twenty times over whenever they approach an area of the labor movement infected by it.

It was Marx's idea that *in socialism* there would be no national conflicts: *in socialism* is here the operative term. If one were to assume that Russia is already a socialist country, that China has already established socialism, then, of course, one would be entitled to conclude that an internationalist socialist society was a phantasm. The truth is that neither Russia nor China are socialist: theirs are the postcapitalist societies which still carry within themselves the heritage of capitalism and contain the elements of an even more backward—feudal and prefeudal—civilization. They carried out their revolutions in isolation from the developed modern civilization of the West, meeting only with the hostility of the Western bourgeoisie and even, to some extent, the Western working classes. The outside world condemned these revolutions to stew in the juice of their backwardness. What is the wonder that tensions persist, conflicts recur, and nationalism raises its head? But it would be a mistake to underrate the strength of the internationalist trend which comes to the fore now and again. It shows itself mainly in the desire to do away with Russian chauvinism and with the domination of one nation by another, and with the striving to establish a genuine international division of labor within the communist bloc. At this moment we are witnessing the disintegration of the old forms of the communist movement, the disintegration of Stalinism, and the revolt against the domination of that movement by any single party. This "centrifugal dispersal" is preferable to the puppet-like existence of communist parties and to their integration in a puppet-like manner. The disintegration of a nonexistent shadow International is in itself a progressive and healthy phenomenon, provided that it is followed by a reintegration of the labor movement on the basis of international socialism.

From this survey of the century of the Internationals we can draw one lesson only: that the idea of internationalism is, after all, more important, more vital, more relevant than the Internationals that succeed each other, flourish, then decay and die away. The Internationals come and go; internationalism remains the vital principle of a new world; and even among the wreckage of the Internationals I still believe that the idea of internationalism will grow and flourish like a plant that grows and blossoms amid ruins.

the tragedy of the polish communist party

Would you throw some light on the key problems of the history of the Polish Communist Party, which I am at present studying? I am particularly interested in the ideological and political currents within the Party, in the background to the formation of its various factions, in the Party's policy during the critical periods of the two interwar decades, and, finally, in its tragic end.

Let us begin with some general reflections and with a remark of a personal nature. When you ask me to speak of the history of the Polish Communist Party you are surely aware of the particular point of view from which I reply. In June 1957, exactly twenty-five years will have elapsed since I was expelled from the Party as an oppositionist. I shall not analyze now the reasons for my expulsion: they have been stated

This interview was originally published in French in Les Temps Modernes, *March 1958. The interviewer was K. S. Karol.*

clearly although tendentiously—and with the passage of time their very bias becomes more and more self-condemnatory—in the documents and statements published at the time by the Party leadership dealing with the "Krakowski affair." (Krakowski was one of the pseudonyms which I was then using.) From 1932 until its dissolution I was in sharp conflict with the Polish Communist Party. Nevertheless, at the time of the dissolution and of the accusations made against its leaders, I stigmatized these actions as an unparalleled crime committed against the working class of Poland and of the whole world. The opposition group to which I belonged was in fact the only group of members or former members of the Polish CP which denounced this crime then and protested against it vehemently.*

It was unquestionably the Polish Communist Party which had the greatest influence on my intellectual and political development. I never doubted that it would be "rehabilitated"—though even the term "rehabilitation" is out of place here. It was a great and heroic party, the only party in Poland which represented the interests of the proletarian revolution, the great Marxist tradition, and a true and living internationalism. In this respect no other Polish party could be compared with it. Unfortunately, up to this day the history of the Polish Communist Party still remains a closed and sealed book. The most recent publications which I have had an opportunity to read are on the whole rather pitiable. They

---

* It is said that at one of the meetings of the Central Committee which took place after October 1956, when Gomulka was relating the story of the Party's dissolution and of the slanders made against its leaders, he was asked whether at that time, in 1938, he himself believed them. Gomulka answered: "No." Why, then, had he not protested? he was asked. "I was not brave enough to do so, or I had not enough self-confidence," he is said to have replied, "but if Lenin had been living in Poland, he would certainly have protested in such circumstances." We must acknowledge Gomulka's sincerity and modesty. Nevertheless it was not necessary to be a Lenin in order to dare to protest. I knew ordinary workers who had no ambitions towards leadership and who understood that their duty was to protest, and acted accordingly.

note the Party's rehabilitation, but do nothing more. There is no real attempt to depict the great periods in the Party's existence—the high flights and decline. What is striking is a tendency—the result of habits acquired in the course of many years—to be satisfied with clichés and writings in the manner of *Lives of Saints.* The only party in Poland which was worthy of bearing the name of a proletarian and Marxist party deserves to have its record studied in a serious, realistic and critical manner. The Polish CP was once buried under a pile of outrageous slanders. Let us not bury it again, wrapped in shrouds of golden legends to the accompaniment of senseless hymns.

I should like to add a remark of a general methodological character. In order to understand the history of the Polish Communist Party, every important phase of it must be considered from a double point of view: from the angle of the class struggle within Poland itself, and from that of the processes which were taking place within the Communist International and the Soviet Union. These two groups of factors acted upon each other continuously. An investigator who restricts himself to an analysis of only one of these will be unable to grasp the essence of the story. As years went by, the processes occurring in the Soviet Union played a more and more important role and weighed more and more disastrously on the fate of the Polish Party. Therefore to see clearly the policy of the Party and its ideological tendencies and also to understand the factional struggle, we must be continuously aware of the class relationship within Poland and of the processes of development taking place within the Russian Revolution.

What were the main internal divisions in the Polish Communist Party at the time it was founded, that is to say, at the end of 1918 and the beginning of 1919?

These divisions followed from the fact that the Polish CP was born from the fusion of two parties: the Social-Democratic

Party of the Kingdom of Poland and Lithuania (Rosa Luxemburg's party, the SDKPiL) and the Polish Left Socialist Party (the PPS Lewica).* Each of these two parties had its own traditions. The Social-Democratic Party grew in opposition to the nationalism and patriotism of the Polish nobility, harking back to the insurrectionist romanticism of the nineteenth century, and placed its main emphasis on proletarian internationalism. The Left Socialist Party had at first adhered to the patriotic-insurgent tradition, and the restoration of Poland's independence had occupied a central place in its program; but later on it came closer to the internationalist attitude of the Luxemburgist Party. The Left Socialist Party had its affinities with the Left Mensheviks; only under the influence of the October Revolution did it move closer to Bolshevism. The Social-Democratic Party adopted—as the proceedings of its Sixth Congress show—an attitude very close to that of Trotsky, remaining independent both of the Mensheviks and the Bolsheviks. At the time of the revolution, the Luxemburgist Party—again like Trotsky—identified itself with Bolshevism. Here we must take note of the differences within the Party between adherents of the Party's official leaders (Rosa Luxemburg, Marchlewski, Jogiches) and the so-called "splitters" (Dzerzhinski, Radek, Unszlicht). This was, however, a discord, not a genuine split. The "splitters" represented a certain opposition to the centralism of the Executive Committee, which operated from abroad. Furthermore, they were somewhat closer to the Bolsheviks. In the Polish Communist Party the SDKPiL tradition was predominant from the beginning. Nevertheless the importance of these differences should not be exaggerated. They were in

---

* The Social-Democratic Party of the Kingdom of Poland and Lithuania was formed in 1893 as a Polish party; the Lithuanian Social-Democrats attached themselves in 1900. From the beginning this party was led by Julian Marchlewski, Leo Jogiches-Tyszka, and Rosa Luxemburg. The Left Socialist Party was formed in November 1906, as a result of a split in the Polish Socialist Party (PPS) and of an opposition, stimulated by the 1905 revolution, to Pilsudski's reformist, terroristic and nationalist leadership.

actual fact restrained and even obliterated by the real unity of the newly founded Party and the conviction of its members that the old divisions were a matter of the past. The Party's ranks were further united by a sharp awareness of their common and unyielding opposition to the nationalist and reformist Poland, to the Poland of the landlords and petty nobility.*

Is it not true that the Communist Party began its political life in independent Poland with a certain moral disadvantage arising from its Luxemburgist tradition, which was opposed in principle to the struggle for national independence?

There is a little truth and a great deal of exaggeration in that. The proof that this is so is seen, for example, in the relative strength of the different parties within the Soviets of the Workers' Deputies which were set up, at the end of 1918, in Warsaw, in Lodz, and in the Dabrowa coalfields. In Warsaw the forces of the Communist Party and of the Socialists were equally balanced and, if I am not mistaken, the Bund† tipped the scales. There was a similar situation in Lodz, although there the Communists had a certain superiority. In the Dabrowa mining district the Communist Party was incomparably stronger than the Socialist Party, and with this is connected the episode of the Red Republic of Dabrowa. One could say that on the eve of independence, the influence of the Polish CP over the working classes in the main industrial

---

* It is a curious fact that the "splitters" and particularly Dzerzhinski and Radek should have made almost the same criticism of Rosa Luxemburg as the latter made of Lenin during the division of the Party into Mensheviks and Bolsheviks. They accused her of applying a policy of ultracentralism in the Party, of enforcing too much discipline, etc. In fact, Rosa Luxemburg's Party was led in a manner very similar to that in which Lenin led the Bolshevik Party. This was due essentially to the fact that both parties were operating illegally.

† The Bund was the Jewish socialist party, which then maintained an intermediate position between socialist reformism and communism.

centers was certainly not smaller than that of the reformist and "patriotic" PPS—it was probably larger.

The situation was complicated. On the one hand, events had *to a certain degree* refuted the assumptions on which Rosa Luxemburg and her comrades had dissented from the "struggle for national independence." On the other hand, however, Luxemburg and her followers had been alone in placing their hopes on revolutions in Russia, Germany, and Austria, the three empires that had subjugated Poland, rather than on an unending repetition of Polish nineteenth-century insurrections. Pilsudskism—and the Polish Socialist Party which in 1918 was almost inseparable from Pilsudskism—had above all proclaimed its skepticism and distrust of the reality of revolution in these empires. Events had given the lie to this skepticism and distrust. Contrary to Rosa Luxemburg's expectations, Poland had regained her independence; but contrary to the expectations of her opponents, Poland had received it mainly from the hands of the Russian and German revolutions. History showed itself to be more cunning than all the parties; and that is why I do not believe that, in comparison with other parties, the Communist Party entered the phase of independence with any particular "moral handicap." Moreover, while the "Luxemburgists" were rotting in tsarist prisons and in exile, the Polish bourgeois parties (especially the "national democrats," who opposed all movements for national independence, but also Pilsudski and the Socialist "patriots") placed themselves at the service of the occupying powers and collaborated with them; after the fall of these powers, this did not prevent the bourgeois parties from adopting hypocritical, ultranationalist attitudes and from seizing power.

After the foundation of the Polish Communist Party did the old controversy over Poland's independence go on within the Party?

Only at the beginning, and to an insignificant degree; later it stopped altogether. The Party was concerned with other problems—its position in the configuration of social forces; the elaboration of its political line; and, of course, the problem of the Russian Revolution and the prospects of world revolution.

Did not the question of boycotting the Constituent Assembly of 1919 mark the appearance of a new division within the Party?

Unless I am mistaken, this question did not give rise to much discussion. On this matter the Polish and the German parties took similar stands, considering elections to the Constituent Assembly as a diversion which had as its aim the liquidation of the Soviets of Workers' Delegates. The Polish *Seym* and the Weimar Constituent Assembly were regarded as the foundations of a bourgeois parliamentary republic, erected on the ruins of the workers' Soviets—the potential organs of the socialist revolution. Undoubtedly, the two parties made a mistake in proclaiming the boycott of the bourgeois parliament, and in both cases this mistake was a result of the ultraleft mood of the period.

How did the Communist Party react to the Polish-Soviet War of 1920?

The Polish Party treated this war—as it had every reason to do—as a war of the Polish possessing classes (or of their decisive elements) against the Russian Revolution, and as an integral part of the capitalist powers' intervention in Russia. The Party felt it was at one with the Russian Revolution and obliged to defend it. The situation became complicated after Pilsudski's retreat from Kiev and at the time of the Red Army's march on Warsaw. The state of siege and the existence of military tribunals reduced to a minimum the Party's open activities; and it was difficult for both leaders and rank and file to express the various nuances of Communist opinion. Nevertheless I should like to draw attention to characteristic differences which appeared among the numerous groups of Polish Communists living in Moscow. When the question of the march on Warsaw came up, this group split in a rather paradoxical manner. On the one hand, the old "Luxemburgists," the "opponents of independence," Radek and Marchlewski,* spared no efforts to convince Lenin and the Russian Politburo that the march on Warsaw should not be undertaken, but that peace should be proposed to Poland as soon as Pilsudski's armies had been chased out of the Ukraine. (They succeeded in winning to their point of view only Trotsky, who was then the People's Commissar for War.) On the other hand, the old supporters of independence, former PPS men like Feliks Kon and Lapinski,† favored the Red Army's march on Warsaw; they maintained that the Polish proletariat was in a state of the utmost revolutionary ferment and would welcome the Red Army as its liberator. I should like to report yet another episode: in 1920 the paper *Rote Fahne*, the organ of the German Communist Party, published a protest against the march on Warsaw signed by Domski, one of the most eminent "Luxemburgist" members of the Central Committee of the Polish Party. By the way, under the conditions of internal democracy, which existed at that time in the Party, the right of a member of the Central Committee to publish such a protest was considered as something quite natural. Domski remained a member of the Central Committee and played a leading role in it for many more years, until 1925 precisely.

* Julian Marchlewski, one of the closest friends of Rosa Luxemburg, was an eminent writer and Marxist theoretician who played an important part in the German socialist left and in the Polish movement. After the October Revolution he stayed in Russia.

† Feliks Kon, a veteran of Polish patriotic socialism, was one of the founders of the Communist Party and with Marchlewski and Dzerzhinski was a member of the "Provisional Communist Government," set up during the Red Army's march on Warsaw. Lapinski belonged to the same group as Feliks Kon, and in the twenties he played an important role in the Comintern.

You asked whether the Luxemburgist tradition was not a moral embarrassment for Polish communism. I have no intention of defending *post factum* Rosa Luxemburg's ideas about national independence. I shall simply say that the Red Army's march on Warsaw was a much more serious and more damaging moral handicap for the Polish CP than had been all of Rosa Luxemburg's real or imaginary mistakes taken together; about these mistakes both her bourgeois opponents as well as Stalin (the latter misusing, in his characteristic manner, quotations from Lenin) have made an enormous amount of noise. However, the mistake made by Lenin in 1920—let us call things by their proper name—was a real tragedy for the Polish CP, because in effect it pushed the Polish proletarian masses towards anti-Sovietism and anti-communism.

Nevertheless, after 1920 the Party rapidly regained its strength—didn't it?

Yes, to a certain extent. That does not alter the fact that the march on Warsaw also had certain permanent effects: it undermined the trust of the Polish working masses in the Russian Revolution. However, after 1920 the workers recovered fairly quickly from their first enthusiasm for Polish national sovereignty, and from the illusions that went with it. In the relatively freer atmosphere which followed the war, the working class had the opportunity to view the events more calmly. It became known that Lenin's government had done everything possible to avoid war between Poland and Russia and that without Pilsudski's march on Kiev there would probably never have been any Soviet march on Warsaw. The Polish working class came to understand that Pilsudski, in 1920, was not fighting so much for Polish independence as for the estates of the big Polish landowners in the Ukraine, and also to satisfy his own dreams of grandeur. The early years of the twenties marked another increase in the influence of the Polish Communist Party, an influence which reached its peak in 1923, particularly in November, at the time of the general strike and the rising of the Cracow workers.

This was the time of the "three W's" leadership, wasn't it?

It was. One of them, Warski, was a former Luxemburgist, and the two others, Walecki and Wera (Kostrzewa), were former Left Socialists. Nevertheless, they formed a united leadership which proved that the old divisions within the party had been overcome. Now, however, we are approaching a particularly critical period, when the development of the class struggle in Poland was complicated once more, and to a certain extent distorted, by the influence of events taking place in the Soviet Union. For many years, I personally believed that in Poland, as well as in Germany, the year 1923 was one of a "missed revolution." Now, after an interval of thirty-five years, I can no longer be so sure that the historical evidence bears out the correctness of this point of view. In any case, we certainly had many elements of a revolutionary situation: a general strike, the rising of the Cracow workers, the army going over to the side of the working class, and more generally, the country in a state of utter ferment. The only factor, it seemed, which was lacking was the initiative of a revolutionary party which might have led the revolution to success. The Polish CP did not show that initiative. In accordance with the resolutions of the International, the Party was then following a policy of united front with the socialists. Up to a certain moment, this policy had produced excellent results, enabling the Party to widen its influence, and introducing more vigor into the class struggle. But at the same time, the Party leadership left the political initiative to the Socialists; and in the critical days of November 1923, this produced unfortunate consequences. The rank and file felt that the Party had allowed a revolutionary situation to pass by without taking any advantage; and they reacted, not without bitterness, against the "opportunism" and the lack of revolutionary initiative of the "three W's."

As I have said, the situation became even more complicated because of events taking place in the USSR. At that time the struggle between the so-called triumvirate (Stalin, Zinoviev and Kamenev) and Trotsky broke into the open. At once it took on extremely violent forms unknown hitherto in the movement. The European Communist parties were deeply disturbed, all the more so as until then Trotsky, like Lenin, had been the International's inspirer and greatest moral authority. In the autumn of 1923 the Central Committees of the Polish, French and German parties protested, in one form or another, to the Central Committee of the Soviet Party against the violence of the attacks on Trotsky. Those who protested had no intention of associating themselves with Trotsky's specific policies. They were simply warning the Soviet leaders of the harm which the campaign against Trotsky was doing to the Communist movement, and they appealed to them to settle their differences in a manner worthy of Communists. This incident had serious consequences. Stalin never forgot or forgave this protest. Zinoviev, who was then president of the International, viewed it as a vote of no confidence in himself. Immediately, the Communist parties of Poland, France and Germany became involved in the internal Soviet conflict. The leadership of the International—in other words, Zinoviev and Stalin—dismissed from their posts the principal leaders of the three parties who had dared "to come to Trotsky's defense." A pretext was provided by the mistakes committed by these leaders, notably by the group of the "three W's" in November 1923; they were expelled for "opportunism, right deviation, and failure to exploit a revolutionary situation."

Does it not follow from your account that those who criticized the "three W's" were justified?

Even if they were justified, that did not authorize the leadership of the International in Moscow to intervene in such a drastic manner in the internal affairs of the Polish Party. I must add that the leadership of the German and French parties was changed in the same way.* In all these cases the changes were brought about as a result of orders from above, and not as a result of decisions taken by the members of the Party in a way corresponding to the principles of internal democracy. This was the first dangerous attack on the autonomy of the Communist Party, the first act, as it turned out, of "Stalinization," although this was done not only by Stalin, but by Zinoviev also. Both played demagogically on the feeling of disillusionment which existed among the rank and file of the Polish and German parties. This feeling was understandable and it turned violently against the "three W's" in Poland (as it did against Brandler in Germany). It is possible that if the Party had been free to decide for itself, it might have changed its leadership. Nevertheless, more important than the fact of the change itself was the manner in which it was carried out: the way was opened to further unscrupulous interference by Stalin in the affairs of the Polish Communist Party, an interference which was to end in the Party's assassination.

How did the Party react to this first act of deliberate interference?

Passively, unfortunately. Many of its members were more or less in favor of the "three W's" being replaced. And even those who weren't did not oppose it. The operation was mild in comparison with the expulsions, purges and forced recantations which were to follow. Stalinism was only in its formative period, and could not yet show its claws. The attack on the displaced leaders was carried on with relative moderation and correctness of form—and this facilitated its acceptance. What was decisive, however, was the Party's psychological attitude—its misguided conception of solidarity with the

* In France, Monatte, Rosmer and Souvarine were dismissed from the leadership of the Communist Party.

Russian Revolution, its belief that any conflict with Moscow must be avoided, no matter at what cost. The moral authority of the Soviet Party, the only one which had led a proletarian revolution to victory, was so great that the Polish Communists accepted Moscow's decisions even when Moscow abused its revolutionary authority. Stalinism was indeed a continuous succession of abuses of this kind, a systematic exploitation of the moral credit of the revolution for purposes which often had nothing to do with the interests of communism but served only to consolidate the bureaucratic regime of the USSR. During the years 1923–24 it was vital for Stalin to attack Trotskyism in the whole International. Warski and Kostrzewa tried to safeguard their own position by dissociating themselves from their own protest against Moscow's anti-Trotsky campaign. Their motives were understandable. In Moscow the majority of the Politburo and of the Central Committee had come out against Trotsky. In view of this, Warski and Kostrzewa decided that they could not support the minority in the Soviet Party and thus expose themselves to the charge of interfering in the internal affairs of the Party. That did not, however, protect the Polish Party from Soviet interference. Thus, although the "three W's" had some sympathy with the views of the Trotskyist opposition, they came, in fact, to support Stalin and Zinoviev and to proclaim their loyalty to them. For this moment of weakness they had to pay dearly later on.

What was the change in the Party's policy after 1923?

What was called "the left" took over the leadership: Domski, Zofia Unszlicht, and Lenski. Both in the International as a whole and also in the Polish Party the new policy presented a sharp reaction from the orientation of the preceding period. This was, in fact, the time of an "ultraleftist" policy. If, in 1923, the Party did not show enough revolutionary vigor, its policy during the years 1924 and 1925 was marked by a false excess of that vigor. This was all the more harmful because after the crisis of November 1923 the objective possibilities of revolutionary action had decreased. During this period the Polish CP rejected the united front tactic completely and dispersed its efforts in futile adventures. The result? It lost its influence and cut itself off from the working masses.

It is worth recalling that, at the beginning of 1924, in local elections, the Polish CP was still stronger than the Socialist Party. This success, however, was no more than a delayed echo of the radicalization of the masses which had taken place in 1923 and it did not foreshadow the rise of a new revolutionary wave. In the following year the Communist Party's influence declined drastically. The Party was unable to lead any mass action. This was not only a Polish phenomenon. The same fluctuations could be seen in all the Communist parties of Europe—all were, in fact, pursuing the same ultraleftist policy with similar results. This was the time of the Fifth Congress of the Comintern; it was called the "Bolshevization Congress," but actually it was the "Stalinization Congress." Henceforth, all parties were subjected to the same treatment; all followed the same "line"; all had recourse to the same tactical tricks; all launched the same slogans without taking into account differences in the class relationships of different countries, in the level and form of class struggle, etc. The movement had reached the stage of bureaucratic uniformity. The Polish Party was affected by this even more painfully than were other European parties because its revolutionary tradition had been deeper and stronger, and it operated in conditions of complete illegality,* appealing continuously to the spirit of revolutionary self-sacrifice and to the heroism of its members, which never failed. Bureaucratic uniformity and revolutionary enthusiasm are a contradiction in terms.

---

* The Polish CP was made illegal at the beginning of 1919, only a few weeks after the proclamation of Polish independence. It remained illegal until 1944.

Nevertheless, at the end of 1925, Warski, Walecki and Kostrzewa returned to the leadership of the Party, didn't they?

Yes. The ultraleftist policy was soon discredited in the eyes of the Party, and that of the "three W's" was almost automatically vindicated. Whatever might be said against Warski and Kostrzewa, they had the gift of feeling the moods of the working class and the ability to strengthen and widen contacts between the Party and the masses. The periods when they led the Party were, in general, those when the Party expanded and conducted its activity on a grand scale, although it frequently lacked—how shall I put it—a revolutionary edge. The return of Warski and Kostrzewa to the leadership of the Polish Communist Party was, again, due more to what was then happening in Russia than to the change of climate in the Polish Party.

In Russia, a new political situation had developed. The triumvirate had broken up. Zinoviev and Kamenev had turned against Stalin, and shortly afterwards they were to ally themselves with Trotsky. Stalin formed a bloc with Bukharin and Rykov and followed what has been called "a rightist line" in the Soviet Party and in the International. What was called the "Polish right," the "three W's," came back into favor for the time being because they had lent support to Stalin and Bukharin. On the other hand, a part of the ultraleftist leadership, Zofia Unszlicht and Domski, sided with Zinoviev; it was for this reason, more than for any mistake they had committed in Poland, that they were removed.* Once more, calculations connected with the struggle in the Soviet Party were decisive. Lenski, in spite of his ultraleft policy, remained in the leadership, sharing influence with the "three W's"; Lenski, unlike Domski and Unszlicht, had come out against the Zinovievist opposition. More than this, he became the leader of the Stalinist nucleus within the

---

* At that time, too, Treint was eliminated from the leadership of the French Communist Party, of which he had been general secretary.

Polish CP, whereas Warski and Kostrzewa, although completely loyal to Stalin, maintained a certain reserve towards him and were closer to Bukharin's group. Later this division within the Polish Party was to be crystallized in the formation of a "minority" faction led by Lenski and a "majority" led by Warski and Kostrzewa. At the beginning of 1926 these two factions shared the leadership and both were responsible for policy, in particular for the "May mistake," that is, the support the Polish CP gave to Pilsudski at the time of his coup d'état of May 1926.

Could you say something more about the "May mistake" and explain its background? Among old Party militants I often find the following thesis: at the time of the coup the Party could not avoid supporting Pilsudski, who had the confidence of the Polish Socialist Party and of the entire left, and whose "putsch" was directed against the so-called Chjeno-Piast government (a coalition of the right-center). The Party, they say, considered that the coup constituted in a certain measure the beginning of a bourgeois revolution, and as such was relatively progressive, because during the previous period only the semifeudal landed proprietors had held power, to the exclusion even of the bourgeoisie.

The "May mistake" is clearly of fundamental importance in the history of Polish communism. I cannot attempt to give you here a detailed explanation of its background. This would require an analysis of the most complicated class relationships and political forces.* Therefore, I shall simply try to sketch in certain broad historical outlines. Again, it is essential to examine the situation on two levels: on the level of the class struggle in Poland and on that of the internal development of the Soviet Party and the Comintern.

Let us begin with the purely Polish aspect. Poland was

---

* Shortly before the war I wrote a large-scale study of the history of working-class movements and class struggles in Poland; unfortunately this manuscript was lost.

going through a crisis of the parliamentary regime. No stable government could be formed on a parliamentary basis, and this reflected the breakdown of the social and political equilibrium outside parliament. All the possibilities of parliamentary alliances had been exhausted. The masses were utterly disillusioned with their regime, which proved incapable of providing employment and of protecting workers from the catastrophic results of the currency devaluation, which had deceived the peasants' expectation of land reform, which had condemned the national minorities to oppression and despair. On the other hand, the propertied classes were equally opposed to parliament and to the "omnipotence of the Diet." They were afraid that the feeble Polish parliamentarianism, unable to ensure stable, let alone "strong" government, might expose the existing social system to the danger of violent attack and revolution. Objectively, the situation was ripe for the overthrow of the parliamentary regime. Theoretically, there were three possibilities. The parliamentary regime might have been overthrown by a fascist mass movement, similar to Nazism or the Italian prototype. This, however, was not the actual prospect. For reasons which I shall not examine here, all attempts to launch such a movement in Poland, attempts repeated more than once both before and after 1926, failed. Our native varieties of fascism or Nazism were little more than comic-opera creations.

The second theoretical possibility consisted in the overthrow of the bourgeois-parliamentary regime by proletarian revolution—for this, one might have thought, the Polish CP should have been preparing. However, during the months preceding the May coup the CP had been preparing for almost everything except revolution. Up to a point, this fact reflected the ebb of the militant mood among the working class, the shock the 1923 disaster had inflicted on them, and, finally, the exhaustion of the movement by the pseudo-revolutionary, sterile "activities" of 1924–25. The Communist movement lacked self-confidence; and when there was little self-assurance in the vanguard, there was, naturally, even less of it in the working class as a whole. Not believing in its own strength, the working class was inclined to place its hope in external forces and to calculate the benefits which it might obtain for itself through the activities of other classes or social groups. Such was the objective political background to the "May mistake."

A remark in passing—the Polish Communist Party's "May mistake" began even before 1926. If my memory does not mislead me, it was Warski who, on behalf of the Communist group, offered an emergency motion in the Diet in the autumn of 1925 on "the dangers threatening the independence of Poland." The motion was as unexpected as it was amazing. It was astonishing that a friend of Rosa Luxemburg should suddenly raise an alarm about the "dangers threatening Poland's independence." In the situation of 1925 it was difficult to see what justified the alarm. The conclusion of this emergency motion was even more amazing. In it, Warski—to meet the "threat to independence"—demanded the immediate return of Pilsudski to the post of commander-in-chief of the armed forces (this at a time when Pilsudski had left the army and was sulking in his retreat in Sulejowek).

The spectacle was tragicomic indeed! Hardly five years had elapsed since Pilsudski had marched on Kiev, mainly in order to return the Ukrainian estates to their landowners, and the Communist Party was now calling back this man of destiny to head the army, in order to safeguard national independence. It is enough merely to describe the situation in these terms—and these are the only realistic (though grotesque) terms—to dispose of the theory according to which the comeback of Pilsudski was supposed to mark the beginning of the bourgeois revolution in Poland. How could the defender of the feudal estates of the *szlachta* (nobility and gentry) have become transformed suddenly into the inspirer of the bourgeois revolution, the main task of which is usually to destroy feudalism, or what is left of it?

I have mentioned three possible solutions to the crisis of the parliamentary regime in Poland. The third solution con-

sisted in the setting-up of a military dictatorship. Pilsudski
was clearly the candidate, the pretender. He had this advantage over other generals: he enjoyed a high reputation. A
legend surrounded him as a fighter for national independence, as former chief of the Polish Socialist Party, as the
antitsarist terrorist of 1905, and as the founder of the Polish
legions in 1914. By clamoring for his return, the Polish CP
blindly and in spite of itself wove a few of its own purple
threads into the fabric of this rather phony legend. The Party
helped to create illusions in the working masses about the
"Granddad" (*Dziadek*), as Pilsudski was called familiarly, and
so to prepare the way for the May coup d'état. How much
more correctly did Adolf Nowaczynski, the talented clown of
the National-Democratic petty bourgeoisie, grasp Pilsudski's
role when he nicknamed him "Napoleon IV, the very small-
est"! How much more appropriate it would have been for
Marxists, who should have learned the art of political analysis
from Marx's *18th Brumaire*, to take this view of Pilsudski!

*It is, nevertheless, true that Pilsudski was opposing a center-
right government, presided over by Witos, which represented
the interests of the petty nobility and gentry. Is it not true
that it was precisely this government which had abolished
parliamentary liberties and begun to set up a fascist regime?
Do not these facts—independently of what happened in
1920—indicate that the Party was right to a certain extent to
support Pilsudski?*

It is undeniable that this is how the situation now appeared
to very many communists—and even more so to socialists.
Nevertheless these were optical illusions; and their spell was
broken only when it was too late. In any case one could not,
without simplifying things too much, define the Witos
government as one representing the interests of the large
landowners. Witos represented a compromise between the
interests of the landed gentry and those of the rich peasantry,
a compromise that had been reached at the expense of the

poor peasants, robbing the latter of the benefits of an agrarian reform. This compromise was clearly the result of the aspirations of the landlords and the kulaks. Moreover, it was not true that the danger of fascism came from this government. The government coalition represented the most reactionary combination of interests and forces that was possible *within the framework* of the parliamentary regime, but it worked precisely within that framework. Outside parliament it did not possess a political force strong enough to be set against the "omnipotence of the Diet." This was the insoluble dilemma of the Polish propertied classes and their traditional parties; they were incapable of maintaining their class domination either by a stabilization of the parliamentary regime under their own auspices or by overthrowing that regime. As in Marx's description of the 18th Brumaire, only the executive, the state machine, could solve this dilemma, at least for a time. Throughout the twenty years between the two wars, the objective conditions favorable to the rise of a real fascist dictatorship did not exist in Poland, if by "fascist" we understand a totalitarian dictatorship based on a strong and clearly counterrevolutionary mass movement. There was no lack of candidates for the role of Hitler or of Mussolini, but in Poland the counterrevolution never succeeded in setting such a mass movement in motion. The counterrevolution could only offer a "dictatorship of the sword." And once again, as in Marx's classic description, we are witnessing the quarrels and the coarse rows between our own pseudo-Napoleon and our own Changarnier, quarrels which were concerned with the question of whose sword was to rule the nation—Pilsudski's or Haller's.* (There are probably few in Poland today who realize that Haller was at one time Pilsudski's most important rival.) And because of the role that the "independence mythology" played in our politi-

---

* General Josef Haller, the commander of the Polish divisions in France during the First World War, was the hero of the extreme right in Poland, and was Pilsudski's antagonist during the 1920s.

cal life and also in our political thinking, the choice of the sword depended on the sheath. Only Pilsudski's sword, sheathed in the legends of the struggle for independence, was considered worthy of exercising power over the people and capable of beheading the feeble body of Polish parliamentarianism.

In other words, Pilsudski expropriated the Polish landlords and bourgeoisie *politically* in order to preserve their *social* domination over the proletariat and the peasantry. When, in May 1926, we saw President Witos, with his trousers half-buttoned, scuttling through the courtyard of the Belvedere Palace in Warsaw, pursued by detachments of Pilsudski's forces, we were witnessing, in fact, an act of political expropriation. To the working class and to its parties this looked like the beginning of economic and social expropriation. But Pilsudski saved the Polish propertied classes in spite of themselves and in spite of their traditional representatives; and he did this with the help of the workers' parties.*

All of this does not yet explain fully the origin of the "May mistake." Even before the May coup, the leaders of the Polish Communist Party had a premonition that Pilsudski was getting ready to seize power and that this augured nothing good for the working classes. Warski, it seems, said so publicly. Indeed, even some of the leaders of the Polish Socialist Party had few illusions on this score. I remember how, as a novice journalist of nineteen, on the first night of the putsch I found myself by chance in Warecka Street, in the office of Feliks Perl, editor of *Robotnik*,† the historian of the Polish Socialist Party, and one of its most eminent

---

* The western reader will see clearly the analogy between this attitude of the Polish Communists and socialists and the illusions which Proudhon, for example, entertained for a time with regard to the person of Napoleon III, or Lassalle with regard to Bismarck. Polish Marxists—especially Rosa Luxemburg's followers—had adopted a very critical attitude towards the traditions and methods of Proudhonism and Lassallism.

† *Robotnik* was the main newspaper of the Polish Socialist Party.

leaders. Perl was very worried and indignant. Every few minutes he grabbed the telephone and demanded to be put through to Pilsudski's headquarters, to General Tokarzewski, if I am not mistaken, and with a sweet-and-sour look on his face asked: "Any news on *our* front, comrade general? How are *our* troops getting on?" Replacing the receiver, he paced nervously up and down, and forgetting that I was there, grumbled to himself: "This adventurer has landed us in the soup ["adventurer" applied to Pilsudski]. If he fails, things will go badly, but if he wins, he'll thrash us." This scene repeated itself several times during the night. Meanwhile, the presses in the *Robotnik* printing shop were turning out an appeal "to the toiling people of the capital" in which the "adventurer" was hailed as a firm friend of the working class and of socialism.

But let us come back to the Polish Communist Party. Its leaders were too good Marxists to be, in normal circumstances, taken in so easily by optical illusions, even when these illusions originated in the peculiar class relationships in the country. There was another and perhaps a weightier reason for the "May mistake," and it should be sought in the ideological atmosphere and in the policy of the Soviet Communist Party and the Comintern. The Polish Party was not alone in making such a "mistake": a similar one on a gigantic scale, which was to have tragic consequences, was committed by the Chinese Communist Party when it blindly supported Chiang Kai-shek and the Kuomintang. And in nearby Rumania, almost at the same time—I think this was also in May 1926—the extremely weak Communist Party supported a similar military putsch carried out by General Antonescu.

This was, we remember, the time of the Stalin-Bukharin bloc. Trotskyism had already been routed; the bitter struggle between the Stalin-Bukharin group and the so-called Leningrad opposition led by Zinoviev and Kamenev was in its full swing. Bukharin for reasons of principle, and Stalin for tactical reasons, had both declared themselves the defenders of small peasant property and of the peasantry in general, which was supposedly threatened by the Leningrad opposition. The actual disagreements were over domestic, economic and social policies but, as usual, Stalin transformed a discussion on specific policies into a great dogmatic battle in which the issue at stake was allegedly the fundamental attitude towards the "middle strata"—the peasantry and the petty bourgeoisie. Stalin and Bukharin accused the Leningrad opposition of hostility towards the "middle strata" and of failing to understand the importance for the proletariat of the alliance with these strata. This discussion formed a sequel to the anti-Trotskyist campaign of 1923–25, during which the most serious accusation made against Trotsky had been that in his theory of the permanent revolution he too had not "appreciated at their true value" the importance of the middle strata, their progressive role, and the need to form alliances with them. Trotsky, it was said, had not understood in 1905 the necessity for a bourgeois revolution in Russia (and in the other backward countries) or had underestimated it; that was why he had proclaimed that in the twentieth century the bourgeois-democratic revolution and the socialist revolution would merge into a single one ("permanent revolution") to be accomplished under the leadership of the proletariat throughout. To try and "skip" the bourgeois stage of the revolution, so the argument ran, was the characteristic aberration of Trotskyism.

I cannot enter here into an analysis of these extremely complex problems; I am concerned now with their repercussions in Poland. The Comintern was just then busy eradicating the Trotskyist and Zinovievist heresies. The distinctive marks of these heresies were defined as an "ultraleftist" and negative attitude towards "alliances with the middle strata," a fundamental unwillingness to make such alliances, and an unwillingness to recognize that bourgeois revolution, especially in the underdeveloped countries, formed a separate stage of the historical development, in which the bourgeoisie played a progressive and even a revolutionary role. The Comintern was as if seized with an obsessional cult of "alliances."

Any sign of skepticism with regard to this cult was stigmatized as Trotskyism. The cult of alliances served a double purpose: within the Soviet Union it justified the "rightist" line of Bukharin and Stalin; internationally it justified Soviet policy in China, which subordinated the Chinese CP to the Kuomintang and placed it under Chiang Kai-shek's orders. The principles and the methods of this policy were soon applied, automatically and bureaucratically, to all the parties of the International, and among them obviously to the Polish Party. Translated into the terms of Polish politics, this line implied an "alliance" with Pilsudski as the representative of the "progressive" forces of the "bourgeois" revolution. Pilsudski suddenly appeared almost as the ideal ally—and only the Trotskyists and the Zinovievists could spurn the ideal.

At this time were there any Trotskyist or Zinovievist groups within the Polish Communist Party?

As I have already mentioned, Domski and Zofia Unszlicht had ideas which brought them close to the Zinovievist opposition. However, by that time, they had been removed from any activity in the Polish Party. Nevertheless, the Party leadership was fully aware of the practical and political questions as well as of the doctrinal issues which had been raised; and it worked under the pressure of the ideological conflicts in Moscow. At this time Warski and Kostrzewa showed a quite extraordinary docility towards Stalin. They cherished the illusion that by paying the price of submissiveness they would buy for themselves freedom of action in their own Party. Handicapped as they were by their double "mistake" of 1923 (their intervention in Trotsky's favor and their "opportunistic" policy in Poland), they were anxious to provide every possible proof of their conversion to the new "Bolshevism" that spoke of the two *distinct* stages in the revolution, the bourgeois and the socialist, the "Bolshevism" that attached so much importance to its alliance with "progressive bourgeois" elements. The whole Party propaganda was carried out in this spirit; and it created certain conditioned political reflexes within the Party which definitely contributed to the "May mistake."

In addition we must examine the effect on the Party's state of mind of the campaign which was carried out with the aim of liquidating what was called the "Luxemburgist heritage." This, by the way, is a problem which so far has not received the attention it deserves in Poland, probably because those who study the Party's history have not been equipped sufficiently to tackle the problem—they lack both method and factual knowledge. The most extraordinary myths have multiplied around the "Luxemburgist heritage." I do not want this statement to give rise to misunderstandings: I do not claim that Rosa Luxemburg was infallible, and I am not a Luxemburgist. Undoubtedly, she made some mistakes, but they were no more serious than those committed by Lenin or even by Marx, and in any case they were in quite a different category than Stalin's "errors." It was, and still is, necessary to analyze these mistakes rigorously and objectively, and to see them in their true proportions. This, however, was not the kind of analysis in which Stalin was interested—nor was Zinoviev in the years 1923-24, when, in the name of the "Bolshevization" of the Polish CP, they declared a holy war on Luxemburgism—that is, on the main ideological tradition of Polish communism. In order to realize what really mattered to Stalin it would be enough to reread his notorious 1931 letter to the editor of *Proletarskaya Revolutsya*. Instinctively, Stalin detected Rosa Luxemburg's affinity with Trotsky. And, even though there had been no Trotskyist opposition within the Polish Party during the 1920s, that party reeked to him of "Trotskyism"; Stalin considered Luxemburgism as the Polish variety of Trotskyism. This provoked the *furor theologicus* with which the Comintern set out to crush the Luxemburgist heritage.

It is undeniable that this heritage was not above criticism. Lenin's attitude on the question of national independence, or rather of the self-determination of oppressed peoples, was more realistic than that of Rosa Luxemburg. As far as the agrarian question was concerned, Rosa Luxemburg and her disciples did not go beyond advocating the socialization of farming, without understanding the necessity, in Russia and Poland, to share out the land of the semi-feudal latifundia among the peasants. This attitude did not allow Polish communism to exercise revolutionary influence over the peasantry in 1920, particularly in the eastern marches. At the time of the anti-Luxemburgist campaign, however, it was not enough to analyze these mistakes critically. The whole way of thinking, which belonged both to Luxemburgism and to Marxism—the traditions of true internationalism, the Party's specifically proletarian and socialist orientation, its healthy suspicion of the leaders (genuine or self-appointed) of the so-called middle strata—had to be rooted out. Thus the Polish CP began to atone for the Luxemburgist "sins" against national independence by belated and absurd demonstrations of its reverence for the fetishes of patriotism; and it began to pay undeserved homage to the "Legends of Independence." From this there resulted the paradoxical spectacle, which I described above, when, in 1925, Warski sent out a cry of alarm at the dangers which faced national independence and demanded the return of Pilsudski to the post of commander-in-chief. On the one hand Warski was prey to the qualms of his own political conscience, and on the other hand he echoed the anti-Luxemburgist exorcisms that came from Moscow. As if to expiate the "antipatriotic" sins of his youth, Warski—and in his person Polish Marxism at large—went to Canossa. On this pilgrimage the Party was once more torn and tormented by bitter misgivings: it paid homage to the would-be dictator, of whom Rosa Luxemburg had said, at the beginning of the century, that his whole "patriotic" ideology was but the sublimation of the dream of a déclassé petty nobleman who, even under tsardom, saw himself as the future gendarme-in-chief of his "own" independent Polish state. Rosa may have been mistaken about the chances of bourgeois Poland regaining independence, but she was not wrong about Pilsudski's ambitions and the nature of Pilsudskism.

Finally, Luxemburgism, like Trotskyism, was charged with the mortal sin of failing to understand the Party's tasks in a bourgeois revolution. In their enthusiasm to fight and defeat the Luxemburgist tradition, the Party leaders suddenly discovered that in Poland history had put on the agenda the bourgeois democratic revolution, and not, as they had thought hitherto, the socialist revolution, which would complete our overdue and unfinished bourgeois revolution. But if the bourgeois revolution was on the agenda, who could be its chief and its leader? Neither in its youth nor in its maturity had the Polish bourgeoisie produced a Danton or a Robespierre. How could it produce one in its old age? But an offshoot of our petty gentry, our "frontiersman-gentry," * could still produce our own parish-pump edition of the 18th Brumaire. It was in him, then, that our Marxists, misled and hopelessly confused by Stalinism, discovered the hero of the bourgeois stage of the revolution. The situation was grotesque precisely because this *bourgeois* revolution was designed to overthrow a government presided over by Witos, the leader of the kulaks, backed by the largest section—the peasant section—of the Polish bourgeoisie. And in retrospect the vicious circle in which the Polish CP moved under Stalinist guidance can be seen even more clearly: in 1926 the Party saw in Pilsudski an ally against the "fascism" of Witos; and a few years later, in the Popular Front period, it greeted in Witos a fighter and an ally in the struggle against Pilsudski's "fascism." Incidentally, without any Stalinist promptings, the Polish Socialist Party was floundering in the same vicious circle.

You have recalled the analogy between the Polish CP's "May mistake" and the support the Chinese CP was giving to

---

* Pilsudski came from the eastern borderlands of the old Poland, famous for the fanfaronades and feuds of its Falstaffian gentry.

Chiang Kai-shek at the same time. Did the Polish CP give its support to Pilsudski on definite orders from Moscow in the same way as the Chinese supported Chiang Kai-shek?

No. Not at all. Stalin's and Bukharin's attitude towards Pilsudski was different from that towards Chiang Kai-shek. In Chiang Kai-shek, then an honorary member of the executive of the International, they saw an ally of the Soviet Union and of Communism. In Pilsudski they saw the enemy of the 1920 war. Not only had Moscow not advised the Communists to support Pilsudski, they immediately took an unfavorable view of the CP's stand in the May coup d'état. Moreover, when the Communist group in the Diet decided to vote in the presidential election for Pilsudski, it was prevented from doing so by the veto of the executive of the Communist International. It was not "orders from Moscow" which were responsible for the "May mistake," but rather a certain political fetishism which spread from Moscow and which was inseparable from that stage of the Stalinization and bureaucratization of the Comintern. Stalin did not prompt Warski to report to Pilsudski's headquarters during the May coup. Yet Stalinism was responsible for the "May mistake," because it had confused the Polish CP, as it had confused other Communist parties, because it had made it impossible for the Party to analyze situations and problems in the Marxist manner, because it had terrorized the Party leaders with cults that did not allow them to work out policies in accordance with the demands of our class struggle and our ideological tradition. One may say what one likes against "Luxemburgism," but within the framework of this "ism" there was certainly no place for anything even remotely resembling the "May mistake." Can anyone imagine Rosa Luxemburg reporting docilely at Pilsudski's GHQ and declaring her Party's support for his coup? It took a luckless disciple of hers, a disciple whose backbone was already hopelessly deformed by Stalinism, to perform the feat.

How long did the Party maintain this policy?

For a very short time. On the day following the coup d'état
or very shortly afterwards as far as I can remember, Communist Party proclamations were circulating in Moscow, brand-
ing Pilsudski as a fascist dictator. Pilsudski himself did not
allow the Party to cherish any illusions; he refused straight-
way to grant an amnesty to the thousands of imprisoned
Communists, he boasted loudly of the "strong arm" government he was going to set up, he repudiated all "social experi-
ments" and reforms, and he sought at once to come to terms
with the big landowners.

There are some mistakes which are committed in a few
days or even hours, but which cannot be repaired in decades.
The "May mistake" was of this kind. In fairness to the Communist Party leaders it must be said that despite Pilsudski's
reactionary and dictatorial manners, the Polish Socialist Party
backed him for two years or more, while the Communists
recovered quickly from their May "intoxication" and began
at once to wage an active struggle against Pilsudski, continu-
ing to do so until the end. Disoriented and knocked off balance as it was, the Communist Party was still the only one to
defend the cause of the proletariat and of the poor peasantry,
and to stand up for democratic liberties, while the declared
upholders of democracy—the socialists—helped Pilsudski to
strengthen his position and to undermine all democratic institutions. Warski tried as best he could to make good the "May
mistake." On this occasion he showed great dignity, militancy, and personal courage. In the name of the Party, he
hurled accusations in Pilsudski's face and for this, on the
dictator's orders and in the dictator's presence, he was
dragged out of the National Assembly by Pilsudski's guards.
In order to realize the effect that Warski's cry, "Down with
the dictator " had, one must bear in mind the cult which
surrounded Pilsudski at that time. Pilsudski himself was as if
taken aback by this cry: this was the first attack on his

legend, the first attempt to tear it to shreds. I also remember the image of Warski at the Theater Square on May 1, 1928. He was marching in the forefront of our huge and illegal demonstration, through the hail of machine-gun fire and rifle shots with which we were greeted by the Socialist Party militia;* while tens and hundreds of wounded were falling in our ranks, he held up his white-gray head, a high and easy target visible from afar; unyielding and unmoved, he addressed the crowd. This was the image of him I had in my mind when, some years later, it was announced from Moscow that he was a traitor, a spy, and a Pilsudski agent.

What responsibility had the different "majority" and "minority" factions for the "May mistake"? Did this split exist even before 1926?

As far as I know these divisions did not exist before 1926. It was, in fact, the "May mistake" which brought them into being; if my memory does not betray me, these two factions first came to the fore at the plenary session of the central committee in September 1926. And, as it happens, the new split was traced back to previous dissensions. Lenski, the leader of the minority, belonged in 1924–25, after the "three W's" had been dismissed, to what was called the "left." Most of those who had belonged to it were now indeed on the side of the minority; and many of those who had belonged to the "right" were now on the side of the majority. Even older antagonisms played a role, for two of the leaders of the majority, Kostrzewa and Walecki, had come from the Left Socialist Party; as for the opposition between Warski and Lenski, an attempt was made to trace it back to the conflicts within the Social-Democratic Party (the Luxemburgists) before the First World War. Nevertheless, it seems to me that these were artificial genealogical trees, and that they were

---

* Shortly afterwards this militia was to break with the Socialist Party and enter Pilsudski's service.

dragged in quite gratuitously. Their irrelevance to the situation of 1926 is proved by the fact that both factions, the majority as well as the minority, were responsible for the "May mistake." At the critical juncture both behaved in exactly the same way. Both supported Pilsudski. Both equally recognized their responsibility for the blunder—the question they quarreled about was which of the factions had contributed more and which had contributed less to the "May mistake."

The majority was particularly identified with the theory of the "two distinct stages of the revolution" and the tactic of the united front, in which the Communist Party marched, or limped, behind the Socialist Party. It was a little more difficult to define the attitude of the leaders of the minority, who themselves did not go to the trouble of defining it. To a large extent they represented a mood of "radicalism" in the Party rather than any precise theoretical concepts. In no instance did they fight against the fetishes which were being imposed on the Polish Party from the Comintern, and which had contributed to the "Bolshevization," or in other words to the bureaucratization of the Polish CP. To that extent they contributed in a greater measure, perhaps, to the moral disarming of the movement. Both factions shared responsibility and each tried, not very effectively, to shift the blame to the other. This was a difficult period. The Party was split from top to bottom and indulged in mutual and sterile recriminations.

The recriminations were sterile because neither of the two factions was in a position to reveal the true sources of the mistake; neither was capable even *post factum* of making a Marxist analysis of the May putsch and of the regime which came out of it. Each faction sought in its adversary the cause for the Party's moral-political disaster; neither dared to look for the cause in the Comintern; neither had the courage to attack the fetishes of Stalinism; neither had the courage to challenge the false "Bolshevization" of the Party. Neither dared to submit to a critical analysis the methods by which the "Luxemburgist heritage" had been fought; neither had the nerve to try to save what had been and still was great and valid in this heritage. Let us hope that the Polish working class will now rediscover this heritage at last. It will find there its own past and its own forgotten greatness. However, it is quite possible that habits of thought, formed not just in these last years but for a good thirty years, will make it difficult for the young as well as for the old generation of Polish Marxists to find a key to that heritage. I should like to add that this cannot be a question of using, for some tactical purposes, a few isolated fragments of Rosa's thinking, such as, for example, her initial doubts about 1917—there is no lack of such attempts to "use" Rosa Luxemburg in present-day Poland. No, the task of Polish Marxists is to assimilate the sum and substance of the ideas of our greatest revolutionary, the ideas which are in full harmony with the enduring achievement of Lenin.

But let us come back to the Polish CP. The Party was then searching exclusively within itself for the causes of its political errors. The leaders hoped to remain at the helm with the support of the ruling circles in the Soviet Union. Warski and Kostrzewa relied more, perhaps, on the support of Bukharin, who was then the moving spirit in the International. As for Lenski, he staked his future on Stalin. The two factions were desperately afraid of the possibility of a conflict with the Russians; they feared that this would amount to a break with the revolution and with the international Communist movement. I am not making here any indictment of the men who led the Polish Party. They had their reasons for behaving as they did. I know from my own experience, as the former member of an opposition which was not afraid of conflict with the Soviet Party and which undertook the struggle in 1932 with full knowledge of what was involved—I know from my own bitter experience that in fact all the groups which did not recoil from this conflict condemned themselves to isolation and political impotence. But the fact that the leaders of the Polish Party had submitted to Stalin did not save them from political impotence either. And it did not save them from leading the working class into a blind alley; it condemned them to intellectual and moral sterility, and the Party—to death.

The conflict between the majority and the minority already presented a sad spectacle of that sterility. It was like a quarrel of damned souls imprisoned within the enchanted circle of Stalinism. There was no endeavor to find an explanation of the situation and to investigate the mistakes made and the tasks ahead; all were merely anxious to display Stalinist orthodoxy and loyalty to the bosses of the Comintern. Each faction used the latest orthodox formula to whiten itself and blacken its adversary. Any student who would now immerse himself in the Party literature of this period would be struck by the scholastic methods of this controversy, by the obsessive repetition of some magic formulas, and by the queer violence of a debate, the object of which remains altogether elusive.

Did you yourself belong to the majority or to the minority?

I did not belong to either, probably because when I joined the Party, at the age of nineteen, the dividing line had already been drawn and I did not really understand what it was all about. However, I remember clearly that in 1926-27 I had a very sharp sense of the futility of the dispute. It seemed to me that the majority carried the burden of a certain opportunism, and that the minority had the more revolutionary dynamic. What disturbed me about the latter was its intellectual crudity and inclination towards sectarianism. It seemed to me that the majority represented a more serious school of thought and a deeper Marxist tradition. This was the predominant view among the group of comrades with whom I mixed, young Communist as I then was. This may have induced me to keep aloof from both factions and to search in a different direction for a way out of the impasse. I am convinced that the history of the Polish Party must be tackled afresh; to approach it from the angle either of the old minority or of the old majority would lead nowhere and would bring no positive result, intellectually or politically.

Which of the factions was dominant in the Party after May 1926?

At the time of the coup d'état the two factions shared the leadership, and this state of affairs lasted almost until the end of 1928. At the beginning of this period, Warski's and Kostrzewa's ascendancy was more marked, if only because the Bukharinist line still predominated in the Comintern. As usual, their influence showed itself in a more "organic" activity of the Party, in a closer link between the Party and the masses, in a greater realism of its agitation, and in its stronger pull on the left elements in the Socialist Party, and also on the rural population and on the national minorities. In spite of the mutual recriminations which weakened it, the Party had in certain respects recovered quickly from its "May mistake." The working class had "forgiven" that mistake. Hadn't the Communists admitted their error sincerely and unambiguously? After all, they all shared the same illusions. The Party was now gaining strength. This was proved, for example, by the results of the municipal elections in Warsaw, where, in 1927, more votes were cast for the CP's illegal list than for the list of any other party. The electors knew that their pro-Communist votes were lost, that none of our candidates would get into the municipal council, but they nevertheless demonstratively voted Communist. This was again a period when in the main industrial centers—Warsaw, Lodz, the Dabrowa coalfields—the CP was stronger than the Socialist Party, in spite of severe police persecution and wasteful interfactional struggle. In 1928 the Communist Party really was leading the working class in its struggle against the Pilsudski dictatorship. The fear which seized the Pilsudskists and a section of the Socialist Party explains the bloody repression of May 1, of which I spoke earlier. (The illegal Communist demonstrations were very often larger than the demonstrations of the Socialist Party, which marched under the double protection of the police and their own armed militia.) In spite of all the handicaps and difficulties, the Party had some chance of going over to the offensive again. Just at this moment, however, it suffered a new blow, which knocked it off its relative balance and rendered it powerless.

Are you referring to the change in the leadership and to the elimination of Warski and Kostrzewa?

Yes. And once again it was not *what* happened that mattered so much as *how* it happened. Whether Warski and Kostrzewa or Lenski was at the helm was less important than the fact that the change was brought about solely from "above," that it bore no relation to the logic of the class struggle in Poland. Once again, the Russian Party and the International weighed on the fate of Polish Communists and the Polish working classes.

At the Sixth Congress of the International, in the summer of 1928, the struggle between Stalin and Bukharin, previously confined within the Soviet Politburo, had burst into the open. Acting under the pressure of the USSR's internal crisis, Stalin was reviving his policy towards the peasantry and preparing the wholesale collectivization. A huge social drama was being enacted in the Soviet Union, and it entailed another drama, less obvious but in its consequences equally grave, for European Communism. Having broken with Bukharin on domestic issues, Stalin set out to eradicate all Bukharinist influence in the Comintern and to change international Communist policy. Automatically, this involved the condemnation of the "majority" in the Polish CP. Warski and Kostrzewa were deprived of all influence. The steering wheel was violently turned "left." In 1929 Molotov put forward the ill-fated conception of a "third period" which, briefly, consisted in this: the capitalist world was entering a directly revolutionary situation, and consequently the Communist movement must go over to an offensive struggle for power; social-democracy, otherwise "social-fascism," was Communism's main and most dangerous enemy; moreover, the left wing of the social-democratic parties was more dangerous than the right wing; the Communists should direct their main fire against that enemy; they were forbidden to enter into any agreements with Socialists, they should set up their own Red Trade Unions (breaking away from the general trade unions) and, with their help, organize general strikes and armed insurrections. The policy of the "third period" was in force from 1929 to 1934. This was the time when Nazism was growing like an avalanche in Germany, and in the face of this threat, to which the Social-Democrats were surrendering anyhow, the Communist Party found itself disarmed. When the Party was told that its main enemy was not Hitler but "social-fascism," and that it had no right to ally itself with social-democracy against Nazism, German Communism, tied hand and foot, was delivered over to the heroes of the swastika.

In Poland the *direct* results of this policy were not yet quite as tragic, but they were grim enough. The simmering conflict between Pilsudski on the one hand, and the Socialist Party and the peasant movement on the other, was nearing the boiling point. These were the years of the Left-Center opposition. Pilsudski seized the leaders of this opposition and had them imprisoned and tortured in the fortress of Brzesc. The anti-Communist terror, too, had grown more intense and reached a climax with the tortures inflicted on Ukrainian Communists imprisoned in Luck. In these conditions the policy and the slogans of the "third period," diligently translated into Polish by Lenski, had all the characteristics of a malignant political diversion. The Party member had to "concentrate the fire" on the victims of Brzesc and not on their executioners; he had to believe that the Party's gravest sin would be to support the struggle of the Left-Center against Pilsudski, or to turn this struggle into a fierce revolutionary contest, which the leaders of the Left-Center neither could nor wished to do.

In conditions incomparably more serious, the Polish CP repeated the whole series of ultraleft mistakes which it had committed in 1924–25. It indulged once more in ultrarevolutionary acrobatics, which consisted in launching revolutionary activities with great energy into an empty space—activities the aims of which became less and less real. Loud and big words were not followed by deeds. The Party operated exclusively within its own ranks—and these were melting away. It cut itself off from the working and peasant masses who had been first aroused and then confounded by the half-hearted struggle of the Left-Center. It lost common language with the mass of workers and found itself driven more and more towards the fringe of politics, towards radical but politically impotent déclassé petty-bourgeois elements (mostly Jewish). The leaders did not, and would not, see the vacuum around the Party and the moral ravages in the rank and file. In the long run a revolutionary party cannot tolerate with impunity a divorce between word and deed; nor can it turn its back on reality and feed on the conventional fictions of a pseudorevolutionary "line" without having one day to pay for all this with the distortion of its own character. This indeed was the price the whole Comintern paid for the policy of the "third period." The Polish Party, in addition, labored under the dictatorship of a faction which—following Stalin's example—dragged its inner-party opponents in the mud, gagged them, and thus stopped all the processes of opinion-formation within the party. These characteristics of the Stalinist inner-party regime, with which Poland was to become so thoroughly acquainted in the 1940s and 1950s, existed by the end of the twenties and had become fully developed in 1932–33. The phenomenon was all the more paradoxical because it did not result from the "corruption of power," which to some degree may be expected in a ruling party, nor did it come about through the growth of a bureaucracy jealous of its social and political privileges. The Polish Communist Party remained the party of the oppressed and the persecuted. Its members and followers continued to crowd Pilsudski's and Rydz-Smigly's prisons. The dream of proletarian revolution and socialism still animated them. It was this dream precisely that made them inclined to accept blindly everything which came from the Soviet Union—the fatherland of the proletariat. Instead of being true to itself, the Party was becoming false to itself. Guided by its devotion to the cause of revolution, it was losing itself as the party of revolution.

In the middle 1930s there took place in the Party a turn in favor of the Popular Front. How did this influence the Party?

At this time, I was already out of the Party. Cut off from it, I could judge the facts from the outside only. Whatever else may be said about it, the policy of the Popular Front undoubtedly rejuvenated and refreshed the Party, which came into contact with reality. This brought new elements within the Party's sphere of influence. The intellectuals, who were then attracted by the Polish Party, now play, it seems to me, an important role in Poland's political life. That is why to the young generation they present this period as idealized and enveloped in a beautifying mist. Nevertheless, we must examine it coolly and objectively.

The Popular Front was the extreme opposite of the policy of the "third period." Yesterday's "social-fascists" turned out to be anti-fascist fighters. Even the right-wing leaders of the peasant movement, like Witos, were recognized as knights-errant of democracy and progress. By comparison with the moderation of the Party's new tactical line, the "opportunism" of Warski and Kostrzewa looked like exuberant ultraradicalism. Yet the slogans of the Popular Front were, in 1935 and 1936, launched by the same leaders (Lenski and Henrykowski) who in the previous year had directed their main fire against the "social-fascists" and who had considered "united front from below" as the only admissible policy, and who had expelled hundreds of militants simply because they had dared to doubt whether social-fascism was really "the main and most serious danger." Once again, what is important is not so much *what* policy was applied as *how* it was applied. No inner party discussion had preceded this violent change of line, which only followed the change of line of the Comintern, a line based in its turn on the calculations of Stalin's foreign policy. The effect which the reversal of policy had on the Party itself was therefore full of contradictions. On the one hand, the break with the "third period" had a stimulating and reviving influence on the Party, and allowed it to escape from its vacuum. On the other hand, the mechanical character of this turn, coming entirely from "above," increased still further the atrophy of political thinking among the cadres of old militants, who had already become accustomed to replace one set of political rituals by another at a single word of command and to consider all political notions and all watchwords as so many conventional phrases with no living content. Cynicism and ideological apathy made serious inroads. The young, who began their political life under the banner of the Popular Front, greeted the new slogans much more seriously and threw themselves with enthusiasm into the thick of anti-fascist activity. Nevertheless, this period was not conducive to the formation of Marxist consciousness in the young; they absorbed only very little of the Party's specifically Communist tradition. The Party propaganda, disseminating the vaguest of "democratic" and antifascist slogans and the most insipid "let's all get together" proclamations, was jettisoning all the criteria of proletarian interest and class struggle. It hardly differed from the routine propaganda of right-wing socialists, except that it markedly lacked any genuineness. Ideological shallowness and a patriotic-democratic vulgarity characterized the Party which once drew its inspiration from Rosa Luxemburg's flaming thought.

I am dwelling on this not in order to tear open old wounds or revive lapsed controversies, but in order to show the state of spiritual weakness in which the Party found itself on the eve of its assassination, and so to explain the passivity and the silence with which in 1938 it received its own death sentence and endured the unparalleled slaughter of its leaders.

A picture presenting the Polish CP as a flourishing, intellectually healthy body, brimming over with strength, which suddenly fell a victim to Yezhov's provocation, would be false and unhistorical. There is no need to resort to such a myth in order to rehabilitate the Party. Moreover, this would transform the very act of rehabilitation into a magic ritual. How did it happen, we must ask, that a Party which had to its credit decades of underground struggle and a long (seventy years long!) and proud Marxist tradition submitted meekly to this horrible outrage—without a protest, without making any attempt to defend its martyred leaders and fighters, without even trying to vindicate its honor, and without declaring that in spite of the death sentence Stalin had passed on it, it would live on and fight on? How could this happen? We must be fully aware of the moral corrosion to which Stalinism had for so many years exposed Polish Communism in order to understand its complete collapse under the blow.

At the time of its dissolution, the Polish CP was charged with being "infected" with Trotskyism and of being an agency of the Polish political police. What in fact was the influence of Trotskyism on the Party?

The Trotskyist opposition in the Party was formed in the years 1931–32. It grouped comrades who had formerly belonged both to the minority and to the majority, and others who had not been connected with either faction. The opposition did not *a priori* take up a Trotskyist stand. It was formed on the basis of a critical view of the policy of the "third period," the slogans about "social-fascism," the "united front only from below," etc., and also of the bureaucratic inner-party regime. Demanding the right of self-determination for the Polish Party, the opposition adopted a critical attitude towards the regime that was prevailing within the International and the Soviet Party. Consequently, the ideas of the Trotskyist opposition in the USSR and particularly the magnificent, though fruitless, campaign which Trotsky waged in exile for a united front against Hitler, had a powerful and decisive impact on our group. At the beginning, the opposition exercised a fairly large influence. In Warsaw, where the Party counted at that time, it seems, hardly more than a thousand members, the opposition had about three hundred members (most of whom had played an important role in the movement), not counting a large circle of sympathizers in the Party organizations. Unfortunately, the deplorable condition in which the Party found itself affected the opposition too. The Party was cut off from the workers in large industry and was relegated to a petty-bourgeois fringe, and this weakness was reflected in the opposition. Although we had attracted many militants in the capital, our influence was much weaker in the provinces, where the pulse of Party life in general had been rather feeble. The bulk of the militants viewed the opposition with much sympathy so long as they did not realize that not only adherence but even mere contact with the opposition would be punished by expulsion from the Party. The new grouping, which did not simply continue the old and sterile quarrel between minority and majority but posed the problem of Party policy on a new plane, was at first greeted with relief. The Party leaders retorted by expelling and slandering us in the best Stalinist style. The same leaders who, a few years hence, were to be liquidated as police agents now branded the opposition as the "agency" of "social-fascism," then simply of fascism, and as a gang of "enemies of the USSR."

By the use of such methods, the leadership succeeded in stifling all discussion and terrorizing Party members to such an extent that they began to shun us with the superstitious fear with which faithful members of the Church used to shun excommunicated heretics. The opposition was hermetically isolated from the Party, and by 1936 had almost no contact with it. Thus the charge that the Polish CP had become a Trotskyist "agency" was sheer invention. But nevertheless, the doubts and ideas that the opposition had sown in the Party continued to germinate. Even while Party members remained conformist, many of them never ceased to listen to the voice of the opposition, and they were influenced by it to a greater or lesser degree—at any rate sufficiently to be skeptical about the holy writ of Stalinism. And since nothing in nature is ever lost completely, the Luxemburgist tradition had not vanished completely either, in spite of the years which had been spent on uprooting it. The opposition's influence and the effect of that tradition was such that even after years of "Bolshevization," the psychological profile of even the most orthodox Polish Communist left much to be desired from the Stalinist point of view. Thus it was in the 1930s; fortunately it was like this also after the Second World War: during this whole period a certain law of continuity had never ceased to operate.

Nevertheless, a question must be posed. We know that Pilsudski had his agents in all the left-wing parties. Surely he must have tried to introduce them into the CP as well?

The theory of these networks of agents which Pilsudski supposedly had created in various left-wing parties is again a crude simplification. No network of secret agents could have enabled Pilsudski to exercise on the Socialists and on a part of the peasant movement the influence he did exercise as a result of his long and above-board connections with these parties. He was one of the founding fathers of the Polish

Socialist Party and was for many years its chief leader and inspiration. He had been the Commander of the Legion, to which men of the patriotic left had rallied. Even after he had left the Socialist Party, he continued to represent something that belonged to its essence: social-patriotism pushed to the extreme. It was that which formed the basis of Pilsudski's "magical" influence. The worship of Polish "statehood," the dreams of the "One and Sovereign" Poland, old loyalties, friendships, and ties of sentiment—these gave birth to those Pilsudskist "networks" in parties of the moderate and patriotic left, which at times of conflict he attempted to destroy from within. There was not, and there could not have been, any similar basis for a Pilsudskist network in the Polish CP. The left-wing socialists who, after 1918, found themselves in the ranks and in the leadership of the Communist Party, had to their credit more than ten years of bitter struggle against Pilsudski. As for the old Luxemburgists, it is hardly necessary to dwell on their attitude towards him. However, even in the moderate, patriotic, left parties (PPS or *Wyzwolenie*) Pilsudski's "agents" achieved very little. Very quickly these parties overcame the confusion and splits provoked by the "networks." Only the Polish CP, if we are to believe Stalin, was *completely* in the hands of Pilsudski's "agents." In 1938, when this accusation was made and one wanted to refute it, one felt overwhelmed by the sheer nonsense of it all. It is true that during the 1930s the Polish Party had suffered particularly from police provocations. The fall in the ideological level of most of the militants, the bitterness of the factional struggles, the ultrarevolutionary policy of the years 1929–35—all this had facilitated to a certain extent the penetration of police agents into the Party. It would in any case have been surprising if the police had had no agents whatsoever in the Polish CP in the same way in which the tsarist Okhrana had had its Azefs and its Malinowskis in nearly all the illegal Russian organizations. However, no one would have had the idea of dissolving the Bolshevik Party or the

Socialist Revolutionary Party for that reason. The Stalinist provocation was a much more serious danger for the Polish CP than all the *agents provocateurs* of the Polish secret police.*

What, then, in your opinion were the reasons for which Stalin ordered the dissolution of the Polish Party? The view which prevails now among old Party militants is that Stalin was already preparing the ground for his 1939 agreement with Hitler and that he liquidated the Polish Party and sent its leaders to their death because he feared that they might obstruct that agreement.

This motive no doubt played a part in Stalin's decision but does not explain it fully. Warski and Kostrzewa, for years cut off from all contact with Poland (and the world), were no longer in a position to offer the slightest resistance to Stalin, even if they had wished to do so. As for Lenski and Henrykowski, I am convinced that they would have remained faithful to Stalin even in a situation as critical for Polish Communism as that of August and September 1939, in the same way as were the leaders of the French Party, not to mention the Germans and others. But here we are dealing with hypotheses. It seems to me that no single motive or sober calculation can explain Stalin's behavior in this matter. His irrational impulses were quite as important as his "rational" calculations; and he was impelled to act as he did by old grudges and ancient phobias, all intensified to the utmost by the persecution mania which gripped him at the time of the great Moscow trials, when he was settling his final accounts with the Leninist old guard. In this frame of mind, Stalin saw the

---

* Azef was a well-known *agent provocateur* who led the terrorist organization of the Russian Social-Revolutionary Party. Malinowski, who was Lenin's friend, a deputy to the Duma, and an influential member of the Bolshevik Central Committee, was finally also exposed as an *agent provocateur*.

Polish CP as the stronghold of hated Luxemburgism—the Polish "variety of Trotskyism"—which had defied him as long ago as 1923; the Party in which some leaders were close to Bukharin and others to Zinoviev; the Party of incurable heresies, proud of its traditions and of its heroism; the Party, finally, which might well in certain international situations become an obstacle on his road. . . . And so he decided to remove that obstacle by the blade of the same guillotine which, working furiously, was already destroying a whole generation of Bolsheviks.

The historian will not end his account of the fortunes of the Polish CP on the act of its annihilation. The epilogue of the story is, in a sense, its most important chapter. The "posthumous" fate of the Polish CP will remain the most striking testimony of its greatness. Crushed, decimated, confounded and outraged, the Party's old cadre was still the spearhead of all of Poland's revolutionary forces. It was that remnant of the old Party which at the end of the Second World War, in the peculiar international situation which favored social revolution, carried this revolution through. The survivors of the Polish CP came forward as the executors of their Party's will, although they had to do so in conditions and by methods that no philosophers dreamed of. And nearly twenty years after the massacre of the Polish CP, its spirit and, if you like, something of its old Luxemburgist tradition, showed themselves in October 1956.

Not only the historian, but also every militant Marxist, must draw certain conclusions from the tragic history of the Polish CP. Here, I must of necessity confine myself to one rather general idea: if the history of the Polish CP and of Poland at large proves anything at all, *it proves how indestructible is the link between the Polish and the Russian revolutions.* This has been proved both negatively and positively. For her attempt to place herself athwart the international revolution which had begun in Russia—the attempt made in 1918-20—Poland had to pay with twenty years of stagnation and backwardness, of provincially narrow and anachronistic social life, and, finally, with the catastrophe of 1939. On the other hand, the revolution, isolated in old and backward Russia, isolated by the world's anticommunist forces (with Poland's eager help), underwent a distortion which affected tragically not only the peoples of the USSR but revenged itself on Poland as well. Already in 1920 Poland had felt something of that revenge. Subsequently, it led to the deformation of the working-class movement in Poland, condemning it to sterility and impotence. Then there came 1939. After the Second World War, the Russian Revolution, in spite of all its distortions, still showed itself to be sufficiently alive and dynamic to stimulate new revolutionary processes in Europe and Asia. Poland once again absorbed from the Russian Revolution its shadows as well as its lights and took over from it, together with the blessings of a progressive upheaval in social relationships, the curse of bureaucratic terror and the Stalin cult. Poland had to pay a heavy penalty for the "miracle on the Vistula" of 1920,* in which she had gloried for twenty years. Having spurned the Russian Revolution in its heroic stage, she had to humble herself before this same Revolution after it had degenerated. Having scorned Lenin and Leninist internationalism, Poland had to prostrate herself before Stalin and Great Russian chauvinism. Only as the Soviet Union was beginning to awaken from the nightmare of Stalinism could Poland free herself from it, and by that very act stimulate processes of recovery in other socialist countries. But only as the Russian Revolution emerges from the sidetracks onto which history had driven it and at last enters the highway of socialist democracy, will the perspectives before People's Poland clear up definitely. At every step

---

* The "miracle on the Vistula" was the name given to the battle of Warsaw, in which Pilsudski's armies inflicted defeat on the Soviet army. At the time of this battle, General Weygand was Pilsudski's adviser.

history demonstrates *ad oculos* how indissoluble are the bonds between the Polish and the Russian revolutions. But whereas hitherto history has again and again demonstrated the indissoluble nature of this bond in a negative manner—by inflicting the most cruel lessons on Poland—in October 1956 it has begun perhaps to demonstrate it in the positive, that is, in the only effective manner. History so far has not always been a good and sensible teacher. The lessons in internationalism which it attempted to teach the Polish masses were singularly involved, badly thought out, and ineffective. During almost every one of these "lessons," history mocked and insulted Poland's national dignity and, in the first place, the dignity and independence of the Polish revolutionary movement. Is it surprising then, that the "pupil" has not been very receptive, and, trying to escape the peculiar "teacher," has sought refuge in the jungle of our nationalist legends? The Polish masses will understand that the bonds which unite their destiny with that of the Russian and other revolutions are indissoluble, but only after they have recovered from the blows and shocks inflicted on them in the past, and when they feel that nothing can ever again threaten their independence and national dignity. Marxists, however, must rise above the shocks and the traumas from which the masses suffer; and they must even now be deeply and thoroughly aware of the common destiny of Poland and other nations advancing towards socialism. Marxists have no right to nourish themselves, nor to feed others, on the spiritual diet of stale and warmed-up myths and legends. Socialism does not aim at the perpetuation of the national state; its aim is international society. It is based not on national self-centeredness and self-sufficiency, but on international division of labor and on cooperation. This almost forgotten truth is the very ABC of Marxism.

You may say that what I am proposing is a new edition of Luxemburgism, slightly amended and adapted to the needs of 1957. Perhaps. You may tell me that this is merely a new version of the theory of "organic incorporation."* Perhaps. But what is at stake this time is the "organic integration" of Poland into international socialism, not her incorporation into a Russian empire.

* In her theory of "organic incorporation," which she formulated in her doctoral thesis, Rosa Luxemburg stated that the struggle for Poland's independence was hopeless and in essence even reactionary because of the "organic" economic ties that linked Poland and Russia; neither the Polish bourgeoisie nor the Polish proletariat were interested in the restoration of a sovereign Poland: the bourgeoisie because Russian markets were more profitable to it, and the proletariat because it strove for international socialism. This conception formed the theoretical basis of the Luxemburgist politics.

an open letter
to wladyslaw gomulka and the central committee of the polish workers party

I am addressing this letter to you in order to protest against the recent secret trials and convictions of Ludwik Hass, Karol Modzelewski, Kazimierz Badowski, Romuald Smiech, Kurón, and other members of your Party. According to all available reports, these men have been deprived of liberty solely because they have voiced views critical of your policy or certain aspects of it, and because they have expressed disappointment with the bureaucratic arbitrariness and corruption which they see rampant in their country. The charge against them is that they have circulated leaflets and a pamphlet containing "false information detrimental to the State and its supreme authorities"—the public prosecutor, it seems, did not accuse them of any crime or offense graver than that.

If this is the accusation, then the persecution of these men is disgraceful and scandalous. Several questions must be asked: Why, in the first instance, have the courts held their hearings *in camera*? Surely, no matter of State security was

This open letter was released on 28 April 1966.

or could have been involved. All the defendants have been academic teachers and students, and what they have tried to do was to communicate their views to fellow students. Why have they not been given a fair and open trial? Why have your own newspapers not even summarized the indictments and the pleas of the defense? Is it because the proceedings have been so absurd and shameful that you yourselves feel that you cannot justify or excuse them; and so you prefer to cover them with silence and oblivion? As far as I know, prosecutor and judges have not impugned the defendants' motives or cast any serious doubt on their integrity. The accused men have proclaimed themselves to be, and have behaved like, devoted nonconformist Communists, profoundly convinced of the truth and validity of revolutionary Marxism.

I know that one of them, Ludwik Hass, was, even before the Second World War, a member of the Communist, so-called Trotskyist, organization of which I was one of the founders and mouthpiece. He then spent seventeen years in Stalin's prisons, concentration camps, and places of deportation. Released in 1957, he returned to Poland so free from all bitterness and so strongly animated by his faith in a better socialist future that he at once decided to join your Party; and he was accepted as a member. No one asked him to renounce his past, and he did not deny his old "Trotskyist" views even for a moment—on the contrary, he upheld them frankly and untiringly. This circumstance alone testifies to his courage and integrity. Do you, Wladyslaw Gomulka, really believe that you have, in your "apparatus" and administration, many people of comparable disinterestedness and idealism? Look around you, look at the crowds of time-servers that surround you, at all those opportunists without principle and honor who fawn on you as they fawned on Bierut, and as some of them fawned even on Rydz-Smigly and Pilsudski. On how many of these bureaucrats can your government, and can socialism, count in an hour of danger, as it can count on the people you have put in prison?

Recently your government claimed with a certain pride that there have been no political prisoners in Poland since 1956. This claim, if true, was indeed something to be proud of in a country the jails of which had always, under all regimes, been full of political prisoners, especially of communist prisoners. You have not, as far as I know, jailed and put in chains any of your all too numerous and virulent anticommunist opponents; and you deserve credit for the moderation with which you treat them. But why do you deny such treatment to your critics on the left? Hass, Modzelewski and their friends have been brought to the courtrooms handcuffed and under heavy guard. Eyewitness accounts say that they raised their chained fists in the old Communist salute and sang the *Internationale*. This detail speaks eloquently about their political characters and loyalties. How many of your dignitaries, Wladyslaw Gomulka, would nowadays intone the *Internationale* of their own free will and accord?

I have been informed that before the trial, during the interrogation, the official who conducted it alleged that Hass and other defendants had worked in contact with me. I do not know whether the prosecutor took up this charge in the courtroom. In any case, the allegation is a complete falsehood. Let me say that if the defendants had tried to get in touch with me, I would have readily responded. But the fact is that I have had no contact whatsoever with any of them. I have not even seen a single one of their leaflets or pamphlets. I judge their behavior solely from reports reaching me by word of mouth or through Western European newspapers.

I ought perhaps to explain that since the Second World War I have not participated in Polish political life in any way, and that, not being a member of any political organization, Trotskyist or otherwise, I am speaking only for myself. I should add, however, that on a few very rare occasions I have broken my self-imposed political abstinence. I protested when you, Wladyslaw Gomulka, were imprisoned and slandered in the last years of the Stalin era. Knowing full well that I could not share all your views, I expressed solidarity with you. Similarly, I do not know whether I can fully approve the views and behavior of Hass, Modzelewski, and their comrades. But in their case, as in yours, I think I can recognize reactionary police terror for what it is and tell slander from truth.

Another occasion on which I allowed myself to have a say on Polish political matters was in 1957, when I explained in a special essay "The Tragedy of Polish Communism between the World Wars." You may remember that your censors, Stalinists of the so-called Natolin group, confiscated the essay when *Polityka* tried to publish it, and that then you, Wladyslaw Gomulka, ordered the essay to be widely distributed among Party members. In those far-off days, just after the "Polish spring in October," you held that Polish Communists ought to know my account of the havoc that Stalin made of their Party, delivering nearly all its leaders to the firing squad. You knew that I had been one of those very few communists who, in 1938, protested against that crime and against the disbandment and denigration of what had once been our common Party. Moscow "rehabilitated" the Polish Party and its leaders only after seventeen or eighteen years; and then you, Wladyslaw Gomulka, apologized for having kept silent in 1938, although you had not believed the Stalinist slanders. I do not believe that you are right now in persecuting and imprisoning members of your own Party and your critics on the left; and I cannot keep silent.

May I remind you of your own words spoken at the famous Eighth Session of the Central Committee in October 1956? "The cult of the personality was not a matter just of Stalin's person," you stated then. "This was a system which had been transplanted from the USSR to nearly all Communist Parties. . . . *We have finished, or rather we are finishing, with that system once and for all.*" (Your italics.)

But are you not to some extent re-establishing that system? Do you wish these trials to mark the tenth anniversary of your own rehabilitation and of that "spring in October," during which you raised so many hopes for the future?

In the name of those hopes and in the name of your own record, the record of a fighter and of a political prisoner under Pilsudski and Stalin, I appeal to you and to your colleagues of the Central Committee: Do not allow this miscarriage of justice to last! Dispel the secrecy that surrounds the cases of Hass, Modzelewski, and their comrades. If you think that they are guilty of grave offenses, then publish the full report of the court proceedings and let it speak for itself. In any case, I appeal to you to order an immediate and public revision of the trial. If you refuse these demands, you will stand condemned as epigones of Stalinism, guilty of stifling your own Party and compromising the future of socialism.

ISAAC DEUTSCHER

London, 24 April 1966

germany and marxism

How do you judge the present trend in Germany towards the possible eruption of a new nationalism, as evidenced by the NPD,* and the electoral successes which the party has scored in several of the Länder? Do you really see in this a genuine, and acute, danger for our young Western democracy?

A genuine danger, yes; an acute one, perhaps not as yet. I remember a remark of Leon Trotsky's: in 1919 or 1920 he said of the Weimar Republic that it would prove to be merely an interval between two dictatorships. One now wonders with real anxiety: is not this—I do not know whether I should say democracy—is not the West German parliamentary regime of the last seventeen or eighteen years, too, merely an interval between two dictatorships, between two waves of

* Nationaldemokratische Partei Deutschlands

This is the translation of an interview Isaac Deutscher gave to Hamburg Television on 23 July 1967, of which he edited the original transcript himself. The English version was first published in New Left Review, *Jan.-Feb. 1968.*

nationalism? There are grounds for this anxiety. Probably the danger is not immediate; the situation may well be similar to that of the years 1927–28, when National Socialism still stood on the fringe of German political life, a marginal phenomenon. That could be the case today as well with the new nationalism. It was in 1929–30 that Nazism first thrust itself, with a sudden leap, into the foreground of German political life. However, it seems to me that a simple rebirth of National Socialism in Germany is unlikely. History never repeats itself in such uncomplicated ways. It is said that generals in every war tend to fight anew the battles of the previous war. Something similar happens in politics too: people imagine new dangers taking old forms. But the waves of nationalism, of reaction, of counterrevolution always assume new forms. In the years of the Weimar Republic, most people on the left thought that democracy in Germany was threatened by a restoration of the Hohenzollerns and of the *ancien régime.* But Hitler's party was republican, and even called itself "socialist." The new wave of authoritarian reaction and of nationalism now appearing on the horizon will most probably also differ in many of its features from National Socialism. Naturally there will be a certain continuity, but it will not be a direct one.

But what do you see as the basis for a possible new wave of reaction?

A great deal depends on the stability of social relations and on the economic situation. Also the problem of the division of Germany remains unresolved; this is a great open wound in the life of the nation, even if it is not at the present moment so painfully sensitive as it might be. Here are contained really dangerous possibilities.

Do you believe then that the NPD is a reservoir for this reactionary wave?

That I do not know. It is hard to say. To take up once again the analogy with the twenties: Nazism was crystallized and formed from various fermenting groups and competing ultra-nationalist sects. Whether a similar development lies ahead of the present nationalistic ferment necessarily remains uncertain. But the thought that the nationalistic insanity—the perennial tragedy of Germany—is once again spreading its shadow must cause us grave anxiety.

But is not the danger of a new nationalistic insanity, as you put it, really banished by our NATO links, and our Friendship Treaty with France? Or do you believe that all these ...

I am afraid those links are quite fragile, if I may say so. No, I believe that a guarantee against this nationalism can only come from a deep inner transformation of Germany, and not through external, diplomatic arrangements.

How do you see this transformation? What do you understand by it?

This is a large and rather difficult question. I think that since the Reformation the tragedy of Germany consists in the fact that it has not advanced with the times, and that Germany has never fought through its own revolution. The French had their great revolution. The English carried theirs through in the seventeenth century and then experienced a long process of reform, democratization and progress. Germany in many respects has remained fixed in the sixteenth century and at the catastrophe of the Thirty Years War. Every revolution has failed. Germany did not merely invent the *ersatz* industrially, it produced it sociopolitically as well: the ersatz-revolution of a Bismarck, the ersatz-revolution of 1918 and the ersatz-revolution of 1945—none of them were made by Germans, but by conquering foreign armies. That is the tragedy, the guilt and the misfortune of Germany.

Of course you were here in West Germany in 1945, as a correspondent for English newspapers. What impression did you have then, and what was at that time your opinion as to what should be done with the German state and people, lying in ruins?

Yes—I was in Germany as correspondent of the *Economist* and of the *Observer*, and wrote quite a lot about this question. During the war, and in the period immediately after the war, I was one of the few in the Anglo-Saxon press who criticized the policy of so-called de-industrialization of Germany, and the Potsdam decisions. In the spring of 1946 I wrote, under the title "The Modern Luddites," a detailed study directed against the Potsdam economic policy. The *Economist* published my essay as a special supplement; later Lord Beveridge brought it out as a pamphlet. At that time, the time of the dismantling, the essay made a real impact in Germany too: it was sold in the streets, on the black-market for almost astronomical sums. I was myself offered a copy of my essay by a street-hawker in Hamburg for the equivalent of almost twenty-five pounds. That impressed on me deeply the misery of Germany, the physical and the moral misery; the terrifying misfortune of a people which had been twice defeated: by its own insane nationalism, and by the foreign armies.

In 1945 did you hope for a revolution of our own, a German revolution, to defeat National Socialism from within? If so, in what form?

I must admit I did not for a minute imagine that Nazism could be defeated otherwise than by a German revolution. I remember that on July 21, 1944, that is to say on the day after the attempt on Hitler's life, I published an article in the *Observer* in which I treated the attempt as "Prelude to the German Revolution." I hoped that July 20 might give the impulse—from above—for a revolution—from below. Of course I was over-optimistic. But in a historical sense my line of thinking was not false: without a revolution from below—well, has National Socialism been defeated in its roots? Here one can discern a certain revenge on the part of history. In the Germany always spurned by its own revolution, the Germany which rejected the socialism of Marx and Engels, of Rosa Luxemburg and Liebknecht—in other words the socialism which was a product of German thought and philosophy—in this Germany a kind of bastard socialism has now been decreed in the East by a Russian army of occupation and by Ulbricht.

Had you ever concerned yourself previously with Germany and German problems?

Yes, naturally, I have always been conscious of the fact that the destiny of Europe and of mankind necessarily depends on what happens in Germany, in the heart of Europe. In my youth, as you know, I was active not only as a writer but also as a Polish communist. I was expelled from the Polish Communist Party in the spring of 1932, because I had published an essay under the title "The Danger of a New Barbarism in Europe," an essay concerned exclusively with the German question. That is how I already termed Nazism in the year preceding Hitler's seizure of power. I called for common action on the part of communists and social-democrats against Nazism in Germany and against the Pilsudski dictatorship in Poland. I wrote that Nazism, should it be victorious, would smash both parties, the Social-Democratic and the Communist, and would raise the specter of a second world war. That was an offense against the current party line. The Party, and the entire Comintern, underrated the destructive dynamic and the totalitarian logic of Nazism, and imagined that Hitler and the Social-Democrats (whom they termed social-fascists) would coexist and reach a compromise. I was the spokesman of an anti-Stalinist group, the first opposition of this kind in the Polish Party; and we considered it as our main task to warn the Party, the Comintern and the working class of the Nazi danger. The official reason for my expulsion from the Party was that I exaggerated the danger from Nazism and spread panic in the workers' movement. In a certain sense that was true: in the years 1931–32 Nazism had cast me into such a state of feverish agitation and anxiety. Those who at that time felt no such "panic" were, of course, blind.

You then came to the forefront, in the period following your expulsion from the Polish Communist Party, as an author. Tell us something about the tasks you set yourself as a writer, and what you wrote.

I set myself the task of being the interpreter of the Russian Revolution, for I was, and still am, convinced that the world had not grasped the full magnitude and the many complex facets of the Revolution. In many writings, but above all in my biography of Stalin, in my three-volume biography of Trotsky and in an as yet unfinished two-volume study on Lenin and Leninism, I have endeavored to make a contribution to the understanding of this, the greatest event of our century. I am glad that these books have met with a friendly and understanding reception in Germany, on the part of many critics.

Tell us something about your home background, the influence which it had upon you, the time in which you grew up, and the intellectual movements which made a Marxist out of you.

I really acquired my lively interest in German questions in my parents' house. I spent my childhood and early years in and around Cracow, in the so-called Three Emperors Corner of Poland. On one side there was Russian Poland, on the other German Poland, and we lived in Austrian Poland—Jews and Poles, among Czechs and Hungarians. A multi-colored corner of our part of Europe. The great year of my childhood was of course 1918, when the three monarchies collapsed. We lived through the landslide of three revolutions. Then came the years of the galloping inflation, of the pogroms, of acute social, political and intellectual ferment, the time of the great confusion. I grew up under the strong influence of my father, but I also differed from him rather violently. My father was an Orthodox Jew, in love with German culture, philosophy and poetry. He had chosen for me the career of rabbi, but I resisted this. I was really brought up in a state of suspension between two orthodoxies, the Jewish and the Roman Catholic. I went to two schools, one Polish and one Jewish-rabbinical. The Polish school and the high school (*Gymnasium*) where I passed my examinations as an external pupil were strongly Catholic. The two orthodoxies neutralized each other in my thinking and reciprocally annihilated each other. I became an atheist. I wrote precociously. My father was always wanting to read German literature and German periodicals with me. He had himself, in his youth, published essays in the *Neue Freie Presse*, the best-known Viennese newspaper; had been correspondent of the Warsaw *Hazefira*, the first daily to appear in the Hebrew language; and had also written a little book in Hebrew about Spinoza, with the Latin title *"Amor Dei Intellectualis."* Spinoza was one of his heroes; Heine the other. My father also had a great respect for Lassalle, but the highest intellectual ideal for him, apart from Hebrew writers, was of course Goethe. I did not share my father's partiality for German poetry. I was a Polish patriot. Mickiewicz and Slowacki were incomparably dearer and closer to me. For this reason I never learned the German language thoroughly either. My father often used to say to me: "Yes, you want to write all your fine poetry only in Polish. I know you will be a great writer one day." For my father had a quite exaggerated idea of my literary talent, and wanted me to exercise it in a "world language." "German," he would say, "is *the* world language. Why should you bury all your talent in a provincial language? You only have to go beyond

Auschwitz"—Auschwitz was just near us, on the frontier—
"you only have to go beyond Auschwitz, and practically
nobody will understand you any more with your fine Polish
language. You really must learn German." That was his ever-
recurring refrain. "You only have to go beyond Auschwitz,
and you will be totally lost, my son." Impatient as I was, I
often interrupted him: "I already know what you are going
to say, father—'You have only to go beyond Auschwitz, and
you will be lost.' " Unhappily my father never went *beyond*
Auschwitz. During the Second World War he disappeared *into*
Auschwitz. Later on I did indeed reconcile myself with the
German language and culture, and what brought about this
reconciliation was precisely the works of Marx and Engels.

Were you hostile to German literature then?

You really must, please, understand that I was a Polish child,
brought up in a Polish school. For us the Germans, like the
Russians, were oppressors, who had robbed us of our independence for a century and a half, and against whom we had
struggled in numerous insurrections. In school we sang the
song of Maria Konopnicka, a great and celebrated poetess,
with the following refrain: "The German will not spit in our
faces, nor will he make Germans of our children." And here
was my father wanting to "make a German of me." This
attempt went against all my sensitivity to Polish lyrical
poetry and all my romantic notions of Polish independence. I
was an adult before I read Marx and Engels, Lassalle and
Bebel, Franz Mehring and Rosa Luxemburg—Rosa Luxemburg who was a Pole too, and who wrote German so wonder-
fully—for the first time. In this way, Marxism reopened for
me the path to German literature, and naturally to German
philosophy too—to Kant, Hegel and Feuerbach, whose heir
Marxism was. As a very young literary critic I was enthralled
by Thomas Mann; I spent many hours with Mann in Warsaw,
in 1926 or 1927 and—in German—discussed his work with
him. When, in an interview, he spoke with high praise of my

understanding for his work, I was quite overcome with pride. Later came the other influences, especially the Russian. After I finally left home at the age of eighteen and came to Warsaw, I associated with a circle of much older people, who were steeped in Russian literature and under the influence of Russian thinkers and revolutionaries. They awoke in me my passionate interest in the Russian Revolution. I began to read the works of Lenin, Plekhanov, Bukharin and then Trotsky too. I first came under the influence of the great English historians very much later. Indeed I first learned English when I was over thirty, after I arrived in England in the year 1939. English historical writing, with Gibbon, Macaulay and Trevelyan, seems to me to be pre-eminent in European literature. Finally, I also found in English my "world language." It gives me great satisfaction when English critics, even those who are politically hostile to me, sometimes compare my prose with that of Churchill or Macaulay, and that the University of Cambridge chose me this year to be its George Macaulay Trevelyan lecturer.

When did your early political involvement really begin?

When I entered the illegal Polish Communist Party as an eighteen-year-old. In that too I was rather precocious, but I was something of an infant prodigy. I was quite well-known as a poet in Cracow, when I was seventeen. Like all infant prodigies, naturally I disappointed the hopes which friends placed in me.

In what way disappointed?

Well—I do not really think that I am still an infant prodigy, nor have I become a prodigy as an old man.

After your expulsion from the Party in 1932, did you withdraw from active political involvement?

I remained active for some years in the independent left in Poland. I was a heterodox communist; I was a Trotskyist. I was seeking a way out of the impasse into which reaction and Stalinism had driven us, and I could not find one. Then I gave up direct party-political activity, in order to devote myself to theoretical and scientific-literary work.

Critics have called you an "unrepentant Marxist." What do you answer to such critics?

I am a Marxist, of course. Those critics who call me "unre-pentant," or say that I "will never learn," are for the most part people who once allowed themselves to be well taught by Stalin, and who later became anticommunists. I did not allow myself to be taught by Stalin, nor by Khrushchev, nor even by Mao Tse-tung, and certainly not by Western anti-communism. Marxism for me is no infallible theory—such a thing cannot exist. However, as a view of the world and a method of analysis, Marxism in my opinion is in no sense outdated or "surpassed." Probably this will happen one day to Marxism too, but we are still a long way away from that. The people who talk today about "anachronistic Marxism" have not yet offered us anything which is intellectually and politically superior to Marxism.

In recent years you were invited to America to take part in a teach-in, a great public discussion on the Vietnam war—you, the "unrepentant Marxist." Is this not in your opinion a notable sign of freedom in so great a democracy as America?

Yes, I often travel to the United States, speak there at mass meetings and give lectures in the universities. I took part in the great debate on the Vietnam War in Washington, in which we spoke directly to an audience of five thousand university professors and lecturers, and hundreds of thousands, if not millions, heard us on radio and television. I have appeared repeatedly as a speaker at the giant rallies of Berkeley students. Last year I opened the nation-wide Socialist Scholars Conference in New York. In the mass meetings, I spoke as an opponent and critic of the American government. I value this freedom of criticism very highly, since it bears witness to how strong, deeply rooted, and vital the democratic tradition is among the people. Perhaps that comes from the fact that the Americans did once carry through their own revolution, and even fought in a Civil War for the abolition of slavery. These experiences have probably remained alive in popular memory; they give nourishment to the democratic tradition, which survived even McCarthyism. I have a great admiration for this other America, the unofficial one, which offers resistance to the official, conservative, neocolonialist America. I believe in the vitality of the American democratic tradition. So I can see the contradiction in the political character of the United States, the clash between the inert conformism of the bourgeoisie and the social and political radicalism of the young intelligentsia. I hope that this radicalism will finally seize the working class too.

So, if I may put it that way, you are politically involved once more. But, coming back to the Vietnam War, what are the basic lines of your criticism?

In the Vietnam War, the great, decisive international conflicts have found their focus, just as was once the case in the Spanish Civil War. This dictates my position on the Vietnamese question. I am on the side of the Vietnamese people, against American imperialism or neocolonialism. I have no doubt about that, just as during the Second World War I had no doubts about which side I was on in the struggle, let us say, between the Yugoslav partisans and the Nazi occupation forces. I believe that the role of gendarme of neocolonialism and counterrevolution which the American ruling class has taken upon itself is catastrophic for America itself, and for the world brings nearer the danger of a nuclear war. But even someone who does not share my attitude, even someone who wishes to consider the situation quite unpolitically, could not help asking himself: "How does it come about that the greatest power in the world is waging a life-and-death struggle against a small, hungry, Asian peasant people, and cannot win it? Where, then, does the strength of the Vietnamese partisans lie? It must, surely, be a moral and political strength—it certainly cannot depend on physical, military factors. Could the partisans generate such a moral strength if they were not supported by the overwhelming majority of the people, of a people inspired with the conviction that it is fighting for a just cause?"

But do you not also think that the military tactics now employed in Vietnam, the tactic of the guerrilla war, the tactic of the jungle, have until now facilitated survival against the great material power of America?

The jungle does not fight. The jungle is neutral. It only assists the partisans because the support of the population permits them to make use of the jungle, while the Americans and their South Vietnamese puppet army cannot do this. In the areas controlled by the partisans, the estates of the big landowners are divided among the peasants. The entire peasantry supports the partisans, since for them the victory of the partisans is *the* guarantee against a return of the feudal landlords. Here a national war is fused with a class struggle—"a war of the cottages against the palaces" to quote Bebel, the great champion of German socialism.

You belong to a tribunal [the War Crimes Tribunal organized by Bertrand Russell], composed of free authors, which concerns itself with so-called war crimes in Vietnam. What do you see as the task of this tribunal?

The tribunal certainly does not consist only of authors. They are probably in a minority. We have seven or eight professors, juridical specialists in international law. Differing points of view and shades of political opinion are also represented within the tribunal. Two or three members belong to small, independent, socialist parties; except for these, we are all without party. We set ourselves the task of ascertaining, on the basis of a thorough analysis of the factual material, whether the United States is guilty of aggression and war crimes in Vietnam. Naturally, we are not a conventional, legal institution. We are able to pass no legally binding sentence. We do not wish to consign anybody to prison or to the gallows. Of course we do not represent a victorious power. We only represent men, who have no power and yet sit in judgment over those who wield power.

Let us take a look into the future. What vision do you have of political development, of social development, from now until the year 2000? How does our world appear in your vision of the year 2000?

Vision—I am afraid that if I reveal my vision to you, it may disconcert our viewers. I imagine that by about the turn of the century something like a United States of Socialist Europe will exist. A timid and conservative prefiguration of these United States is naturally the Common Market, for even conservative, bourgeois politicians are beginning to sense that the nation state, at least in Europe, if not in Asia and Africa, has become an anachronism. In order to live, Europe must unite in an international body, but not on the basis of imperialism, not on the basis of a capitalist economic expansion of one empire or another, but on the basis of the equality of socialist peoples. I am convinced that this will come about. The United States of Socialist Europe will probably be closely linked with the Soviet Union. I assume that the Soviet Union by then will have entirely overcome the heritage of Stalinism, that in fact a free socialism will have developed there, and that economic and cultural progress will by then have made possible a working day of three or four hours and higher education for all. I believe that the Soviet Union and

Socialist Europe will then live together in real equality, and will perhaps be able to help the peoples of Asia and Africa too to come together in such "united states." I hope that such a development will not drive Europe and the rest of the world into a conflict with the United States of America, although I am afraid that—if the United States becomes petrified in a state of social conservatism—certain theoreticians, let us say in Harvard, will have to construct a theory of "capitalism in one country," just as once the theory of socialism in one country was proclaimed in Russia. But that was only a phase in Russian development, and in the same way capitalism in one country would only be a phase of American development. Since mankind has embarked on the conquest of interplanetary space, it must unite on its own planet; and I can see no other social and moral power which could unite mankind, other than a socialism based on freedom.

the roots
of bureaucracy

I

We are presently witnessing an obvious tendency toward
the increasing bureaucratization of contemporary societies,
regardless of their social and political structure. Theorists in
the West assure us that the momentum of bureaucratization
is such that we now live under a managerial system which
has, somewhat imperceptibly, come to replace capitalism. On
the other hand, we have the huge, stupendous growth of
bureaucracy in the postcapitalist societies of the Soviet bloc
and especially in the Soviet Union. We are justified in attempting to elaborate some theory of bureaucracy which
would be more comprehensive and more satisfying than the
fashionable and to a large degree meaningless cliché:
"managerial society." It is not, however, easy to come to
grips with the problem of bureaucracy; in essence it is as old

*At the beginning of 1960 Isaac Deutscher delivered three lectures on
the subject of bureaucracy to a graduate seminar at the London School
of Economics. This essay, originally published in the Fall 1969 issue of*
Canadian Slavic Studies, *is a shortened version of these lectures.*

as civilization, although the intensity with which it has appeared before men's eyes has varied greatly over the ages.

If I have undertaken to discuss the roots of bureaucracy, it is because I believe we have to dig down to find the deepest causes—the initial ones—of bureaucracy, in order to see how and why this evil of human civilization has grown to such terrifying proportions. In the problems of bureaucracy, to which the problem of the state is roughly parallel, is focussed much of that relationship between man and society, between man and man, which it is now fashionable to describe as "alienation."

The term itself suggests the rule of the "bureau," of the apparatus, of something impersonal and hostile, which has assumed life and reigns over human beings. In common parlance we also speak about the lifeless bureaucrats, about the men who form that mechanism. The human beings that administer the state look as if they were lifeless, as if they were mere cogs in the machine. In other words, we are confronted here in the most condensed, the most intensive, form with the reification of relationships between human beings, and with the appearance of life in mechanisms, in things. This, of course, immediately brings to mind the great complex of fetishism: over the whole area of our market economy man seems to be at the mercy of things, of commodities, even of currencies. Human and social relationships become objectified, whereas objects seem to assume the force and power of living elements. The parallel between man's alienation from the state and the representatives of the state—the bureaucracy—on the one hand, and between his alienation from the products of his own economy, on the other, is obviously very close, and the two kinds of alienation are similarly interrelated.

There is a great difficulty in getting beyond mere appearance to the very core of the relationship between state and society, between the apparatus that administers the life of a community and the community itself. The difficulty consists in this: the appearance is not *only* appearance, it is also part of a reality. The fetishism of the state and of the commodity is, so to say, "built into" the very mechanism in which state and market function. Society is at one and the same time estranged from the state and inseparable from it. The state is the incubus that oppresses society; it is also society's protective angel without which it cannot live.

Here again some of the most hidden and complex aspects of the relationship between society and state are clearly and strikingly reflected in our everyday language. When we say "they," meaning the bureaucrats who rule us, "they" who impose taxes, "they" who wage wars, who do all sorts of things which involve the life of all of us, we express a feeling of impotence, of estrangement from the state: but we are also conscious that without the state there would be no social life, no social development, no history. The difficulty in sifting appearance from reality consists in this; the bureaucracy performs certain functions which are obviously necessary and indispensable for the life of society; yet it also performs functions which might theoretically be described as superfluous.

The contradictory aspects of bureaucracy have, of course, led to two contradictory and extremely opposed philosophical, historical and sociological views of the problem. Apart from many intermediate shadings, traditionally there have been two basic approaches to the question of bureaucracy and the state: the bureaucratic and the anarchist approach. The Webbs liked to divide people into those who evaluated political problems from the bureaucratic or from the anarchist point of view. This is, of course, a simplification, but nevertheless there is something to be said for it. The bureaucratic approach has had its great philosophers, its great prophets, and its celebrated sociologists. Probably the greatest philosophical apologist of the state was Hegel, just as the greatest sociological apologist of the state was Max Weber.

There is no doubt that old Prussia was the paradise of the bureaucracy, and it is therefore not a matter of accident that the greatest apologists for the state and for bureaucracy have come from Prussia. Both Hegel and Weber, each in a different way and on different levels of theoretical thinking are, in fact, the metaphysicians of the Prussian bureaucracy, who generalize from the Prussian bureaucratic experience and project that experience onto the stage of world history. It is therefore necessary to keep in mind the basic tenets of this school of thought. To Hegel, the state and bureaucracy were both the reflection and the reality of *the* moral idea, that is the reflection and the reality of supreme reason, the reality of the *Weltgeist*, the manifestation of God in history. Max Weber, who is in a way a descendant, a grandson of Hegel (perhaps a dwarf grandson), puts the same idea into his typically Prussian catalogue of the virtues of bureaucracy:

> Precision, speed, unambiguity, knowledge of the files, continuity, discretion, unity, strict subordination, reduction of friction and of material and personal costs— these are raised to the optimum point in the strictly bureaucratic administration, and especially in its monocratic form ... bureaucracy also stands ... under the principle of *sine ira ac studio.**

Only in Prussia perhaps could these words have been written. Of course, this catalogue of virtues can very easily be invalidated by a parallel catalogue of vices. But to me it is all the more surprising and in a sense disquieting that Max Weber has recently become the intellectual light of so much of western sociology. (Professor Raymond Aron's gravest reproach in a polemic against myself was that I write and speak "as if Max Weber never existed.") I am quite prepared to admit that probably no one has studied the minutiae of bureaucracy as deeply as Max Weber; he catalogued the various peculiarities of its development, but failed to understand its full meaning. We all know the characteristic feature of that old German so-called historical school which could

* Hans H. Gerth and C. Wright Mills, eds. and trans., *From Max Weber: Essays in Sociology* (Oxford University Press; New York, 1953).

produce volumes and volumes on any particular industry, including the bureaucratic industry, but could rarely see the mainstream of its development.

At the other extreme we have the anarchist view of bureaucracy and the state, with its most eminent representatives—Proudhon, Bakunin and Kropotkin—and with the various derivative liberal and anarcho-liberal trends. Now this school, when you look at it closely, represents the intellectual revolt of the old France of the bourgeoisie and of the old Russia of the *muzhiks* against their bureaucracies. This school of thought specializes, of course, in composing catalogues of bureaucratic vices. The state and the bureaucracy are seen as the permanent usurpers of history; they are seen as the very embodiment of all evil in human society, evil which cannot be eradicated other than by the abolition of the state and the destruction of all bureaucracy. When Kropotkin wanted to show the depths of the moral deterioration of the French Revolution, he described how Robespierre, Danton, the Jacobins, and the Hébertists changed from revolutionaries to statesmen. In his eyes, what vitiated the revolution was bureaucracy and the state.

In fact each of these approaches contains an element of truth because in practice the state and bureaucracy have been the Jekyll and Hyde of human civilization. They have indeed represented the virtues and the vices of human society and its historical development in a manner more concentrated, more intense, than any other institution. State and bureaucracy focus in themselves this characteristic duality of our civilization: every progress achieved so far has been accompanied by retrogression; every advance that man made has been bought at the price of regress; every unfolding of human creative energy has been paid for with the crippling or stunting of some other creative energy. This duality has been, I think, very striking in the development of bureaucracy throughout all social and political regimes.

* * *

The roots of bureaucracy are indeed as old as our civilization, or even older, for they are buried on the border between the primitive communistic tribe and civilized society. It is there that we find the remotest and yet the very distinct ancestry of the massive, elaborate bureaucratic machines of our age. They show themselves at the moment when the primitive community divides into the leaders and the led, the organizers and the organized, into the managers and the managed. When the tribe or the clan begins to learn that division of labor increases man's power over nature and his capacity to satisfy his needs, then we see the first germs of bureaucracy which become also the very earliest signs of a class society.

The division of labor begins with the process of production, with which the first hierarchy of functions appears as well. It is here that we have the first glimpse of the gulf that was about to open in the course of civilization between mental work and manual labor. The organizer of the first primitive process in cattle breeding might have been the forebear of the mandarin, of the Egyptian priest, or the modern capitalist bureaucrat. The primary division between brain and brawn brought with it the other manifold sub-divisions, between agriculture and fishing, or trade and craft and seafaring. The division of society into classes followed in the course of fundamental processes of historic development. In society, from the threshold of civilization to our own day, the basic division has been not so much that between the administrator and the worker as between the owner and the man without property, and this division absorbed into itself or overshadowed the former one. Administration has been, in most epochs, subordinated to the owners of property, to the possessing classes.

One could broadly categorize the various types of relationship between bureaucracy and basic social classes. The first one might call the Egyptian-Chinese type; then comes the Roman-Byzantine type with its derivative of an ecclesiastic hierarchy in the Roman Church; then we have the Western European capitalist type of bureaucracy; the fourth would be the postcapitalist type. In the first three types, and especially in the feudal and slave-owning societies, the administrator is completely subordinate to the man of property, so much so that in Athens, in Rome and in Egypt it is usually from among the slaves that the bureaucracy is recruited. In Athens the first police force was recruited from among the slaves because it was considered beneath the dignity of the free man to deprive another free man of freedom. What a sound instinct! Here you have the almost naively striking expression of the dependence of the bureaucrat on the property owner: it is the slave who is the bureaucrat because bureaucracy is the slave of the possessing class.

In the feudal order the bureaucracy is more or less eclipsed because the administrators either come directly from the feudal class or are absorbed into it. Social hierarchy is, so to say, "built into" the feudal order, and there is no need for a special hierarchical machine to manage public affairs and to discipline the propertyless masses.

Later, much later, bureaucracy acquires a far more respectable status and its agents become "free" wage earners of the owners of property. Then it pretends to rise above the possessing classes, and indeed above all social classes. And in some respects and up to a point bureaucracy indeed acquires that supreme status.

The great separation between the state machine and other classes comes, of course, in capitalism, where the earlier clearly marked hierarchy and dependence of man on man, so characteristic of feudal society, no longer exists. "All men are equal"—the bourgeois fiction of equality before the law makes it essential that there should function an apparatus of power, a state machine strictly hierarchically organized. Like the hierarchy of economic power on the market, so the bureaucracy, as a political hierarchy, should see to it that society does not take the appearance of equality at its face value. There grows a hierarchy of orders, interests, administrative levels, which perpetuates the fiction of equality and yet enforces inequality.

What characterizes the bureaucracy at this stage? The hierarchical structure in the first instance; then the seemingly self-sufficient character of the apparatus of power enclosed within itself. The tremendous scope, scale and complexity of our social life make the management of society more and more difficult, we are told; only skilled experts who possess the secrets of administration are able to perform the organizing functions. No, indeed, we have not moved a very long way from the time when the Egyptian priest guarded the secrets which gave him power and made society believe that only he, the divinely inspired, could manage human affairs. Self-important bureaucracy, with its mystifying lingo which is to a very large extent a matter of its social prestige, is, after all, not far removed from the Egyptian priesthood with its magic secrets. (Incidentally, is it not also very close to the Stalinist bureaucracy with its obsessive secrecy?)

Many decades before Max Weber, who was himself so impressed by the esoteric wisdom of bureaucracy, Engels saw things in a more realistic and objective light:

> The state is by no means a power imposed upon society from the outside. . . . It is rather the product of society at a certain stage of development. It is an admission that this society has involved itself in an insoluble contradiction with itself, that it has become split in irreconcilable contradictions. . . . In order that . . . classes with conflicting economic interests should not consume themselves and society in fruitless struggle, a power had become necessary which seemingly stands above society, a power that has to keep down the conflict and keep it within bounds of "order." That power emerging from society but rising above it and becoming more and more estranged from it is the State.

Even the welfare state, we may add, is, after all, only

the power that emerges from society but rises above it and becomes more and more estranged from it. Engels goes on to say: "In possession of public force and power and of the right to levy taxes, the officials now stand as the organs of society above society." He describes the process of the emergence of the state from the primitive community:

> They [the officials] are not content with the free and willing respect that had been paid to the organs of a tribal community.... Holders of a power estranged from society, they must be placed in a position of respect by means of special laws which assure them the enjoyment of a special halo and immunity.*

However, there is no use being angry with bureaucracy: its strength is only a reflection of society's weakness, which lies in its division between the vast majority of manual workers and a small minority which specializes in brain work. The intellectual pauperism from which no nation has yet emancipated itself lies at the roots of bureaucracy. Other fungi have grown over those roots, but the roots themselves have persisted in capitalism and welfare capitalism, and they still survive in postcapitalist society.

II

I would like to redefine my subject of discussion more rigorously. I am not interested in the general history of bureaucracy, nor do I wish to give a description of the varieties and modalities of bureaucratic rule that can be found in history. The focus of my subject is this: What are the factors that have historically been responsible for the political supremacy of bureaucracy over society? Why has no revolution so far succeeded in breaking down and destroying the might of the bureaucracy? On the morrow of every revolution, regardless of its character and the *ancien régime* which

---

* Marx and Engels, *Werke* (Berlin, 1962), XXI: *Der Ursprung der Familie*, pp. 165-66. Engels, *The Origin of the Family* (Lawrence & Wishart; London, 1942), pp. 194-95.

preceded it, a state machine rises like a phoenix from the ashes.

I have already pointed out—with some overemphasis—the perennial factor working in favor of bureaucracy, namely, the division of labor between intellectual work and manual labor, the gulf between the organizers and the organized. This contradistinction is in fact the prologue to class society; but in further social development that prologue seems to become submerged by the more fundamental division between the slave owner and the slave, between the serf owner and the serf, between the man of property and the propertyless.

The real, massive ascendancy of bureaucracy as a distinct and separate social group came only with the development of capitalism, and it did so for a variety of reasons, economic and political. What favored the spread of a modern bureaucracy was market economy, money economy and the continuous and deepening division of labor of which capitalism is itself a product. As long as the servant of the state was a tax farmer, or a feudal lord, or an auxiliary of a feudal lord, the bureaucrat was not yet a bureaucrat. The tax collector of the sixteenth, seventeenth, or even eighteenth century was something of an entrepreneur; or else he was a servant of the feudal lord or part of his retinue. The formation of bureaucracy into a distinct group was made possible only by the spread and the universalization of a money economy, in which every state employee was paid his salary in money.

The growth of bureaucracy was further stimulated by the breaking down of feudal particularism and the formation of a market on a national scale. Only on the basis of a national market could national bureaucracy make its appearance. By themselves these general economic causes of the growth of bureaucracy explain only how bureaucracy in its modern form became possible, but they do not yet explain why it has grown and why, in some definite historical circumstances, it has acquired its political importance. To these questions one should seek an answer not in economic changes but in socio-political structures. We have, for instance, the striking fact that England, the country of classical capitalism, was the least bureaucratic of all capitalist countries, while Germany, until the last quarter of the nineteenth century the underdeveloped capitalist country, was the most bureaucratic. France, which held a middle position, also held a middle position with regard to the strength of bureaucracy in political life.

If one were to seek certain general rules about the rise and decline of bureaucratic influence in capitalist society, one would find that the political power of bureaucracy under capitalism has always been in inverse proportion to the maturity, the vigor, the capacity for self-government of the strata constituting a given bourgeois society. On the other hand, when in highly-developed bourgeois societies class struggles have reached something like a deadlock, when contending classes have lain as if prostrate after a series of exhausting social and political struggles, then political leadership has almost automatically passed into the hands of a bureaucracy. In such situations the bureaucracy establishes itself not only as the apparatus regulating the functioning of the state, but also as the power imposing its political will on society. The real cradle of modern bureaucracy was, of course, the pre-bourgeois absolute monarchy—the Tudors in England, the Bourbons in France, or the Hohenzollerns in Prussia—the monarchy which was maintaining the uncertain equilibrium between a decaying feudalism and a rising capitalism. Feudalism was already too weak to continue its supremacy, capitalism was still too weak to establish its domination; a stasis in the class struggle, as it were, between feudalism and capitalism left room for the absolute monarchy to act as the umpire between the two opposed camps.

The stronger the opposition of feudal and bourgeois interests and the more paralyzing the stalemate between them, the more scope was there for the bureaucracy of the absolutist monarchy to play the role of arbiter. Incidentally, England (and also the United States) was the least bureaucratic of all capitalist countries precisely because very early in history that feudal-capitalist antagonism was resolved through the gradual merger of the feudal and capitalist interests. The feudal-bourgeois notables, the great aristocratic English families, assumed some of the functions which on the continent were exercised by the bureaucracy. In a sense, the *embourgeoisé* feudal elements administered the state without becoming a distinct and separate social group. The United States too was in its history free from that strife between feudal and capitalist interests, the strife which acted as a stimulus for the growth of bureaucracy.

Quite a different and peculiar case was Russia, where the great power of state and bureaucracy resulted from the underdevelopment of both social strata: neither the feudal element nor the bourgeoisie was ever strong enough to manage the affairs of the state. It was the state that, like the demiurge, created social classes, now inducting their formation and expansion, now impeding and thwarting it. In this way its bureaucracy became not only an umpire but also the manipulator of all social classes.

*   *   *

If I were to give a sub-title to my further remarks it would probably be a very general one: on bureaucracy and revolution. At this point I would like to clear up some confusion, and I fear that in the process I shall clash with several established historical schools. As this is unavoidable in any case, I shall pose the problem in its most provocative form: Was the English Puritan Revolution a bourgeois revolution? Was the great French Revolution bourgeois in character? At the head of the insurgent battalions there were no bankers, merchants or shipowners. The sans-culottes, the plebs, the urban paupers, the lower-lower middle classes were in the forefront of the battle. What did they achieve? Under the leadership of "gentlemen farmers" (in England) and lawyers, doctors and journalists (in France) they abolished the absolutist monarchy and its courtier bureaucracy and swept away feudal institutions which were hindering the development of bourgeois property relations. The bourgeoisie had become strong enough and sufficiently aware of its power to aspire to political self-determination. It no longer wanted to accept the tutelage and the dictates of the absolutist monarchy; it wanted to rule society by itself. In the process of the revolution the bourgeoisie was driven forward by the plebeian masses—on the morrow the bourgeoisie attempted by itself to rule society at large.

The process of the revolution with all its crises and antagonisms, with the constant shifting of power from the more conservative to the more radical and even to the utopian wings of the revolutionary camp—all these led to a new political stalemate between the classes which came freshly to the fore: the plebeian masses, the sans-culottes, the urban poor were tired and weary; but the victorious, now dominant class—the bourgeoisie—was also internally divided, fragmented, exhausted from the revolutionary struggle and incapable of governing society. Hence in the aftermath of bourgeois revolution we see the rise of a new bureaucracy somewhat different in character: we see a military dictatorship, which outwardly looks almost like the continuation of the prerevolutionary absolutist monarchy or an even worse version of it. The prerevolutionary regime had its centralized state machine—a national bureaucracy. The revolution's first demand was the decentralization of this machine. Yet this centralization had not been due to the evil intentions of the ruler but reflected the evolution of the economy, which required a national market, and this "national soil," as it were, fed the bourgeois forces which in their turn produced the revolution. The aftermath of the revolution brings renewed centralization. This was so under Cromwell; this occurred under Napoleon. The process of centralization and national unification and the rise of a new bureaucracy was so striking that Tocqueville, for example, saw in it nothing more than the continuation of prerevolutionary tradition. He argued that what the French Revolution had done was merely to carry further the work of the *ancien régime*, and had the revolution not taken place this trend would have gone on all the same.* This was the argument of a man who had his eyes fixed on the political aspect of the development only and completely ignored its social background and deeper social motives; he saw the shape but not the texture or the color of society.

Political centralization after the revolution went on as before, yet the character of the bureaucracy had completely and thoroughly changed. Instead of the courtier bureaucracy of the *ancien régime*, France now had the bourgeois bureaucracy recruited from different layers of society. The bourgeois bureaucracy established under Napoleon survived the Restoration and in the end found its proper head in the Citizen King.

The next phase in which we see another rise of bureaucracy and a further promotion of centralistic tendencies of the state occurs again at a moment of political paralysis of all social classes. In 1848 we find a situation in which different class interests are again opposed to each other; this time it is the interest of the established bourgeoisie and that of the nascent proletariat. To this day nobody has described this process of mutual exhaustion better than Karl Marx, especially in the *18th Brumaire*. He also demonstrated how the prostration of all social classes secured the triumph of the bureaucracy, or rather of its military arm, under Napoleon III. At the time this situation was characteristic not only of France but also of Germany, especially Prussia, where the deadlock was many-sided: between the feudal and semi-feudal interests of the Junkers, the bourgeoisie, and the new working class. And in Prussia it resulted in the rule and dictatorship of Bismarck's bureaucracy. (Incidentally, Marx and Engels described Bismarck's government as a "Bonapartist" regime, although outwardly there was, of course, very little or nothing of the Bonaparte in Bismarck.)

---

* Alexis de Tocqueville, *The Old Regime and the French Revolution*, trans. Stuart Gilbert (Doubleday; New York, 1955), pp. 32-41.

III

I am well aware that because of the vastness of the subject I can do no more than indicate schematically the main points which need further elaboration. I am not going to deal with reformist socialism and bureaucracy. This, important though it is politically, especially in England, presents from my viewpoint very little theoretical interest. To my mind it is part of "capitalism and bureaucracy." The bulk of the economy remains capitalist whether or not fifteen percent or twenty-five percent of industry is nationalized, and here quantity also determines quality. The whole background of social life is capitalist, and ordinary capitalist bureaucratic spirit permeates all industries including the nationalized ones. We hear a lot of grumbling about "bureaucracy on the railways" or in the coal mines. During a recent strike television presented some railwaymen who said "things are not as they used to be": before the nationalization of the railways they could maintain a more personal relationship between themselves and their employers, while now the industry has become so anonymous that there is no personal link between the workingmen and this vast nationwide enterprise. This "personal link" was, of course, a figment of the workers' imagination. What sort of personal relationship was there between the footplate man and the boss of one or another of the five huge railway companies? But politically it was important that this railwayman really believed that in the Southern or Midland or Western Railway he was more than a mere cog Now he feels "alienated" from that vast entity into which he has to fit, for which he has to go to work. And this "alienation," as the word goes, is a problem common to all sorts of bureaucratic establishments, no matter what their broader social framework, and I would be the last to deny that there are certain common features between bureaucracy in a capitalist and in a postcapitalist system.

Now I would like to touch upon those special problems of bureaucracy which arise in a fully nationalized industry after a socialist revolution, under a regime which, at least in its beginnings, is in every sense a proletarian dictatorship. Clearly this problem affects one-third of the world, so it is weighty enough; and I am pretty sure that it will acquire validity over at least two-thirds of the world.

As I looked through some of the classical Marxist writings on bureaucracy I was struck by how relatively optimistically—one might say lightmindedly—Marxists approached the problem. To give one illustration: Karl Kautsky once asked himself whether a socialist society would be threatened with all the evils of bureaucracy. In *The Foundations of Christianity* Kautsky discusses the process by which the Christian Church was transformed from a faith of the oppressed into a great imperial bureaucratic machine. This transformation was possible against the background of a society which lived on slave labor. The slaves of antiquity, devoid of any active class consciousness, were liable to become slaves of bureaucracy. But the modern working class, mature enough to overthrow capitalism, maintained Kautsky, will not allow a bureaucracy to rise on its back. This was not just an individual judgment of Kautsky, who for over two decades between Engels's death and the outbreak of the First World War was the most authoritative spokesman of Marxism and was considered a real successor to Marx and Engels. Engels himself in various of his works, and especially in *Anti-Dühring*, committed himself to a view which almost ruled out in advance the possibility of bureaucracy under socialism:

> The proletariat seizes the State power and turns the means of production in the first instance into State property. But in doing this it puts an end to itself as proletariat, puts an end to all . . . class antagonism. . . .*

Former societies needed the state as an organization of the exploiting class, as a means of holding down the class that was exploited—slaves, serfs, or wage laborers. In socialism the

* F. Engels, *Anti-Dühring* (Lawrence & Wishart; London, 1943), p. 308.

state, when it becomes truly representative of society as a whole, makes itself superfluous. And with the full development of modern productive forces, with the abundance and superabundance of goods, there will be no need to keep men and labor in subjection.

I think it was Trotsky who used a very plain but very telling metaphor: the policeman can use his baton either for regulating traffic or for dispersing a demonstration of strikers or unemployed. In this one sentence is summed up the classical distinction between administration of things and administration of men. If you assume a society in which there is no class supremacy, the bureaucracy's role is reduced to the administration of things, of the objective social and productive process. We are not concerned with the elimination of *all* administrative functions—this would be absurd in an industrially developing society—but we are concerned with reducing the policeman's baton to its proper role, that of disentangling traffic jams.

When Marx and Engels analyzed the experience of the Commune of Paris they were as if half-aware of the bureaucratic threat that could arise in the future, and they were at great pains to underline the measures that the Commune had taken in order to guarantee a socialist revolution against the recrudescence of bureaucratic power. The Commune, they stressed, had taken a number of precautions which should serve as a pattern and a model for future socialist transformations: it was elected in a general election and established an elected civil service, every member of which could be deposed at any time at the demand of the electorate. The Commune abolished the standing army and replaced it by the people at arms; it also established the principle that no civil servant could earn more than the ordinary worker. This should have abolished all privileges of a bureaucratic group. The Commune, in other words, set the example of a state which was to begin to wither away as soon as it was established. It was no matter of chance that only a few weeks before the October Revolution Lenin made a special effort to restore this, by then almost forgotten, part of Marxist teaching about state, socialism and bureaucracy. He expressed his idea of the state in that famous aphorism: under socialism or even in a proletarian dictatorship the administration should become so simplified that every cook should be able to manage state affairs.

In the light of all the painful experience of the last decades it is all too easy to see how very greatly the representatives of classical Marxism had indeed underrated the problems of bureaucracy. There were, I think, two reasons for this. The original founders of the Marxist school never really attempted to portray in advance the society which would emerge after a socialist revolution. They analyzed revolution, so to say, in the abstract; in the same way as Marx in *Das Kapital* analyzed not any specific capitalist system but capitalism in the abstract, capitalism *per se*; they also thought of socialist or postcapitalist society in the abstract. If one considers that they carried out their analysis so many decades before the actual attempt, their method was scientifically justified. The other reason is, so to say, psychological. They could not help viewing the future revolution on the pattern of the greatest revolutionary experience in their own life, that of 1848. They saw it as a chain reaction of revolutions, as 1848 was, spreading at least over Europe more or less simultaneously. (Here was the germ of the idea of permanent revolution, which in this respect was not the original creation of Trotsky; it was indeed very deeply embedded in the thought of classical Marxism.) An all-European socialist revolution would have been relatively secure immediately after its victory. With very little social tension there would be hardly any civil strife, and without wars of intervention there would have been no need for the re-creation of standing armies which are an important factor of bureaucratization. They also assumed that, at least in the highly industrialized societies of Western Europe, the very considerable proportion of the working class would provide a strong mass support for the revolutionary government. They also trusted that once the majority of the European working class had been won for the revolution it would, as it were, remain faithful and loyal to the revolution. This, together with the existing democratic tradition, would form the strongest guarantee against any revival of the bureaucratic machine or the formation of a new one.

When we are tempted to reproach the founders of the Marxist school with underrating the dangers of bureaucracy in postrevolutionary society, we must bear in mind the fact that they took the abundance of goods as the first condition, a precondition and *raison d'être* of a socialist revolution. "The possibility of securing for every member of society, through social production, an existence not only fully sufficient materially ... but guaranteeing to all the free development and exercise of their physical and mental faculties—this possibility is now ... here. ... *it is here*," * stated Engels emphatically in his *Anti-Dühring* nearly ninety years ago. It is only in the middle of this century that we are faced with attempts at socialist revolution in countries where a desperately insufficient production makes any decent material existence quite impossible.

There was undoubtedly in Marxism an ambivalent attitude toward the state. On the one hand—and this Marxism had in common with anarchism—there was a conviction based on a deeply realistic historical analysis that all revolutions are frustrated as long as they do not do away with the state; on the other, there was the conviction that the socialist revolution has need of a state for its own purpose, to smash, to break the old capitalist system and create its own state machine that would exercise the proletarian dictatorship. But that machine, for the first time in history, would represent the interests not of a privileged minority but of the mass of toilers, the real producers of society's wealth. "The first act by virtue of which the state really constitutes itself the representative of the whole of society"—the taking possession of

* Ibid., p. 311.

the means of production—"is at the same time its last independent act as a state."* From then on the interference of
the state in social relations becomes superfluous. The government of persons is replaced by the administration of things.
The political function of the state disappears; what remains is
the direction of the process of production. The state will not
be abolished overnight, as the anarchists imagine; it will
slowly "wither away."

The reality of the Russian Revolution was in every
single respect a negation of the assumptions made by classical
Marxism. It was certainly not revolution in the abstract—it
was real enough! It did not follow the 1848 pattern, it was
not an all-European upheaval; it remained isolated in one
country. It occurred in a nation where the proletariat was a
tiny minority and even that minority disintegrated as a class
in the process of world war, revolution and civil war. It was
also an extremely backward, poverty-stricken country where
the problem immediately facing the revolutionary government was not to build socialism, but to create the first preconditions for any modern civilized life. All this resulted in at
least two political developments which inevitably led to the
recrudescence of bureaucracy.

I have described how the political supremacy of
bureaucracy always followed a stalemate in the class struggle,
an exhaustion of all social classes in the process of political
and social struggles. Now, *mutatis mutandis*, after the
Russian Revolution we see the same situation again: in the
early 1920s all classes of Russian society—workers, peasants,
bourgeoisie, landlords, aristocracy—are either destroyed or
completely exhausted politically, morally, intellectually.
After all the trials of a decade filled with world war, revolution, civil wars and industrial devastation no social class is
capable of asserting itself. What is left is only the machine of
the Bolshevik Party which establishes its bureaucratic
supremacy over society as a whole. However, *cela change et*

* Ibid., p. 309.

ce n'est plus la même chose: society as a whole has under-
gone a fundamental change. The old cleavage between the
men of property and the propertyless masses gives place to
another division, different in character but no less noxious
and corrosive: the division between the rulers and the ruled.
Moreover, after the revolution it acquires a far greater force
than it had before when it was as if submerged by class
distinction and class discord. What again comes to the fore is
the perennial, the oldest split between the organizers and the
organized. The prelude to class society appears now as the
epilogue. Far from "withering away" the postrevolutionary
state gathers into its hands such power as it has never had
before. For the first time in history bureaucracy seems
omnipotent and omnipresent. If under the capitalist system
we saw that the power of bureaucracy always found a
counterweight in the power of the propertied classes, here we
see no such restrictions and no such limitations. The bureaucracy is the manager of the totality of the nation's resources;
more than ever before it appears independent, separated,
indeed set high above society. Far from withering away the
state reaches its apotheosis, which takes the form of an
almost permanent orgy of bureaucratic violence over all
classes of society.

Let us now go back for a moment to the Marxist
analysis of the revolution in the abstract and see where and in
what way the picture of postrevolutionary Russia contradicts
this analysis. Had there been a European revolution in which
proletarian majorities would have won swiftly and decisively
and spared their nations all the political and social turmoil
and slaughter of wars and civil strife, then very probably we
would not have seen that fear-inspiring apotheosis of the
Russian state. Nevertheless the problem would still have
existed to a degree which classical Marxism did not envisage.
To put it in a nutshell: it seems that the thinkers and theoreticians of the nineteenth century tended to telescope certain
stages of future development from capitalism to socialism.
What classical Marxism "telescoped" was the revolution-

and-socialism as it were, whereas between the revolution and socialism there was bound to lie a terribly long and complicated period of transition. Even under the best of circumstances that period would have been characterized by an inevitable tension between the bureaucrat and the worker. Some prognosis of that tension can be found in Marxism, however. In their famous *Critique of the Gotha Programme* Marx and Engels speak about two phases of communism, the lower and the higher.* In the lower one there still prevails the "narrow horizon of bourgeois rights" with its inequality and its wide differentials in individual incomes. Obviously, if in socialism society, according to Marx, still needs to secure the full development of its productive forces until a real economy of wealth and abundance is created, then it has to reward skill and offer incentives. The bureaucrat is in a sense the skilled worker, and there is no doubt that he will place himself on the privileged side of the scale.

The division between the organizers and the organized acquires more and not less importance precisely because, the means of production having passed from private to public ownership, the responsibility for running the national economy rests now with the organizers. The new society has not developed on its own foundations, but is emerging from capitalism and still bears all the birthmarks of capitalism. It is not yet ripe economically, morally and intellectually, to reward everyone according to his needs, and as long as everyone has to be paid according to his work the bureaucracy will remain the privileged group. No matter what the pseudo-Marxist terminology of present Russian leaders, Russian society today is still far from socialist—it has only made the very first step on the road of transition from capitalism toward socialism.

The tension between the bureaucrat and the workers is rooted in the cleavage between brain work and manual labor.

* Karl Marx, *Critique of the Gotha Programme* (Lawrence & Wishart; London, 1933), p. 106.

It simply is not true that today's Russian state can be run by any cook (although all sorts of cooks try to do it). In practice it proved impossible to establish and maintain the principle proclaimed by the Commune of Paris which served Marx as the guarantee against the rise of bureaucracy, the principle extolled again by Lenin on the eve of October, according to which the functionary should not earn more than the ordinary worker's wage. This principle implied a truly egalitarian society—and here is part of an important contradiction in the thought of Marx and his disciples. Evidently the argument that no civil servant, no matter how high his function, must earn more than an ordinary worker cannot be reconciled with the other argument that in the lower phase of socialism, which still bears the stamp of "bourgeois rights," it would be utopian to expect "equality of distribution." In the post-revolutionary Russian state with its poverty and its inadequate development of productive forces the scramble for rewards was bound to be fierce and ferocious, and because the abolition of capitalism was inspired by a longing for egalitarianism, the inequality was even more revolting and shocking. It was also inequality on an abysmally low level of existence, or rather inequality below subsistence level.

Part of the Marxist theory of the withering away of the state was based upon a certain balance between its centralistic organization and the universal element of decentralization. The socialist state was to have been a state of elected communes, local municipal councils, local governments and self-governments, yet they were all to form a unified organism which was necessary for a rational nationalized mode of production. This concept also presupposed a highly developed society, which Russia at the beginning of the century was not.

In the development of postcapitalist society the tension between the worker and the bureaucrat may yet prove to have some essentially creative elements. The worker and the bureaucrat are equally necessary for the transition toward socialism. As long as the working masses are still in that stage of intellectual pauperism left over from the centuries of oppression and illiteracy, the management of the processes of production must fall to the civil servant. On the other hand, in a truly postcapitalist society the basic social class is the workers, and socialism is the workers' and not the bureaucrats' business. The dynamic balance between the official and the worker will find its counterpart in the authority of the state and the control of the masses over the state. This will also assure the necessary equilibrium between the principle of centralization and that of decentralizaton. What we have seen in Russia has been an utter disequilibrium. As a result of objective historic circumstances and subjective interests, the balance swung heavily, decisively, absolutely to the side of bureaucracy. What we have seen in Hungary and Poland in 1956 was a reaction against this—Stalinist—state of affairs with an extreme swing of the pendulum in the other direction and the workers' passionate, violent, unreasoning revolt against bureaucratic despotism—a revolt no doubt justified by all their experiences and grievances, but one which in its consequences led again to a grave and dangerous imbalance.

How then do I see the prospects and how do I see the further development of that tension between the worker and the bureaucrat?

I have indicated before all the faults of the historical perspective in the classical Marxist view of bureaucracy. Yet, I think that basically and fundamentally this view helps to cope with the problem of bureaucracy far better than any other I have encountered.

The question we have to answer is this: has the bureaucracy, whose apotheosis after the revolution I have described, constituted itself into a new class? Can it perpetuate itself as a privileged minority? Does it perpetuate social inequality? I would like first of all to point out one very obvious and important but often forgotten fact: all the inequality that exists in today's Russia between the worker and the bureaucrat is an inequality of consumption. This is undoubtedly very important, irritating and painful; yet with all the privileges which the bureaucrat defends brutally and stubbornly, he lacks the essential privilege of owning the means of production. Officialdom still dominates society and lords over it, yet it lacks the cohesion and unity which would make of it a separate class in the Marxist sense of the word. The bureaucrats enjoy power and some measure of prosperity, yet they cannot bequeath their prosperity and wealth to their children. They cannot accumulate capital, or invest it for the benefit of their descendants: they cannot perpetuate themselves or their kith and kin.

It is true that Soviet bureaucracy dominates society—economically, politically and culturally—more obviously and to a greater extent than does any modern possessing class. Yet it is also more vulnerable. Not only can it not perpetuate itself, but it has been unable even to secure for itself the continuity of its own position, the continuity of management. Under Stalin one leading group of bureaucrats after another was beheaded, one leading group of managers of industry after another was purged. Then came Khrushchev who dispersed the most powerful center of that bureaucracy: all the economic ministries in the capital were scattered over wide and far-flung Russia. Until this day the Soviet bureaucracy has not managed to acquire that social, economic and psychological identity of its own which would allow us to describe it as a new class. It has been something like a huge amoeba covering postrevolutionary society with itself. It is an amoeba because it lacks a social backbone of its own, it is not a formed entity, not a historic force that comes on the scene in the way in which, for example, the old bourgeoisie came forth after the French Revolution.

Soviet bureaucracy is also hamstrung by a deep inherent contradiction: it rules as a result of the abolition of property in industry and finance, as a result of the workers' victory over the *ancien régime;* and it has to pay homage to that victory; it has to acknowledge ever anew that it manages industry and finance on behalf of the nation, on behalf of the workers. Privileged as they are, Soviet managers have to be on their guard: as more and more workers receive more and more education, the moment may easily come when the managers' skill, honesty, and competence may come under close scrutiny. They thrive on the apathy of the workers who so far have allowed them to run the state on their behalf. But this is a precarious position, an incomparably less stable foundation than that sanctified by tradition, property, and law. The conflict between the liberating origin of bureaucracy's power and the use it makes of that power generates constant tension between "us" the workers and "them" the managerial and political hierarchy.

There is also another reason for the lack of stability and cohesion in the managerial group no matter how privileged it has become. Over the last decades Soviet bureaucracy has all the time been in a process of stupendous expansion. Millions of people from the working class and to a lesser extent from the peasantry were recruited into its ranks. This continuous expansion militates against the crystallization of the bureaucracy not only into a class but even into a cohesive social group. I know, of course, that once a man from the lower classes is made to share in the privileges of the hierarchy, he himself becomes a bureaucrat. This may be so in individual cases and in abstract theory, but on the whole the "betrayal of one's class" does not work so very simply. When the son of a miner or a worker becomes an engineer or an administrator of a factory he does not on the morrow become completely insensitive to what goes on in his former environment, in the working class. All surveys show convincingly that in no other country is there such a rapid movement from manual to non-manual, and to what the Americans like to call "elite strata," as there is in the Soviet Union.

We must also realize that the privileges of the great majority of the bureaucrats are very, very paltry. The Russian administrator has the standard of living of our lower middle classes. Even the luxuries of the small minority high on top of the pyramid are not especially enviable, particularly if one considers the risks—and we all know how terrible these were under Stalin.

Of course, even small privileges contribute to the tension between the worker and the bureaucrat, but we should not mistake that tension for a class antagonism, in spite of some similarities which on closer examination would prove to be only very superficial. What we observe here is rather the hostility between members of the same class, between, say, a skilled miner and an unskilled one, between the engine driver and a less expert railwayman. This hostility and this tension contain in themselves a tremendous political antagonism, but one that cannot be resolved by any upheaval in society. It can be resolved only by the growth of the national wealth in the first instance, a growth which would make it possible to satisfy the minimum needs of the broadest masses of the population and more than that. It can be resolved by the spread and improvement of education, because it is the material and intellectual wealth of society that leads to the softening of the age-old division—now renewed and sharpened—between the organizers and the organized. When the organized is no longer the dumb and dull and helpless muzhik, when the cook is no longer the old scullion, then indeed the gulf between the bureaucrat and the worker can disappear. What will remain will be the division of functions, not of social status.

The old Marxist prospect of the "withering away" of the state may seem odd to us. But let us not play with old formulas which were part of an idiom to which we are not accustomed. What Marx really meant was that the state should divest itself of its oppressive political functions. And I think this will become possible only in a society based on nationalized means of production, free from slumps and booms, free from speculations and speculators, free from the uncontrollable forces of the whimsical market of private economy. In a society in which all the miracles of science and technology are turned to peaceful and productive uses; in which automation in industry is not hampered by fear of investment on the one side and fear of redundancy on the other; in which working hours are short and leisure civilized (and completely unlike our stultifying commercialized mass entertainment!); and—last but not least—in a society free from cults, dogmatism, and orthodoxies—in such a society the antagonism between brainwork and manual labor really will wither away, and so will the division between the organizers and the organized. Then, and only then, it will be seen that if bureaucracy was a faint prelude to class society, bureaucracy will mark the fierce, ferocious epilogue to class society—no more than an epilogue.

ideological
trends in the ussr

A survey of current Soviet trends in party and ideology may take as its starting point the political crisis which developed in the Soviet Union in the second half of the year 1964 and led to Khrushchev's downfall. The crisis was a rather complex affair with many issues, trends and attitudes involved, and it did not lead to any clear-cut solutions. The situation which has developed since Khrushchev's downfall has remained as ambiguous as that which had preceded it. By dissociating itself from its leader, the Soviet ruling group acknowledged tacitly the fiasco of the Khrushchevite policies and ideological conceptions; but they refused to make the acknowledgement explicit or to draw conclusions. Their reticence was not accidental. It reflected the profound embarrassment with which Khrushchev's successors viewed the discomfiture of his policies. Khrushchevism, to put it in a nutshell, had proved itself unable to cope with the many

This essay was written for a conference on "The Soviet Union 1917–1967" at the State University of New York at Binghamton and was originally published in The Socialist Register 1968, *Ralph Miliband and John Savile, eds. (Merlin Press; London, 1968).*

issues posed in the process of de-Stalinization. To have posed those issues was Khrushchev's historic merit; to leave them unsettled, unclarified and, in many cases, even aggravated was his sad destiny. The legacy of the Stalin era defeated him, and it still overshadows the Soviet scene today.

It is now very nearly a commonplace that Stalinism was the product of a postrevolutionary, isolated, underdeveloped, largely preindustrial society engaged in "primitive socialist accumulation," that is, in a process of rapid industrialization and modernization carried out under the aegis of the state, on the basis of public ownership of the means of production. As a system of government and an ideology, Stalinism represented both the backwardness of its national environment and the progressive transformation of that environment. Hence the duality in the character of Stalinism and its Janus-like appearance. Hence its crude violence and primitive, isolationist, ideological outlook on the one hand, and on the other, its historic élan and determination in replacing Russia's archaic mode of production and way of life by a modern planned economy and extensive mass education. Admittedly, the whole phenomenon of Stalinism cannot be explained by these factors alone, but they do account for its most essential features. Stalinism was thus a phenomenon of social transition and not (as its adherents and also most Western anticommunist Sovietologists once maintained) the quintessence or the final shape of the postcapitalist or socialist society. The very success which Stalinism attained in changing and modernizing the social structure of the USSR turned it into an anachronism and made de-Stalinization a historic necessity. Khrushchevism, though it proclaimed this necessity, was unable to act as its effective agent.

To take the economic problem first: the Stalinist method of economic planning, with its bureaucratic rigidity and overcentralization, dated back to the early phases of industrialization, which were characterized by an overall scarcity of productive resources, skilled labor, technological know-how, and educational facilities, not to speak of con-

sumer goods. As these scarcities were being gradually overcome and as Soviet society entered upon a more advanced
stage of economic expansion and educational progress, Stalinism lost its relative *raison d'être*. It was a relic of the past
even in the early fifties, and it became a formidable obstacle
to further advance.

The Khrushchev period brought important and positive
changes, a radical reduction of coercion in economic as well
as political life, easier labor relations, and a more rational
outlook in the management of industry. It failed, however, to
rationalize the system of planning as a whole. What it produced in this field was a purely administrative decentralization of industrial management. Khrushchev disbanded the
central ministries that had exercised absolute rule from
Moscow over all branches of the economy. This was his pana-
cea, but it did not work. By 1964 it had become obvious that
the new administrative regime had resulted in a slowing down
of industrial expansion and in a lower rate of growth of the
national income. As these setbacks coincided with a whole
series of bad harvests and a slump in agricultural output, the
improvement in the popular standard of living also came to a
halt. Thus, just as Stalinist bureaucratic rigidity and over-
centralization had proved obsolete in the early fifties, so the
Khrushchevite patchwork of decentralizing reforms lagged
behind the needs of the early sixties.

However, despite this slowing down—this should not be
forgotten—the expansion and transformation of the social
structure proceeded on a vast scale—and this called for reforms far more radical and comprehensive than anything
Khrushchev and his colleagues envisaged. In the fourteen
years since Stalin's death, the urban population of the USSR
has nearly doubled. It has grown by about fifty million
people, mostly rural immigrants who have been absorbed
by industry. This gives us a measure of the momentum of
the social-economic advance and of the demands it put on
the leadership of party and state. The mere overhaul of the
administrative mechanism could do no justice to those

demands. The Khrushchevite decentralization was in fact a narrow, one-sided, bureaucratic reaction to Stalin's over-centralization. Its effects were probably beneficial in some cases but harmful in others, and on balance inadequate. What Khrushchev's successors have since been trying to do is to substitute economic decentralization for the purely administrative one. This is the meaning of the latest industrial reform with its emphasis on the autonomy and profitability of each industrial concern. Incidentally, the novelty of this reform is far less startling than it appears to most Western observers. And, although it too may have its beneficial effects and stimulate productivity temporarily, it is not likely to alter the bureaucratic character of economic management.

The issue of centralized versus decentralized management is, in my view, only part of the problem of the rationalization of the Soviet economy, and not its most essential part. The dilemma between centralization and decentralization is inherent in any planned economy. It cannot be resolved dogmatically or one-sidedly, and it cannot be conjured out of existence. The dialectics of planning consists precisely in this—that the planner must constantly search for a balance between the opposites and for their unity, as he must also search for an equilibrium between the general social needs and the profitability of particular concerns, between supply and demand, and between production and consumption. There can be no single prescription for achieving the equilibrium. The scales may and, indeed, must tilt one way and the other, and it is the planner's task to control the oscillations and correct them.

If in the Stalin era the equilibrium was upset by over-centralization, in recent years, Soviet (and Yugoslav and Eastern European) economists, reacting against the past, have undoubtedly overemphasized, in varying degrees, the principle of decentralization. Their almost exclusive concentration on the autonomy and profitability of each industrial unit may swing the pendulum much too far in that direction, at the expense of the social interests and of the coherence of planning. Some reaction against this trend is already making itself felt. Nevertheless, this is not, in my view, the main issue. It is at least premature to see in this trend a revival of a truly market-oriented economy or any tendency towards the restoration of capitalism. The Soviet economy was incomparably more market- and profit-oriented during the NEP period of the 1920s than it is likely to become, if and when the present reform is completed. But there was a far cry from NEP to a restoration of capitalism. Not even Libermanism spells economic liberalism.

The crucial issue posed by the failure of Khrushchevism is neither administrative nor economic in character but sociopolitical. The main cause of the economic disarray revealed in the last years of Khrushchev's government lay in a crisis of morale, in the persistent discord between rulers and ruled, in the "we" and "they" conflict, that is, in the feeling of workers and intellectuals that "they," the bureaucrats, "do what they like anyhow," regardless of "our" needs, demands and wishes. Bureaucratic arbitrariness, though it is less severe than it was in Stalin's days, prevents the mass of producers and administrators from identifying themselves with the national interest. That is why purely administrative or economic remedies cannot cope even with the economic and administrative difficulties; and neither Khrushchev nor his successors have been able or willing to deal with the moral-political aspects of the situation. It was because of this that Khrushchevism suffered defeat after defeat, nationally and internationally, and that it ran into a deadly impasse.

Nationally, Khrushchevism was unable to fill the political and ideological void left by Stalinism. Having analyzed this question elsewhere* I shall say here only that Khrushchev and his colleagues, the present Soviet leaders, have dealt with the legacy of the Stalin era in a manner which

---

* See, e.g., "The Failure of Khrushchevism" in my *Ironies of History* (Oxford University Press: London, 1966), pp. 121–46; and *The Unfinished Revolution* (Oxford University Press; London, 1967), chapter 6.

could only produce confusion and frustration. Brought up in the Stalinist school of thought, and ever mindful of their own stake in Stalinism, they merely sought to cover up the void by means of bureaucratic manipulations. They conducted even de-Stalinization in a Stalinist manner. Imbued with the characteristic Stalinist belief in the omnipotence of the trick, a belief which has with them the force of an ineradicable superstition, Khrushchev and his colleagues in the end turned de-Stalinization itself into a trick, into a huge and elaborate essay in deception and make-believe. They denounced Stalin's hypocrisy but sought to protect the hierarchical structure on which it had rested. They exposed his crimes and did what they could to conceal their own participation in them. They discredited the "cult of the personality" but clung to the orthodoxy the cult had epitomized. They cried out against Stalin's prodigious despotism but were anxious to save most of his canons and dogmas. They freed the Soviet people from his massive and ubiquitous terror but tried to keep the body politic in the shape it had taken on under the press of that terror. They sought to preserve the monolith and to keep Soviet society in that amorphous and atomized condition in which people cannot think for themselves, express themselves, arrive at nonconformist opinions, and voice them.

Yet the huge trick, with all the evasions, subterfuges, and contradictions, did not work. Underneath the monolithic surface, deep down in the mass of the people, and even higher up in the ruling group, ferments were released which were bound to escape control. Some people saw through the evasions and contradictions and began to press for a more radical and genuine de-Stalinization. Others, especially among the bureaucracy, took fright at the ideological drifting and called for an end to the desecration of the old idol; many reacted simply with disgust and cynicism. Some were raising the demand for the mitigation or abolition of various forms of administrative control and thought control, the demand for more freedom; while others, again among the bureaucracy, afraid that popular discontent and criticism might rise in a flood, were anxious to close the gates. Khrushchev maneuvered uneasily and clumsily between the conflicting pressures until he exhausted his moral credit. In 1956 he used Stalin as the colossal scapegoat for all the sins of the Soviet bureaucracy. In 1964 the bureaucracy quietly made Khrushchev the scapegoat. But the men who took over from him inherited all his dilemmas without having any new program or any new idea on how to resolve them. Their chief advantage over Khrushchev was that they could afford to mark time, as he could not.

The division between the de-Stalinizers and the Stalinist die-hards or crypto-Stalinists has lain on the surface of Soviet politics. It showed itself in Khrushchev's struggle against Molotov, Kaganovich, and their followers, and it has been widely reflected in Soviet literature. It corresponded broadly to the division between those elements in the ruling group that favored a gradual and limited liberalization of the regime and those inclined to uphold the disciplinarian and authoritarian routines in the management of party and state. Khrushchev, attempting always to be all things to all men, in the end antagonized all. The crypto-Stalinists never forgave him his speech at the Twentieth Congress. The bureaucrats were eager to avenge themselves on him for his pogrom of the central economic ministries; and the disciplinarians resented the latitude he allowed the critics and muckrakers who exposed not only Stalin's rule but the heavy remnants of Stalinism surviving in every sphere of Soviet life. On the other hand, to the critics and muckrakers, the liberals and the radicals, Khrushchev's benevolence was only too whimsical and deceptive. They knew only too well that every one of his liberal gestures made in public concealed many acts of repression. The writers and the artists resented his censorship and his attempts to impose on them his crude and uneducated tastes. In 1964 the anti-Stalinists and the crypto-Stalinists, the liberalizers and the authoritarians, for a moment joined hands against him, each hoping to gain from his downfall.

These hopes too have been frustrated. Khrushchev's successors have not identified themselves with either of the opposed groupings. They have rather tried to do what Khrushchev had done, only to do it with greater discretion and caution. They have pursued a middle line and have tried hard to keep the "extremes" at bay.

The division between the de-Stalinizers and the crypto-Stalinists, and between the liberalizers and the authoritarians, forms only part of the picture, its most conspicuous and superficial part. Overshadowed by it there is another division, largely latent and even inchoate but, in the long term, perhaps more essential, namely, the division between right, left and center. The reappearance of this classical division follows naturally from the cracking up of the monolith, the essential of which consisted precisely in suppressing the dialectics inherent in any live movement or party and in preventing any spontaneous differentiation of opinion, both within the party and without. The last time the Soviet Union witnessed any open struggle between right, left and center was in the middle and late 1920s. The present redifferentiation resumes to some extent, but only to some extent, the trends of the 1920s but it does so spontaneously, almost unconsciously, and confusedly. And in view of the change in the social circumstances and in the political context, the continuity of these trends can be only partial. That the tendency to a division between right, left and center is at work in the international Communist movement is now clear enough, even though that division is blurred and distorted by many-sided bureaucratic manipulation, and even though each trend *tends* to be identified with a particular national interest and school of thought—the left or "ultraleft" with Maoism, the center with predominant Soviet policy, and the right with Titoism and its multiple national varieties. However, a *tendency* towards this differentiation is discernible within each Communist party as well, even though each tries to maintain the official facade of its monolithic unity. This makes it often difficult to see and evaluate the hidden processes of division.

But when the facade happens to be suddenly and dramatically blown off, as it has been in China recently, the reality of the division asserts itself. The Soviet party is hardly more monolithic or more united than the Chinese was just before the outbreak of the so-called cultural revolution. Here and there many indications point to the submerged pattern of differentiation—I repeat, to an inchoate or, at best, half-potential and half-actual division between right, left and center. The division cannot become fully actual as long as the groupings involved in it are not free to express themselves and formulate their ideas or programs, for it is precisely in the process of self-expression that ideological trends and political groupings become conscious of themselves and find their identity.

I should, perhaps, clarify here to some extent my criteria and explain what attitudes I describe as "left" or "right" in the context of Soviet social life and Soviet politics at this time.

The specific crucial issues over which the divisions tend to arise are those of egalitarianism versus privilege; of workers' control, or workers' participation in control, over industry versus strictly managerial control; of freedom of expression and association versus bureaucratic dictatorship and monolithic discipline; and last, but not least, of socialist internationalism versus nationalism. Any careful student of Soviet affairs, indeed any attentive reader of Soviet literature and periodicals, familiar with its Aesopian idiom, will have little or no difficulty in tracing the conflicting attitudes as they reflect themselves in Soviet writings or as they refract themselves in the zigzags of official policy. These divisions were potentially there even in Stalin's days, but in those days society was atomized, and the human atoms were absolutely unable to combine or coalesce into groups. They led an existence like that of Leibnitz's monads, closed within themselves, isolated from one another, unable to communicate. When communication did occur, it was a mixed dialogue between two atoms only, like the one Yevtushenko reports in his *Precocious Autobiography*, where he describes his ideological wrangling with a fellow poet, a bard of the establishment, a Great Russian chauvinist, antisemite and fervent authoritarian, a Stalinist descendant of the prerevolutionary Black Hundreds, against whom Yevtushenko whispered, in hints only, his feelings about the Jews, his internationalism, his vague longing for an outlook broader than the official ideology, and his instinctive distaste for bureaucratic privilege.*

No doubt such dialogues between two atoms went on in various places and you can detect in them the germ of a controversy between left and right. But the germ could not germinate and grow. What has been new in these post-Stalinist years has been the slow, hesitant movement and coalescence of like-minded atoms into groups, whether in the party hierarchy or in literature, among the sculptors and painters, the philosophers, sociologists, historians, scientists, and almost certainly also at the factory bench and in the *kolkhoz* community. People of similar ideological and political disposition recognize one another and are drawn toward one another. Where previously only bureaucratic cliques could exist, surrounded by a political vacuum, now groupings and trends form themselves, though they are still very far from crystallization. We know of the groupings among the writers who now engage in public, semi-public, and private controversy. Such groupings tend to form themselves in other occupations as well in all walks of life, on all social levels, in all milieus. But we do not hear about them because those milieus are, of course, not as vocal and articulate as men of letters normally are. This is largely still a molecular process, though it is sometimes more than that. And officialdom, of course, does all that it can to slow down the process and obstruct it.

It is in this way that the new right and the new left have begun to stir. Trying to face the features of the emerging

---

* E. [Y]evtushenko, *A Precocious Autobiography* (Collins; London, 1963).

political types, one is inclined to melancholy reflections about the price the Soviet Union is still paying, in spiritual and intellectual terms, for the forcible interruption by Stalinism of all open ideological and political confrontation. The level of political thinking and expression is lamentably low. The profile of a man of the right in the 1960s is simple enough. He usually defends privilege, favors wide discrepancies in scales of wages and salaries, and tends to be a Great Russian chauvinist and power politician; he is contemptuous of the small Soviet nationalities and of such poor relations as Poles and Hungarians, but, above all, of the Chinese, against whom he will even vent racial prejudice. More often than not, he is an antisemite. Next to him stands a more moderate and educated man of the right, who may combine anti-egalitarianism and distrust of the masses with a certain cosmopolitanism, with an eagerness for close relations with the West, and with an intense fear of any Russian involvement in class struggles abroad or in anti-imperialist wars of liberation. Western observers often come across this political type among Soviet diplomats, journalists and industrial managers; but more plebeian versions of the type also abound.

The man of the Soviet left is more often than not an intellectual, a philosopher, sociologist, or party historian; but he may also be a worker at the factory bench. He criticizes the present distribution of the national income, the wide wage differentials, and bureaucratic privilege. He attacks—sometimes even in public—the secrecy with which the earnings of the various "income groups" are surrounded, and presses for a radical narrowing of their discrepancies. He favors shorter working hours in the factories and demands better and wider educational facilities for working-class children. That pressure on all these points has been effective is evidenced by the concessions which the ruling group has again and again had to make in regard to them. This new egalitarianism, inherently hostile to the Stalinist tradition, is also critical of the social implications of the new economic policy, with its heavy emphasis on profitability and the "laws of the market." The man of the left recalls that socialism has aspired and should still aspire to transcend gradually the laws of the market, not by means of rigid bureaucratic direction, but by a rational economic policy and the producers' participation in control over the economy. In ideology and politics, the elements of the left seek to pick up the threads of the revolutionary tradition where Stalinism broke them, and to restore the true history of the revolution and of Bolshevism, for they feel that only if the ground is cleared to the end of the rubble of Stalinist legends and myths will a new socialist consciousness develop in the people. In foreign affairs men of the left try to grasp the significance of recent social-revolutionary events in the world, of Cuba and Vietnam, and of China's internal conflicts; and they attempt to relate these to Soviet policy. They are, no doubt, perturbed by the decline of international solidarity in the USSR and by the quasi-isolationist mood that characterizes both official policy and the popular frame of mind.

I do not undertake, I don't think anyone can undertake, to judge the relative strength and weight of these opposed currents of thought and feeling. Even the characterization of the types is, of necessity, fragmentary and patchy. Yet it is based on the internal evidence of the events, and on a wide range of philosophical, economic, sociological and literary indications. These are the hidden or half-hidden conflicting pressures under which, I think, Soviet policy finds itself and by which it is to some extent shaped. Official policy is, of course, centrist, cagey, and is trying to keep at a safe distance from the extremes or to reconcile the contradictions. But in the long run the basic trends seem more important; they are likely to become more effective as time goes on; they make up the submerged bulk of the Soviet iceberg.

The two patterns of the ideological and political division, the division over Stalinism and the conflict between right and left are not coincidental. They overlap and produce cross-currents. Among the adherents of de-Stalinization there are some with a rightist and others with a leftist bias. In the early years after Stalin, Khrushchev sought to rally the support of both wings; and therein lay his strength. In his later years, his own policy showed a markedly rightist bias in both domestic and foreign affairs. This circumstance undoubtedly brought a measure of discredit upon de-Stalinization. Occasionally, it lent color to the Maoist accusation that, by undermining the Stalinist orthodoxy, Khrushchev released or stimulated latent reactionary forces, within the Soviet Union as well as without, in Eastern Europe, in Hungary, Poland and elsewhere.

Thus, paradoxically, the opposition to de-Stalinization, which at first came only from a rather narrow conservative bureaucratic milieu, found itself gradually strengthened by a spreading disappointment with various aspects of Khrushchevism. Seeing that de-Stalinization in Khrushchev's policy was, in his last years, associated with anti-egalitarianism, with a virtual wage freeze, and agricultural failure, and further with the Russo-Chinese feud and the disintegration of the Soviet bloc, quite a few people inclined towards egalitarianism and internationalism and became fearful of the implications of Khrushchevism. Critical, well-informed observers reported, for instance, in the years 1963 and 1964, the spread of something like a spontaneous, nostalgic Stalin cult among Soviet factory workers, a mood which expressed itself in biting popular witticisms contrasting some of Khrushchev's failures with Stalin's wisdom and foresight. "Do you know what was the greatest of Stalin's crimes?" went one popular joke, "it was this, that he did not lay up a stock of grain that would last us longer than five years of Khrushchev's rule." What a paradox! Who would have thought in 1956 that anyone in the Soviet Union would only a few years later look back nostalgically to the Stalin era.* But this was, in fact, the outcome of half-hearted, hypocritical and

* In January 1968 the literary monthly *Oktyabr* published a poem by Feliks Chuyev expressing hope and belief that after some time Stalin's name would again be honored and respected by the Soviet people.

"rightist" de-Stalinization. One consequence of that state of affairs—one would like to hope an ephemeral one—is that the progressive, anti-Stalinist intelligentsia found itself frequently isolated from the mood in the working class. Another is that before the recent uproar and commotion in China, Maoist criticism struck more chords in the Soviet Union than Soviet officialdom was ready to admit.

Seen against this background the task of Khrushchev's successors has not been an easy one. They were not well equipped to deal with the conflicting trends and cross-currents. They represent—in this respect the Maoists are right—Khrushchevism without Khrushchev. When they turned against their former leader, they held that his policies had been basically correct, but that he had distorted and compromised them by his temperamental outbursts, eccentricities, and excesses. There was a grain of truth in that, but not more. Khrushchev's behavior became increasingly erratic as his policies were leading him into an impasse. He tried to get out of it by alternate overemphatic gestures of conciliation and by aggressive vituperation, by attempts to ingratiate himself with his opponents at home or abroad, and by loud fist-banging or shoe-banging.

There is, in any case, a curiously repetitive logic in all this. It had been Khrushchev's strongly held view that Stalin's policy had, over many years, been basically correct until Stalin spoiled everything by his morbid lust for power and his excesses. Khrushchev, as it were, appealed from the latter-day insane Stalin to the alleged sanity of the earlier Stalinism. Now Brezhnev and Kosygin react in the same way to Khrushchevism. They seek to rescue it from Khrushchev's latter-day distortions.

They began by moving on tiptoes and trying to hush discordant voices around them. There were to be no further drastic exposures of Stalinism, no more talk about the terrors of the concentration camps of the past; but there was to be no rehabilitation of Stalinism either, and no repudiation of the Twentieth and Twenty-second Congresses. There was to be no further liberalization; but neither was there to be any drastic curtailment of Khrushchev's semi-liberal reforms. There was to be no more voicing of egalitarian demands—the emphasis was and is on incentive payments and rewards; but neither was there to be any campaign against the egalitarians. In foreign affairs, Kosygin and Brezhnev decided to put an end to personal diplomacy *à la* Khrushchev, but reasserted their faith in his interpretation of "peaceful coexistence." They tried to restore the unity of the Communist parties and to mend the bridge with China; but they are not willing to make any concessions of substance to the Chinese. Kosygin's first journey, on assumption of the office of Prime Minister, was to Vietnam and China; but since this journey yielded no positive results, Moscow decided to lapse into silence over China, a silence which it maintained for about two years. To undo the harm that Khrushchev had done to Vietnam, by declaring just before his downfall that the Soviet Union had no interest in defending Southeast Asia, his successors reaffirmed Russia's interest in that area; but they have been rather careful in doling out aid to the North Vietnamese and the Vietcong. At the Twenty-third Congress, Kosygin and Brezhnev declared that the Soviet aid to the Vietnamese amounted to half a billion roubles, a negligible sum compared to the many billion dollars spent by the United States on the war in Vietnam. In a word, theirs was to be the good old middle-of-the-road Khrushchevism, not the one drifting more and more to the right, Khrushchevism without Khrushchevian excesses, Khrushchevism combined with silence, which is golden, and with wait and see.

It seems that the waiting game is drawing to a close. Brezhnev, Kosygin, and their colleagues are discovering that Khrushchev's "excesses," distortions, and drifting were not accidental or caused merely by his temperamental disposition. The point is that one cannot be afraid of radical, egalitarian, and democratic socialist and internationalist trends indefinitely without lapsing into bureaucratic conservatism and drifting to the right. Brezhnev and Kosygin are indeed finding it more and more difficult to maintain a cautious, noncommittal, centrist position. The conflicting pressures from left and right have been mounting, even if left and right are not any organized groupings but more or less diffused tendencies and moods.

And so, after an interval of silence, all controversies are resumed, even though they are as a rule conducted behind closed doors. But there they are conducted with a vehemence of which the echoes reaching the Soviet public or the Western world give only a faint idea. Egalitarian and antiegalitarian voices are heard again, even though the former are muffled, and speak less openly than the latter. And in the background one can discern the renewed, though unfocused, discord between nationalism and internationalism, and, on a different level, the clash between various interpretations of peaceful coexistence.*

On all these issues, official policies are slowly but perceptibly drifting again to the right. The government tries to stem the anti-Stalinist mood of the intelligentsia that keeps breaking through. Hence the heavy censorship of recent months. It also attempts to enhance the position of the managers vis-a-vis the workers, although the relative pro-consumer bias of the economic reform may have its anti-bureaucratic implications as well. But it is, above all, in foreign policy that, after a period of reticence and immobility, Brezhnev and Kosygin are driven to follow in Khrushchev's footsteps. The silence over the conflict with China is broken; and the controversy is again conducted in public, though the Russian contribution to it has not yet risen to the high pitch it had reached in Khrushchev's last days. True, the relentless vehemence and vituperation of the Maoists and the so-called cultural revolution have provoked the new ex-

---

* (Footnote of July 1967.) This was, of course, said a few months before the crisis in the Middle East and the Arab-Israel war of June 1967. A few days after that war *Krasnaya Zvezda* wrote that it was perhaps time to revise the official Soviet conception of "peaceful coexistence."

changes. All the same, the renewal of controversy inevitably strengthens the nationalist mood in the USSR and brings out its faintly racial undertones. In diplomacy, the embarrassed *immobilisme* of 1964 and 1965 is giving place to a new period of active maneuvering. The Soviet Prime Minister has in recent months indulged quite freely in that personal diplomacy which he and Brezhnev had censured not so long ago.* The return to Khrushchevian diplomacy and to the Khrushchevian interpretation of peaceful coexistence has been strikingly exemplified by the recent signature of the Soviet-American agreement on withholding nuclear weapons from outer space. What is important here is not so much the agreement itself, which is of course unobjectionable, as its timing; coming at the moment of intensified American escalation of the war in Vietnam, this act has certainly been considered as ill-timed by some military "hawks" in Moscow; and it is not only the hawks who feel uneasy over the USSR's role in the Vietnamese conflict. Obviously recent events have done much to aggravate the quarrel with China even further. The logic of the situation had led the present leaders to do what Khrushchev had done; namely, to try and rally foreign Communist parties against China and to obtain from them a formal condemnation of Maoism. That the Communist parties have apparently proved as reluctant to respond as they were in Khrushchev's days is all the more remarkable, as the Chinese had in the meantime done their best, or their worst, to enhance the Soviet position in the Communist movement.

It seems to me that Soviet policy is indeed heading for an impasse very similar to that of 1964. At home Khrushchevism without Khrushchev cannot contain or stop the growing momentum of the contending trends. It is doubtful whether any government or party leadership not willing to allow those trends to come back into the open can break the

---

* This was also said before the Glassboro meeting between President Johnson and Premier Kosygin, which resumed, though not without some timidity, the line of "personal diplomacy."

domestic deadlock. No government can do this that is not resolved to carry de-Stalinization to a democratic socialist consummation, that is, to an open confrontation of the now submerged ideological and political currents. These currents can be tested only in an open, nationwide debate, which would enable Soviet society to achieve its ideological self-determination. Similarly, in foreign affairs, no government or party leadership addicted to the sacred national egoism in which Stalin bred the present generation of leaders can cope with the disintegration of the Soviet bloc. The centrifugal forces now at work in communism can be overcome, if at all, only on the basis of a democratically oriented socialist inter-nationalism. Whether the forces that might work towards such a way out are strong enough, I cannot undertake to judge. The war in Vietnam and the outcome of the crisis in China will undoubtedly have their impact on developments in the USSR and influence the ideological balance. In any case, we need not take at its face value the apparent uneventful-ness of the post-Khrushchevian period. In this respect, as in many others, the upheaval in China teaches a lesson. Who would have thought two years ago that so much turmoil was pent up behind China's monolithic facade and that so many contradictions, some of them highly "antagonistic," were just about to explode in Mao's face? I am not claiming that I know that the Soviet political barometer is also set on storm. It may well be that current difficulties may just prolong the chronic post-Stalinist crisis in which the Soviet Union has lived since the end of Stalin; but they may also bring it to a sharp and dramatic turn.

on socialist
man

I have been asked to address you on "Socialist Man." This is a theme so wide, and requiring so many approaches from various angles, that I must beg you to excuse me if what I am going to say resembles a somewhat rambling *causerie* in form, rather than a systematic lecture.

Marxists have as a rule been reluctant to speak about socialist man; and I must confess that I myself felt something of that reluctance when the subject for this lecture was first suggested to me. Any attempt to give a positive description of socialist man, i.e., to portray the member of the future classless society, is bound to have a utopian flavor about it. This was the domain of the great visionaries of socialism, especially of Saint-Simon and Fourier, who, like the French rationalists of the eighteenth century, imagined that they—and through them Reason—had at last discovered the ideal

This speech, given to the second Socialist Scholars' Conference in New York in 1966, was published in pamphlet form by Merit Publishers (New York, 1967).

man and that once the discovery had been made, the realization was bound to follow. Nothing was further from Marx and Engels and the outstanding Marxists of later generations than such a thought. They, indeed, did not tell mankind: "Here is the ideal, go down on your knees before it!" Instead of giving us a blueprint of the society that is to come, they devoted their work to a profoundly realistic analysis of society as it was and is, of capitalist society; and, facing the class struggles of their time, they committed themselves irrevocably to the cause of the proletariat.

In attending to the needs of their age, however, they did not turn their backs upon the future. They did try at least to guess the shape of things to come; but they formulated their guesses with remarkable reserve and they did so only incidentally. In all their voluminous writings Marx and Engels have left us only a few scattered hints about the subject of our discussion, hints meaningfully interrelated and suggesting immense new horizons, but only hints. No doubt Karl Marx had his conception of socialist man, but this was an analyst's working hypothesis, not a visionary's brainwave; and although he was convinced of the historic realism of his anticipations, he treated them with a certain dose of skepticism.

Marx scrutinized, to paraphrase his own saying, the embryo of socialism within the womb of capitalism—he could therefore see only the embryo of socialist man. At the risk of disappointing some of you, I must say that this is all that we can do even now. After all the revolutions of our age and despite all that we have learned about society since Marx, we are not at all ahead of him in this respect: in discussing socialist man we cannot yet go beyond the rudiments of the problem. Anything we can say about it is bound to be very general, fragmentary and, in a sense, negative. We can easier see what socialist man cannot be than what he will be. To the extent, however, that negation implies also assertion, our negative characterization of socialist man foreshadows some of his positive features as well.

Marxism has seen the chief contradiction of bourgeois

society, the deepest cause of its anarchy and irrationality, in the conflict between the growing socialization of the modern productive process and the unsocial character of the control that private property exercises over that process. Modern technology and industry tend to unite society, while private property in the means of production disunites it. The socialized productive process, that rudimentary element of collectivism contained within the capitalist, and, if you like, within the neocapitalist economy, needs to be released from the bourgeois property relations which constrict and disorganize it. For more than a century bourgeois economists were blind to this contradiction, until Keynes and his followers recognized it in their own eclectic way, thus paying an unavowed tribute to the Marxist critique.

But all that Keynesianism and neocapitalism, more than ever haunted by the specter of communism, have tried to do is to introduce, on the basis of private property (i.e., of monopolistic capitalist corporations) a kind of pseudosocial control over the socialized productive process. This is not the first or the last time that men have desperately struggled to ensure the survival of archaic institutions or ways of life into an age that has no need and no use for them. I once saw in my native country, Poland, a peasant who by chance acquired an old motor car and then insisted on harnessing his horses to it. Keynesianism and neocapitalism are keeping the horses of private property harnessed to the nuclear-driven vehicles and space ships of our time—and they threaten to shake heaven and earth to prevent us unharnessing them.

To return to my proper subject: our idea of socialism is not an arbitrary intellectual construction but a careful extrapolation and projection into the future of those elements of rational social organization that are inherent in capitalist society but are constantly thwarted and negated by it. Similarly our idea of socialist man is but a projection of the social man who already exists within us potentially, but is distorted, crushed and stultified by the condition in which he lives. (The germ of socialist man is present even in the alienated worker of our time in those rare moments when he rises to a genuine awareness of his role in society and to class solidarity and when he struggles for his emancipation.) It is here that our aspirations are rooted in the realities and are sustained by them, but all too often are also imprisoned in them.

We know, I repeat, what socialist man cannot be and will not be: he cannot be the product of antagonistic society; he cannot be the collective producer who is controlled by his product and social environment instead of controlling them. He cannot be the plaything of the blind forces of the market, nor the robot of a state-managed neocapitalist war economy. He cannot be the alienated and cowed proletarian of earlier days, nor the dull counterfeit copy of the petty bourgeois into which our so-called welfare state is turning the worker. He can be himself as collective worker only in a most highly developed and collectivist society. Only such a society will enable him to reduce his socially necessary labor to the unburdensome minimum which the new technology already permits. Only in such a society will he be able to satisfy his material and spiritual needs securely, not haphazardly; rationally, not whimsically. Only in such a society will he guide himself in the satisfaction of his needs and the use of his leisure by educated discernment and intelligent choice, not by any silent or vociferous persuaders of commercial advertisement. Only in a socialist community will man be able to develop all his biological and spiritual capacities, to expand and integrate his personality, and free himself of the dark heritage of millenial material scarcity, inequality, and oppression. Only in such a community can man overcome finally the divorce between physical and intellectual labor, the divorce that has been at the root of man's estrangement from man, of mankind's division into rulers and ruled and into antagonistic classes—the divorce that our advanced technology even now is rendering superfluous while capitalism and neocapitalism do what they can to perpetuate it. Socialist man can rise to his full stature only at the summit of our culture and civilization, a summit which is within our sight but toward which our property relationships, our social institutions, and deeply ingrained inertia do not allow us to advance as firmly and rapidly as we might advance.

Our idea of socialist man has often been criticized for its unabashed optimism. We are told that we too are utopians and that our historical-philosophical and psychological assumptions are untenable. We are told that the "paradise on earth" of which propagandists of socialism have spoken is as unattainable as was the paradise in heaven the theologians had promised. We must listen with open minds to these criticisms—we sometimes find grains of truth in them. We must admit that we have more than once taken too optimistic a view if not of socialism itself, then of the roads leading to it. But we must also realize that many of these criticisms express only the sense of doom permeating bourgeois society and its ideologues, or else irrational forms of disillusionment in our own camp.

Thus some of the existentialists tell us that we are trying to escape from the basic predicaments of the human condition and that we are glossing over the inherent absurdity of our destiny. It is extremely difficult to engage in any fruitful debate with opponents who argue *sub specie aeternitatis* and from purely teleological premises. The pessimistic existentialist asks the old question: What is the purpose or the aim of man's existence and activity when set against the infinity of time and space? To this question we have, of course, no answer—nor has the existentialist. But the question itself is absurd, for it postulates the need or necessity of an ultimate, metaphysical purpose of human existence, a purpose valid for all eternity. We have no such purpose, and we have no need for it. We see no metaphysical sense in our existence and therefore we see no absurdity in it either—absurdity and sense are only the obverse sides of the same coin: only when you postulate sense can you speak of absurdity.

The human condition with which we are concerned is not man's loneliness in the infinity of space and time—in that infinity even the terms "loneliness" and "absurdity" are meaningless. We are concerned with man's condition in society—which is his own creation and which he is capable of changing. The argument from *sub specie aeternitatis* is philosophically arid and socially reactionary; it is as a rule an argument for moral indifference and political quietism, an argument for resigned acceptance of our social conditions as they are. Happily, existentialists, as Sartre's remarkable example shows, can be philosophically inconsistent and can accept the idea of socialist man despite their view of the absurdity of the human condition.

More specific to some extent is the criticism of socialist and Marxist aspirations that Sigmund Freud makes in *Civilization and its Discontents*. To our view of what man can and probably will be in a classless and stateless society, Freud replies with the old adage: *Homo homini lupus.* Human beings, he says, will always remain aggressive and hostile to each other; their aggressive instincts are biologically predetermined and are not significantly affected by any changes in the structure of society. "The communists," Freud says, "believe that they have found the path to deliverance from our evils. According to them, man is wholly good and well-disposed to his neighbor, but the institution of private property has corrupted his nature. The ownership of private wealth gives the individual power and with it the temptation to ill-treat his neighbor; while the man who is excluded from possession is bound to rebel in hostility against his oppressor. If private property were abolished, and wealth held in common, and everyone allowed to share in the enjoyment of it, ill will and hostility would disappear among men. Since everyone's needs would be satisfied, no one would have any reason to regard another as his enemy; all would willingly undertake the work that was necessary."

Before I proceed, let me first check whether Freud's summary of the Marxist view is correct. Do we really consider man to be "wholly good" by nature and "well-disposed to his neighbor"? Freud, who was rather ill-informed about

Marxist theory, certainly came across some such statements in the popular communist or social-democratic propaganda, where they did indeed occur. Serious Marxist theory, however, does not make any such assumptions about human nature—at the most such assumptions may be traced in Marx's youthful, Feuerbachian writings. I remember that this problem occupied me strongly when, as a very young man, I was acquainting myself with Marxist theory and was trying to obtain clarity about the conception of human nature underlying it. Working through the writings of Marx, Engels, Kautsky, Plekhanov, Mehring, Rosa Luxemburg, Lenin, Trotsky and Bukharin, I arrived at the conclusion that their assumptions about human nature were essentially, so to speak, neutral. They did not see man as "wholly good" or "wholly evil," as "well-disposed" or "ill-disposed toward his neighbor"; they refused to accept the metaphysical notion of an immutable human nature unaffected by social conditions. I still think that the conclusion I then drew forty years ago was correct.

Man is the creature of nature, but more particularly of that part of nature which, as human society, distinguishes itself from nature and partly opposes itself to it. Whatever the biological basis of our being, social conditions play the decisive part in shaping our character—even the biological factors refract themselves through, and are partly transformed by, our social personality. To some extent man's nature, including his instincts, has so far been submerged and distorted by his social conditions, and only when these conditions lose their oppressive and distorting quality may we be able to take a clearer and more scientific view than we have had so far of the various biological and social elements in man's nature.

The main criticism of Freudianism that a Marxist is bound to make—and I am speaking as one who wholeheartedly recognizes Freud's fundamental and revolutionary contribution to our understanding of psychology—is that Freud and his disciples all too often fail to make allowance for this refraction and transmutation of man's instinctual drives through his changing social identity—and yet it is Freud who has made us aware of the processes which are nothing but the mechanisms of sublimation! Psychoanalysis has so far been able to deal only with bourgeois man, the bourgeois man of the epoch of imperialism, whom it has tended to present as man at large, treating his inner conflicts in a supra-historical manner as conflicts besetting human beings in all epochs, under all social orders, as conflicts inherent in the human condition. From this point of view socialist man can be seen only as a variation of bourgeois man. Freud himself makes this point: "In abolishing private property we deprive the human love of aggression of one of its instruments, certainly a strong one, though certainly not the strongest; but we have in no way altered the differences in power and influence which are misused by aggressiveness nor have we altered anything in its nature."

Then Freud makes this even more categorical assertion: "Aggressiveness was not created by property; it reigned almost without limit in primitive times, when property was still very scant, and it already shows itself in the nursery almost before aggressiveness has given up its primal, anal form. . . . If we do away with personal rights over material wealth, there still remains prerogative in the field of sexual relationships, which is bound to become the source of the strongest dislike and the most violent hostility among men who in other respects are on an equal footing." Thus we are warned that socialist man will be, not less than bourgeois man, aggressive and hostile toward fellow beings, and that his aggressiveness will show itself even in the nursery.

Note that while Freud recognizes in private property a strong instrument of aggression, he asserts in the most dogmatic manner that it is not the strongest of those instruments. How does he know it? How does he measure the relative strength of the various instruments of aggression? We, Marxists, are more modest here and less dogmatic: we do not claim to have made such precise comparative measurements as would allow us to weigh sexual drives and instinctual aggression against social needs, interests, and compulsions. The instinctual drives will undoubtedly be there in socialist man as well—how could it be otherwise?—but we do not know how they will refract themselves through his personality. We can only guess that they will affect him in a different manner than they affect bourgeois man. (I even suppose that socialist man will offer the psychoanalyst far richer and more reliable material for research and conclusions, because in him a future Freud will be able to watch the working of the instinctual drives directly, not through a glass darkly, not through the distorting prisms of the analyst's and the patient's class psychology.) Nor is Freud right in saying that property is only an instrument of our aggressive instincts—on the contrary, property often uses those instincts as its instruments and generates its own varieties of aggressive drives. After all, throughout history men organized into armies have slaughtered each other over property or claims to property; but they have not so far, except in mythology, fought wars over "prerogative in the field of sexual relationships."

And so when Freud maintains that the abolition of property will not alter "the differences in power and influence which are misused by aggressiveness" and will not "alter anything in the nature of human aggression," he simply begs the question. And when he goes on to say that "aggressiveness . . . reigned almost without limit in primitive times, when property was still very scanty," he does not even suspect that it was precisely the scantiness of property, i.e., material scarcity, that destroyed the unity of primitive society, by giving rise to savage scrambles over scanty resources, scrambles that split society into mutually hostile classes. That is why we maintain that socialist man is conceivable only against the background of an unprecedented abundance of material and cultural goods and services. This is the ABC of Marxism. A friend of mine, an old and wise psychoanalyst, often says with a sigh: "Oh, if only Freud had read Engels's *The Origin of the Family, Private Property, and the State*—he would have avoided so many false trails and errors!" He might also have avoided supplying ammunition to people for whom *homo homini lupus* is the battle cry against progress and socialism, who operate the bogey of the *eternal* human *lupus* in the interest of the real and bloody *lupus* of *contemporary* imperialism.

We may well grant that the aggressiveness of socialist man will show itself in the nursery "in its primal, anal form" and in other more developed manifestations. Yet much will depend, *inter alia*, on the character of the nursery: do we imagine it as an individual nursery within the family unit as we know it? Or as a communal nursery after the dissolution of this family unit? In our hypothesis about socialist man we assume that he will not live within anything like the present family, with its money nexus and its dependence of woman and child on father. We suppose that socialist man will in childhood be far less subjected to paternal authority than his predecessors have been, or that he will not know it at all; and that as an adult he will be free in his sexual and erotic life, or, at any rate, that he will be incomparably freer than bourgeois man is to follow his emotional urges and need of love without coming into conflict with society. His instinctual drives will be refracted through his personality in a manner which we cannot predict but which certainly will not be the manner Freud takes for granted.

Should one, for instance, take it for granted that socialist man will be subject to the Oedipus complex? Will this complex that has worked so powerfully in our psyche, at least since matriarchy gave place to patriarchal society, still be there if and when mankind has moved beyond the bourgeois form of the patriarchal family? And one may wonder what the superego may be like in socialist man, the superego that works in us as our unconscious moral censor and our father within us? Freud, who confuses fatherhood, which is a biological category, with paternal authority, which is a social institution, takes it for granted that the superego and the

Oedipus complex and other reflections of paternalistic society in the individual's mind, are there forever.

True, he seems to have had a momentary premonition of other possibilities. He says: "If we were to remove this factor too [i.e., prerogative in the field of sexual relationships] by allowing complete freedom of sexual life and thus abolishing the family, the germ cell of civilization, we cannot, it is true, easily foresee what new paths the development of civilization could take." He cannot, however, visualize the prospect, for the monogamous family is to him the indispensable germ cell of civilization, and even in his thought he cannot detach himself from his patient, the bourgeois, monogamous man lying in front of him on the couch. And so, although he grants uneasily that we cannot foresee what new paths the development of civilization could take without the present family unit, he is sure that the indestructible aggressiveness of human nature will pursue socialist man beyond class, society, state, and family.

Here again we, Marxists, prefer a certain amount of agnosticism. We are, of course, concerned in the main with the cruelty and oppression which are generated directly by poverty, scarcity of goods, class society, and man's domination by man. Whenever Freud ventures into the fields of sociology and history, he lays himself open to the reproach that he speaks willy-nilly as an apologist for existing society. We have nevertheless learned from him something important about the reality of the destructive and aggressive elements in human nature. It is, of course, true that emperors, kings, warlords, dictators, governments, and leaders of all sorts would not have been able to make men behave as aggressively as they have behaved if aggressiveness had not been there in human nature—our rulers have always appealed and still appeal to man's base instinctual drives. But the question of how much of the biologically or sexually conditioned aggressiveness will affect the non-biological relationships of socialist man must be left open.

We do not maintain that socialism is going to solve all predicaments of the human race. We are struggling in the first instance with the predicaments that are of man's making and that man can resolve. May I remind you that Trotsky, for instance, speaks of three basic tragedies—hunger, sex, and death—besetting man. Hunger is the enemy that Marxism and the modern labor movement have taken on. In doing so they have naturally been inclined to ignore or belittle man's other predicaments. But is it not true that hunger or, more broadly, social inequality and oppression, have hugely complicated and intensified for innumerable human beings the torments of sex and death as well?

In fighting against social inequality and oppression we fight also for the mitigation of those blows that nature inflicts on us. I think that Marxism has tried and is trying to tackle from the right end the tasks confronting our society. The Freudians have concentrated on sex and ignored or belittled man's social problems. And what is the result? For all the theoretical importance of psychoanalysis, the practical benefits of its therapy are in our society available only to a tiny privileged minority. Our vision of socialist man, on the other hand, has inspired a huge segment of mankind; and although we have fought with varying success and suffered terrible defeats, we have nevertheless moved mountains, whereas all the psychoanalysis of the world cannot reduce by a single iota the aggressiveness with which our world is boiling over.

Yes, socialist man will still be pursued by sex and death; but we are convinced that he will be better equipped than we are to cope even with these. And if his nature remains aggressive, his society will give him immeasurably greater and more varied opportunities than bourgeois man has for sublimating his instinctual drives and turning them to creative uses. Even if socialist man may not be quite "free from guilt or pain" as Shelley dreamed he would be, he may be still "scepterless, free, uncircumscribed, but man equal, unclassed, tribeless, and nationless, exempt from all worship and awe." The average member of socialist society may yet rise, as Trotsky anticipated, to the stature of Aristotle, Goethe, Marx, who, whatever their sexual instincts and aggressive drives, embody some of mankind's highest achievements so far. And we assume that "above these heights new peaks will rise." We do not see in socialist man evolution's last and perfect product, or the end of history, but in a sense only the beginning of history. Socialist man may indeed feel the *Unbehagen*, the unease and discomfort, that civilization imposes upon the beast in man. Moreover, this may, indeed, be the most essential of his own inner contradictions and tensions that will impel him to evolve further and scale heights which are beyond our imagination.

These views are or ought to be truisms for any Marxist, and I ought perhaps to apologize for stating them at a Socialist Scholars' Conference. Unfortunately, in the present condition of the labor movement and of socialist thinking certain elementary truths need to be restated, for all too often they are forgotten or falsified for the sake of some dubious political convenience. I have heard it said, for instance, that the proper subject of my analysis ought to be the socialist man living in the USSR or China today. I would take this view only if I held that those countries have already achieved or that they have nearly achieved socialism. I do not accept this assumption and I do not think that the typical or even the advanced member of Soviet or Chinese society today can be described as socialist man.

We all speak, of course, colloquially about the USSR, China and the associated and disassociated states as "socialist countries," and we are entitled to do so as long as we intend merely to oppose their regimes to the capitalist states, to indicate their postcapitalist character or to refer to the socialist origins and inspiration of their governments and policies. But here I am concerned with a theoretically correct description of the structure of their society and the nature of human relationship evolving within that structure. You may remember that over thirty years ago Stalin proclaimed that the

Soviet Union had completed the building of socialism; and until now, despite the so-called de-Stalinization and the demolition of so many Stalinist myths, this has remained a central tenet of official Soviet ideology. Moreover, Stalin's successors allege that the Soviet Union is now engaged in the transition from socialism to communism, or that it is entering into that higher stage of classless society that is to complete the cycle of socialist transformation opened up by the October Revolution.

Spokesmen of the People's Republic of China have been making similar claims for their country. Now, the Stalinist dogma about the achievement of socialism in the Soviet Union has significantly affected and changed the popular image of socialist man and even the thinking of quite a few socialist scholars. Yet one thing is, or ought to be, immediately obvious: the typical man of Soviet society, whether under Stalin or his successors, presents so striking a contrast to the Marxist conception of socialist man that either we must refuse to consider him as socialist man or we must throw the Marxist conception overboard, as the Stalinist school of thought has tacitly done. This is not a squabble over the letter of the Gospel, but an issue of the greatest theoretical and practical importance for us. If our aim is socialist man then our conception or image of him is vital to our theoretical thinking, to the moral-political climate of the labor movement, and to our own ability or inability to inspire our working classes.

Now, socialist man was envisaged by Marx, and all his followers up to Stalin, as a free associated producer working, even in the so-called lower phase of communism, under a rationally planned economy, no longer a buyer or seller trading products in the markets, but someone who turns out goods for society at large and receives them for personal consumption from society's common pool. By definition socialist man lives in a classless and stateless society, free from social or political oppression, even though he may at the beginning still carry a burden—a steadily diminishing burden—of inherited social inequality. The society in which he lives has to be so highly developed, so wealthy, educated and civilized that there is no objective need or necessity for it to allow any recrudescence of inequality or oppression.

This is what *all* Marxists before Stalin took for granted. This is the ideal that has inspired generations of socialists; without it socialism would have never come to life as the dynamic force of the century. Marxism has demonstrated the realistic character of this ideal by showing that the whole development of modern society with its technology, industry, and increasingly socialized productive process tends toward this outcome. Now, the socialist man that Stalin and his successors have shown the world is a pitiful parody of the Marxist image of socialist man. True, the Soviet citizen has lived in a society where the state, not the capitalists, owns the means of production, and this circumstance is already reflected in certain progressive features of his mentality. Even the most backward of Soviet workers takes the social public ownership of the means of production for granted. Private ownership of a factory or of a coal mine seems to him to be a revolting relic of some barbarous past. He shudders at the mere thought of it. He looks upon it very much as the average member of any modern bourgeois society looks upon slavery, as a social condition degrading to man. But nevertheless these progressive features in the outlook of Soviet man— although they are there—are not the dominant features of his social psychology.

Soviet society has suffered and is still suffering from material scarcity, an extreme scarcity of consumer goods in the first instance, which has over the decades led to an inevitable recrudescence and aggravation of social inequalities, to a deep division between a privileged minority and a deprived majority, to a spontaneous reassertion of the economic forces of the market, and to a revival and a terrifying growth of the oppressive functions of the state.

The socialist man Stalin presented to the world was the hungry, ill-clad, ill-shod or even barefoot worker or peasant, selling or buying a shirt, a piece of furniture, a few ounces of meat or even a piece of bread on black or gray markets, working ten or twelve hours a day under a barracks-like factory discipline and, sometimes, paying for any real or alleged offense with years of forced labor in a concentration camp. He did not dare to criticize a factory manager, let alone a party boss. He had no right to express any opinion on any major issue affecting his and the nation's destiny. He had to vote as he was ordered; and to let his dignity and personality be mocked by the so-called personality cult. These are the facts, now officially so described by the Soviet leaders and reflected in a vast Soviet literature with all the emphasis of authenticity. Although in recent years the conditions have been greatly mitigated, the poverty, the inequality, the lack of political and intellectual freedom and the bureaucratic terror are still there.

My purpose in recalling all this is not polemical, if only because I see the main cause of these conditions not just in the rulers' ill will, though there has never been any lack of this, but in objective circumstances, in the terrible inherited poverty that the Soviet Union (and now China) has had to overcome in isolation, amid blockades, wars, and armament races. It was out of the question that a country like this should be able to achieve socialism in such circumstances. It had to devote all its energies to "primitive accumulation," that is, to the creation under state ownership of the most essential economic preliminaries to any genuine building of socialism. Consequently the Soviet Union is even today a transitional society, finding itself some way between capitalism and socialism, combining features of the one and of the other, and showing marks even of its more primitive precapitalist heritage. The same is unfortunately true of China, Vietnam, North Korea, and most of Eastern Europe. We in the West bear a heavy responsibility for the predicaments of those countries—our failure to promote socialism in the West has been the ultimate cause of their failure. But if we are to face our task anew and enable a new generation of socialists to resume the struggle, we must clear our own minds to the end of the misconceptions and myths about socialism that have grown up in the past decades. We must dissociate socialism once and for all not from the Soviet Union or China and their progressive achievement, but from the Stalinist and post-Stalinist parody of socialist man.

I cannot go here into the motives of dogma and prestige that led Stalin and his associates to proclaim that the Soviet Union had achieved socialism and that still cause his successors to keep up this pretense. I am concerned here only with the impact this dogma or boast has had on socialism in the West. That impact has been disastrous. It has demoralized our labor movement and confused socialist thinking. Our working classes have watched in their own shrewd way developments in the Soviet Union and have drawn their own conclusions. "If this is the ideal of the socialist man," they have said in effect, "then we will have nothing to do with it." Many of our socialist intelligentsia have reacted likewise or have become so entangled in Stalinist mythology and scholasticism that they lost the élan and power of socialist conviction and have so disarmed themselves spiritually that they have been unable to struggle against the disillusionment and apathy in the working classes.

It was once said of the Jesuits that, having failed to raise earth to heaven, they dragged heaven down to earth. Similarly, Stalin and Stalinism, unable to raise a poverty-stricken and miserable Russia to socialism, have dragged down socialism to the level of Russian misery. It may be argued that they had to do it. Even if that were so, we have to do something else: We have to raise socialism back to its own height. We have to explain to our working classes and intelligentsia why the Soviet Union and China have not been able to produce and could not produce socialist man, despite their remarkable achievements which give them a right to our recognition and solidarity. We must restore the image of socialist man to all its spiritual splendor. We must restore it in our own minds first and then, fortified in our conviction and rearmed politically, we must carry socialist consciousness and the socialist idea back into the working class.

At this point a letter from Herbert Marcuse was read. Marcuse put forward the thesis that the conclusions of traditional Marxism were outmoded and needed to be revised; in particular, he suggested that the working class could no longer be considered the agent of revolution. After a panel discussion followed by questions and comments on Marcuse's letter from the audience, Deutscher addressed himself to Marcuse's thesis in his closing remarks.

Mr. Chairman, I think you exaggerated when you said that I was now going to reply. I'm still recovering from the painful surprise at the first half, at least, of our discussion. One learns even at my age; one learns all the time.

I am grateful to the last two speakers who somehow restored my sense of reality. I can agree or disagree with them, but we can argue. Nevertheless, I feel that I ought to devote most of my answer to the speakers who took part in the first half of the debate, because I see in the first half of the debate a disquieting symptom of this otherwise creative intellectual ferment that is going on in the minds of the American intelligentsia, in the young generation of American scholars. But there are strange by-products of it which seem to me very, very dangerous indeed.

And I am almost nonplussed by the statement which Professor Marcuse sent us. As the first speakers were really forming a sort of supporting chorus to their absent inspirer, I must, unfortunately, concentrate on Professor Marcuse's statement. He raises three or four important points, but he puts these in so vague and elusive a form that this also makes discussion somewhat difficult.

First of all he states that we are far ahead of Marx and Marxism, that our advanced Western society has rendered Marxism obsolete, and that consequently from Marxism we must move somewhere ahead. I'm always inclined to say yes when people tell me that Marxism is surely not the last word in the development of human thought, that we have to advance from Marxism. This is a very Marxist objection to Marxism and I'm inclined to applaud it. But one must also reflect for a moment in what respect Marxism is really so obsolete and whereto we are supposed to move from Marxism.

I must first ask the question: has the basic contradiction of capitalist society, as Marxism has analyzed and diagnosed it, the contradiction between the socialized process of production and the unsocial character of control over production by private property—has this basic contradiction been overcome? Or is it becoming deeper and deeper, more and more irrational, with every decade that passes?

We are told that advanced American society has rendered the Marxist analysis of capitalism obsolete. But has this society, which maintains its balance and keeps its production going with the help of almost permanent warfare, really done so?

I simply don't understand the logical or illogical processes of reasoning by which people can arrive at such a conclusion. We are told that surely in 1966 we cannot hold a diagnosis, which was made on the basis of the technology of 1867, as still valid. We are told that we have therefore left Marxism far behind.

My argument is that, on the contrary, Marx was intellectually so much ahead of his time—ahead of the society in which he lived—that we are even now in many respects still behind him. And if anyone wanted a confirmation of this, he had only to listen to our debate.

The fact is that a hundred years ago Marx postulated as the premise of socialism a society so highly developed technologically, a society capable of producing such an abundance of goods, that really for his age even the vision of such a society was almost utopian. If one were to analyze the statistics of production per head in the most advanced capitalist states of the nineteenth century, one would arrive at the conclusion that if socialism had won then, it would really have won in what by our present standards was an under-developed society. This is the criticism one can make of Marx—that he ran intellectually so far ahead of his age, and incidentally even of our age, that we haven't yet caught up with him.

Marx, we are told, did not foresee a society in which cybernetics, in which machines would do the work of men on the scale on which they are doing it now—computers and all that. Marx had not foreseen a society in which scientists and the proto-class of scientists would be so important. But, on the contrary, Marx always assumed that his society was already on the point of becoming such a society, and there he was mistaken. It is all right to say that surely a theory formulated a hundred years ago must have been obsolete in some respects, although most who say so tell us usually in the end—if they don't advise us to take drugs to "liberate" ourselves from the oppression of this society—most often they advocate a return to some pre-Marxist ideas, sometimes to Christianity which is two thousand years older than Marxism.

Or, at the most, when we have to deal with very educated and very sophisticated critics of Marxism, then they offer us the return, the regression—not an infantile regression though—to utopian socialism or to eighteenth-century rationalism. Yet there are certain revolutions in human thought which are irreversible. Nobody can go back to the pre-Copernican systems of cosmology although the development of the human mind has led from a Copernicus to Einstein; but it did so only after two hundred fifty years or so.

I don't think that Marxism will really be outdated in its broad criticism of the capitalist system as long as the system, no matter how it is further developed, remains with us. Our impatience with certain familiar formulas and truisms of Marxism does not render these truisms false or useless.

Well, some people think that it's enough to go back to the young Marx and to declaim, in and out of context, his very early and even his immature reasonings about "reification" and alienation, and to repeat them in circles, to solve the problems of our age. But they don't go beyond Marxism, they go back from the mature to the immature Marx, to the almost adolescent Marx.

But even the adolescent Marx was a very mature thinker compared with those who now exhibit, as one of the speakers said, that tendency to infantile regression.

I see only one respect, one major issue, on which Marxism, the Marxist prognostication of socialism, has so far really to some extent been falsified by developments. And that is that socialism has so far won not in any of the advanced capitalist societies but in the backward ones, in which a feudal structure was beginning to collapse under the impact of capitalism and where the feudal-capitalist systems collapsed under the impact of primitive bourgeois and socialist revolutions.

And so we have a legacy of this historical development, an historical development which really differs from the Marxist prognostication: we have a tremendous discrepancy and gulf between East and West, a gulf that tends, unfortunately, to perpetuate itself to the detriment of both East and West.

And for Marxists, for socialists, for socialist scholars, whether in this country or elsewhere, the great problem of our age, the great problem of the movement towards our goal, towards socialist man, towards a socialist society, is how to overcome this gulf between the separate, divergent historical roads that East and West have taken. That is the real problem from which you cannot run away into any utopias or into any "liberating" drugs.

I wish I could share the enthusiasm of my comrade on the right side [of the auditorium] for what is going on in China. I wish I could do so because I recognize the great revolutionary idealism and the international value of certain revolutionary innovations which the Chinese have made.

Unfortunately, it will do us no good to show such sovereign idealistic contempt for the realities of China's material situation, for the industrial and cultural backwardness of a society that has had the heroism to initiate a socialist revolution amid its appalling poverty and backwardness. These factors, unfortunately, influence the policies of the Chinese government and lead the Red Guards to repudiate not only Russia's so-called revisionism, but even Beethoven and Shakespeare as the useless rubbish of a degenerate bourgeois culture.

I cannot accept this as socialism. I cannot accept this as a liberating experience. Nor can I accept the Maoist cult as being any better than the Stalinist cult, although it is in some respects more excusable.

All these developments deepen and widen the tragic gulf between the advanced capitalist societies of the West, including their working classes, and the postcapitalist revolutionary societies of the East. The historic precedent of which one thinks is the gulf that developed, during the wars of religion, between the Catholic countries and the Protestant ones.

Protestantism, too, began as a liberating movement, as a protest against the oppressiveness of the Catholic Church; but then in the process of the struggle Protestantism too developed its own oppressive features. And then, after decades and centuries of struggle, the situation became stabilized; and the line of division between Catholic and Protestant countries was not to be obliterated.

A historical coexistence between two rival religious creeds, behind which there were also great social movements, became a fact. Something like it has happened in our lifetime: we have witnessed the actual coexistence—this is an antagonistic, hostile coexistence—of two relatively stabilized systems, the Western capitalist-imperialist system and the Eastern postcapitalist, semi-socialist one.

I think, however, that this historical analogy may be misleading, is misleading, in one respect. Protestantism and Catholicism could coexist in the long run. The world in the era after the religious wars, in the seventeenth and eighteenth centuries, was not yet one world. It was not yet a world unified by technology and industry. It was a world broken up into many units of young nation states, of feudal, semifeudal, principalities and particularistic units.

The world today *is* one world potentially and even actually; technology and the development of the productive forces make of mankind one indissoluble unit, crying out for integration. Either mankind will be integrated within socialism or it is bound to perish. And therefore, the kind of a stabilization of the lines of division that existed after the religious wars is impossible today. The world will become one and must become one. And only socialism can unify it. Capitalism can only keep it disunited and heading for disaster.

But the question is: which is the way to that unification of the world? Can, in the meantime, the class struggle in the world become a single process?

Marx spoke of the history of mankind as the history of class struggle. But of course it wasn't so that class struggle throughout history went on with the same intensity all over the world, over the ages. The transition from capitalism to socialism, we know now, is a matter of very many generations.

I do not feel so much discouraged by the fact that the class struggle has been running at a very low level in our Western society as to give up the Marxist analysis and prognostication. That our working classes, especially the older age group in those working classes, have allowed themselves to be confused, demoralized and corrupted by the meretricious advantages offered them by our so-called welfare state is, of course, true. Yet, I think that the problem that the late C. Wright Mills posed, the problem of who remains the agency of socialism—the working class or elites of the intelligentsia— that this problem needs, especially in America, a thorough discussion and a thorough analysis because nowhere does it pose itself with the same gravity.

It is sixty years now since a great Russian Marxist, Leon Trotsky, said that Western Europe exported its two major products in two different directions. It exported its most advanced ideology, Marxism, to Russia. It exported its most advanced technology to the United States.

But the Russia which received Marxism as an import from Western Europe was technologically and industrially backward, the most backward of the great nations of Europe.

The United States which has so advanced technologically has, unfortunately, remained backward in political thinking. To this day (I am sorry to say this) it has remained a most backward country in political thinking.

And I believe, I would like to believe, that the great teach-in movements of these last two years and meetings like the present one are proof that the United States is trying, is beginning to shake off its backwardness in matters of ideology and political thinking. But how much still remains to be shaken off!

I think it is a great weakness of this movement that you have an American scholars' conference here which takes place without arousing any interest in your working class. And you shouldn't—you have no right to—complain about it because so many of you American socialist scholars—I wouldn't like to generalize—so many of you show no interest in your working classes.

I am not one to deprecate or belittle movements of protest generating in the intelligentsia. I always remember that throughout the nineteenth century the Russian intelligentsia carried on their weak shoulders the tremendous burden of the struggle against the Russian autocracy, the whole tremendous burden of the Russian Revolution.

Generation after generation of the Russian intelligentsia, in the nineteenth century, smashed their heads heroically, self-sacrificingly, against the walls, the iron walls, of the Russian tsarist autocracy and perished. But they didn't perish in vain. They prepared the future, they worked for the future.

I believe that you too are working for the future, for socialist man. The Russian intelligentsia in the nineteenth century—they were then very isolated, the peasantry didn't respond to them, the industrial working class hadn't yet come into being—the intelligentsia were isolated and because of this, because they fought alone, they developed a certain megalomania; and the great epic of the revolutionary struggle of nineteenth-century Russia is full of pathetic, eccentric interludes. Because intellectuals, when they don't have a live contact with the working masses of their own nation, tend to develop their own eccentric self-centeredness and tend to produce goodness knows what fantastic nostrums for society.

Our discussion has revealed something of a similar weakness in present-day America. Excuse me if I go away from my subject, socialist man, but we have to discuss the man who has to pave the way for socialist man. And that is you.

I am convinced—and this is not a matter of dogmatic faith but an analysis of society, of the Marxist analysis of society—that your working class remains the decisive agency of socialism, just as the Russian working class proved itself to be the decisive agent of socialism after generations of the intelligentsia had fought alone.

You too may be fighting alone. It depends on you for how long. Perhaps only for a few years if you find a way to your working class. Or for decades if you try to ignore your working class. You may smash your heads against goodness knows how many iron walls if you ignore your working class. Because every movement of protest, every movement of opposition to powerful capitalist oligarchies, is bound in the long run to be impotent, if it doesn't get a firm grip on the productive apparatus of the nation.

It's true that your scientists now have a much firmer grip on the productive apparatus of the nation than they had in any previous generation. But the great mass of producers are still—whatever you say about cybernetics and the great vision of a supracybernetic future—the great mass of producers in your society are the workers. And I don't believe that they have much more reason to be satisfied with this society, with their alienated condition in it, than the men of your intelligentsia, than you young American scholars have to be satisfied with this society.

Do you really take such a contemptuous view of your working classes that you think that you alone are so sensitive or so noble as to be dissatisfied with this degrading society and that they cannot find it in themselves to be dissatisfied? Do you really believe that they are so much more prone, and by nature conditioned, to be corrupted by the meretricious advantages of this war-flourishing capitalism than you are?

I know, I know that the older age groups of the American working class are almost certainly corrupted. They compare their present condition with what they knew in the 1930s. But surely the head of the young American worker hasn't turned and become confused by the fact that in his parental home he finds a television set and that he can have a car. He takes these things for granted. They are a part of the standard of living which he finds as he enters adult life. He's surely not corrupted by that and he has enough reason to be dissatisfied. I am sure that behind his outward political apathy there are layers and layers of doubt and discontent and a feeling that he has to earn his living by working for death, by working for war.

Can't you approach this young worker and tell him that the way to live is to work for life and not for death? Is it beneath American scholars to try and do that?

Professor Marcuse tells us that we shouldn't count on the working class anymore, but he doesn't tell us on whom we should count. We should count, he says, on the young people who voice their discontent with the sexual conventions of this society. Of course, we should count on them also. After all, it was Engels who wrote about the origins of the family and exposed the family as an institution belonging only to a phase, or phases, of society's history; and he exposed the conventions of bourgeois morality built up around the family.

We should not ignore this discontent with family and sexual conventions among our young people, but sometimes I think that those venerable old teachers like Professor Marcuse are playing some jokes on us, are simply amusing themselves at our expense. He says first that Marxism wasn't utopian enough; then he goes on to say that the actual development suggests that the idea of a socialist revolution in the advanced industrial societies was or is unrealistic and is obsolete, just as obsolete as the idea of a gradual transformation of capitalism into socialism.

Now please add two and two together. Revolution, he says, is an obsolete idea and reformism is also an obsolete idea. That is, there is no road from capitalism to socialism, whether revolutionary or reformist. Why then talk about socialism?

What Professor Marcuse tells us is that socialism was utopian and then he says that socialism wasn't utopian enough. How an old and respected teacher can commit so many non sequiturs and so many illogicalities and play about with such vague irresponsible generalities within five brief paragraphs beats me.

In many respects this discussion has been for me a sad experience. But I remain an inveterate optimist. I believe that these are the incidental costs of a creative intellectual ferment in your midst. I wish you clarity of thought and honesty of thought, and I wish that you should concentrate on the essentials instead of allowing yourselves to be diverted into some circus-like operations that have nothing to do with serious political thinking.

You cannot run away from politics. Men live not by politics alone, true enough. But unless you have solved for yourselves in your own minds the great political problems posed by Marxism, by the contradictions of capitalist society, by the mutual relationship of the intellectual and the worker in this society, unless you have found a way to the young age groups of the American working class and shaken this sleeping giant of yours, this sleeping giant of the American working class, out of his sleep, out of the drugs—out of this sleep into which he has been drugged, unless you have done this, you will be lost.

Your only salvation is in carrying back the idea of socialism to the working class and coming back with the working class to storm—to storm, yes, to storm—the bastions of capitalism.

discovering
das kapital

The conditions in which a young Polish intellectual studied *Das Kapital* in the 1920s or 1930s were very different from those prevailing in most countries of the West. To us, the Marxist forecast of the collapse of capitalism was not an apocalyptic vision related only remotely to the realities of our daily life. The old social order was crumbling before our very eyes. This was the overwhelming fact of our existence. We could not escape it. My own childhood and adolescence were shaken by it again and again. I grew up in Cracow and in a little town halfway between Cracow and Auschwitz, wedged in a tip of land between the frontiers of three empires. As a boy of ten and eleven I watched the downfall of the dynasties of the Romanovs, Hapsburgs and Hohenzollerns. Overnight there vanished ancient powers, sanctities and fetishes that had held our people in awe for many generations. We felt the hot breath of the Russian Revolution.

This is a transcript of a broadcast given on the Third Programme of the British Broadcasting Corporation in October 1967, to mark the centenary of the first publication of Das Kapital.

Then, just across the frontier, the Commune of Budapest flared up and was drowned in blood. At thirteen I absorbed from the adults the tense mood in which they watched the news of the Red Army's advance on Warsaw. For years we lived almost constantly on the brink of civil war, amid galloping inflations, mass unemployment, pogroms, abortive revolutions and futile counterrevolutions.

But even before these cataclysms, in the remote and spuriously idyllic pre-1914 era, Marxism had been, in our parts, the accepted ideology of almost the entire labor movement. Our right-wing social democrats, no less than our communists, still considered *Das Kapital* as the "bible of the working class"; like the old Bible, it was dusty and unread but revered. Portraits of Marx and Lassalle stared at us from the walls of every trade-union local and socialist youth organization and even of many Zionist clubs. I got my first inkling of historical materialism from older schoolmates, and although my own middle-class and Orthodox Jewish upbringing inclined me against it, the shakiness of our social existence made me reluctantly receptive to some of the revolutionary ideas in the air.

I tried to read *Das Kapital* in late adolescence, but I did not persevere. It seemed too hard a nut to crack, and I was not really interested in political economy. I had precociously started out as a poet and literary critic, and was in search of a philosophical approach to art. I was therefore interested primarily in the broad lines of the Marxist *Weltanschauung*. Turning away from *Das Kapital*, I tried to grasp these lines from Marx's and Engels's minor works and from the writings of Plekhanov, Lenin, Mehring, Bukharin, and others. But their philosophical theories always pointed back to the socio-economic realities underlying the multiple forms of human consciousness. And so I found myself scanning *Das Kapital* again and swallowing more popular expositions of its economic doctrine. I found these convincing enough, and I felt that they equipped me quite adequately for further literary and philosophical work and for political struggle. It was even with a hint of irritation that I read Marx's warning in one of his prefaces to *Das Kapital* that science knows no straight and broad highway and that "only those have a chance of attaining its clear summits who will not dodge the toil of climbing up its steep pathways." I wondered whether Marx had not made those pathways just a little too steep. Sometimes his dialectical subtleties seemed to me a trifle overelaborate in an old-fashioned manner, and I wondered just how relevant they were. His exposition seemed to me too slow and leisurely for someone like myself, who was impatient to understand the world and to change it quickly. I was relieved to hear that Ignacy Daszynski, our famous member of parliament, a pioneer of socialism, an orator on whose lips hung the parliaments of Vienna and Warsaw, admitted that he too found *Das Kapital* too hard a nut. "I have not read it," he almost boasted, "but Karl Kautsky has read it and has written a popular summary of it. I have not read Kautsky either; but Kelles-Krauz, our party theorist, has read him, and he summarized Kautsky's book. I have not read Kelles-Krauz either, but that clever Jew, Herman Diamand, our financial expert, has read Kelles-Krauz, and has told me all about it." Unlike the great Daszynski, I had at least read Kautsky and a host of other popularizers. Meanwhile I had committed myself politically: I had joined the outlawed Communist Party. For years I was busy editing literary journals, writing political commentaries, illegal manifestoes and leaflets, addressing workers, organizing even peasants, conducting as a soldier underground propaganda in Pilsudski's army, and all the time dodging the gendarmerie and the political police. In these circumstances I could not even dream of tackling *Das Kapital* seriously.

The time for that came a few years later, in 1932, when I was expelled from the party as spokesman of an anti-Stalinist opposition. I felt the need to re-examine my own political thinking and the principles of communism and Marxism. I decided to take nothing for granted. Could Stalinist policy and practices be justified in terms of Marxism? Has

Marx's analysis and critique of capitalism stood up to the events of our time? These were the questions that troubled me. I made up my mind to plow through the whole of *Das Kapital*, all three volumes of it, and also the many-volumed *Theorien über den Mehrwert*, Marx's history of economic doctrines. I was determined to scrutinize this whole intellectual structure coolly and skeptically and to keep my eyes open to its possible flaws and cracks. The *esprit de contradiction* got hold of me; at moments I was almost bent on proving Marx wrong. Perhaps because of this intense involvement, or because of my greater intellectual maturity, I did not this time find "the steep pathways" at all forbidding. In the next three or four years I read and re-read the great work in its entirety five or six times. I also plunged into the vast economic literature to which Marx referred, studied his bourgeois, academic and social democratic critics, and acquainted myself with the varying interpretations and developments of *Das Kapital* offered by Kautsky, Lenin, Hilferding, Luxemburg, Bukharin and others. I had left my starting point, poetry and aesthetics, far behind and invested all my intellectual passions in monetary doctrines, the trade cycle, land rent, capital concentration in agriculture, the falling profit rate, the impoverishment of the working class, and other aspects of the dismal science. From explorations of Ricardo, Sismondi, Sombart, Böhm-Bawerk and the early Keynes, I returned again and again to *Das Kapital* and was ever captivated afresh by the richness of its theoretical and historical texture and the crystal clarity of the analysis. The toil of the uphill climb was transformed into sheer excitement. I shall never forget the thrill with which from the "summit" I then viewed the boundless horizons on society that Marx, I felt, opened to me. No other work has ever impressed me with comparable force.

But what about those flaws for which I had been on the lookout? Try as I did, I could not detect them. Every time I reread the opus, I found it more rigorously argued and more convincing than I had thought it to be. I saw where in the opening chapter one might dissent from Marx and follow the theorists of marginal utility. That theory, however, failed to satisfy me—I could not accept it as an alternative to Marx's conceptions of value, commodity and labor. And once I had accepted his premises, I could not help following him all the way through to his conclusions. I was aware that Marx analyzed capitalism in its "pure form," as the chemist analyzes his elements, whereas in reality capitalism has absorbed and carries within itself the wreckage of all previous social orders. Yet no one underlines this more emphatically than Marx himself, and no one has elucidated the structural complexities of our society with anything approaching his historical realism. It is true that he dealt with *laissez faire* and not with later quasi-monopolistic forms of capitalist organization. This, I reflected, did not render his analysis obsolete, for he shows precisely how the monopolistic forms grow out of *laissez faire;* and he reveals, as no one else does, the organic connection between these phases of economic development. Even as early as in his *Poverty of Philosophy*, published twenty years before *Das Kapital*, while he argued against Proudhon's idealization of free competition, he demonstrated how free competition tended towards monopoly, its dialectical opposite. Then, in *Das Kapital*, he dramatically extrapolated the process of concentration of capital to describe the "historical tendency of accumulation" leading to the expropriation of many entrepreneurs by ever fewer "magnates of capital." But even when, for the sake of the argument, he assumed perfect competition, he did it only in order to prove that that competition was necessarily self-destructive. And so I could not (and I still cannot) help being puzzled by those of his academic critics who argue that Marx was unaware of the "imperfect competition" of our time. In truth, all later treatises on monopoly capital, non-Marxist and Marxist alike, including those by Hilferding and Lenin, are but illustrations of the manner in which economic evolution has on this point confirmed Marx's predictions.

More important still, Marx shows how, in relation to the

workers, even *laissez faire* capitalism was never anything but monopolistic. There never was nor could there be any perfect competition between capital and labor, for even under the most "just" wage system, in conditions of an ideal exchange of equivalents between employer and worker, capital alone is in command of the means of production, and it alone appropriates surplus value. As long as this is so, I concluded, Marx's theory cannot be outdated, no matter how much the secondary features of the social order may be modified.

Even at that time, thirty or thirty-five years ago, I saw the essence of Marx's theory not in this or that aspect of his analysis of the trade cycle, or even in his views on the impoverishment, relative or absolute, of the working class, important though these views were politically. Admittedly, he left some issues unresolved and some loose ends. But for me the essence of his analysis lay in what he says about the central contradiction of our social system, the conflict between the socialized process of production and the unsocial character of the control which capitalist ownership exercises over that process. Inherent in this is the worker's estrangement from his own labor, from the products of his labor, and from the structure of society which his labor perpetuates. Our "welfare state" has, on the face of it, toned down this estrangement, but only by deepening it; and it has cruelly aggravated the individual worker's alienation from other workers, that is, from his own class.

The study of *Das Kapital* did not merely confirm me in my Marxist conviction, including my sense of its incompatibility with the tortoise nature of social democratic reformism. It also revealed to me the full depth of the gulf that lay between classical Marxism and the cynical expediencies, the dull scholasticism, and the inquisitorial methods of Stalinism. Ever since, it has seemed to me as incongruous to blame Marx for Stalin as it would be to blame the Bible and Aristotle for the dogmas of the medieval church and the Inquisition. It was as a Marxist that I went on opposing Stalinism.

Slowly at first, but then irresistibly, I was entranced by the style of *Das Kapital*. It set what has remained in my eyes the highest standard of reasoning and expression, a standard none of Marx's disciples, not even the greatest, has ever attained. While I realized that it would be unfair to apply this standard to other thinkers and writers, *Das Kapital* seems to have left me with something like a heightened sensitivity to the *style* of all reasoning on social and political problems. I thought that I could recognize the quality of any socialist or communist statement by its language and form. For a long time it was usually my aesthetic sense that was first offended by any piece of counterfeit or phony Marxism; only after that would I proceed to examine its political, philosophical, or economic content. Even now it is usually a kind of aesthetic discomfort that first puts me on guard against any pretentious piece of pseudo-Marxist argumentation. I often experience this discomfort when I follow fashionable debates between the meta-Marxists, para-Marxists, existentialists and structuralists on subjects such as alienation, the young and the mature Marx, the "humanization" of Marxism, and the categories of dialectical reason.

Reading *Das Kapital*, I realized why its author never bothered to offer his readers a systematic exposition of the principles of dialectics, although occasionally he threatened to do so. He evidently preferred to apply these principles rather than expound them; and how right he was! The fact is that attempts to formulate the rules of dialectics usually result in arid scholasticism. Dialectics is indeed the grammar of Marxist thinking. But just as one shows one's mastery of grammar not in reciting its rules, but in living speech, so one shows one's grasp of dialectics not in mulling over its formulas, but in coming to grips with specific, large and vital issues in history and contemporary affairs. No doubt, the rules of dialectics have to be learned; a good manual, like a good grammatical textbook, has its uses. But a one-sided preoccupation with abstract methodology is often a form of ideological escapism, even if those who indulge in it love to dwell on "Praxis" and spell "Praxis" with a capital "P". *Das Kapital* is the supreme example of the dialectical mind in action, of the dialectical mind using all its power of abstraction to plow up layer after layer of empirical social experience. Marx was, of course, greatly concerned with the problems of his philosophical workshop as well, and with the nature of his intellectual tools, those he had inherited from others and those he himself invented. But the workshop and the tools were not ends in themselves—they were there to process the economic and socio-political raw material and to turn out the finished product.

Last but not least, *Das Kapital* was for me a memorable artistic experience. I realized that, like a few other epoch-making discoveries, it was the result not merely of rigorous reasoning and heroic research, but of a creative imagination which had harnessed reasoning and research for one of its tremendous leaps. In science such leaps have produced new visions of the universe, of the structure of matter, and of the emergence and growth of the species. Copernicus, Newton, Darwin and Einstein, each of them must have been endowed with an extraordinary capacity of image-making to be able to see the world in a startlingly new shape, perspective and light, hidden from predecessors and contemporaries. A withdrawn artistic genius lived in each of these giants of science. The same, I think, is true of Marx. For how otherwise would he have been able to focus his thoughts and ideas into that image of society's past and that vision of its future which have ever since inspired one section of mankind and haunted another?

Marx's artistry is more directly evident in the massive and classically pure architecture of *Das Kapital,* in the force and suppleness of his language, in his grave dramatic pathos, his satire and his imagery. I know that what I am saying may baffle those who have tried to tackle *Das Kapital* in translation and have found Marx's prose involved and cumbersome. Unfortunately Marx's style and language cannot be easily Anglicized, although the existing translations are far more clumsy and stiff than they need have been. I once had a similar experience with Shakespeare, whom I first read in wretched Polish translations. Only after I had learned English and heard his lines spoken from the English stage did I succumb to the full force of his poetry. *Wer den Dichter will verstehen, muss im Dichters Lande gehen.* As to the merits of the original, I would like to recall that Franz Mehring, a fastidious literary critic and Marx's bitter opponent before he became his follower, devoted a special essay to the poetic quality of Marx's writing. He analyzed the similes and metaphors of *Das Kapital*, underlining their rare combination of imaginative inventiveness and conceptual precision, and he found a parallel for them only in Goethe's metaphors and similes. For a German literary critic this was, of course, the supreme tribute.

One final remark: For over thirty years after I had studied *Das Kapital*, I never went back to it, although all its volumes reposed on my shelves. During all this time I merely glanced at its pages on a few very rare occasions to find a passage I intended to quote. Only in the last weeks have I begun reading it anew. I have so far gone through the first three chapters, those reputed to be exceptionally involved and abstruse—Marx himself was slightly apologetic about their "abstract and Hegelian" style. I find myself still fascinated by the old familiar pages; but what strikes me about them now, as it never did before, is their essential simplicity.

was the revolution betrayed?

The other day I received by post the latest issues of two Soviet journals, *Kommunist* and *Voprosy Istorii*, together with a new cheap English edition of Leon Trotsky's *The Revolution Betrayed*. It was enough to scan the two journals for a few moments to see how much the ghost of Trotsky is once again haunting the ruling circles of the USSR. *Kommunist* attacks Shepilov for the indulgence he has shown towards "revisionists" in literature and the arts and says that Shepilov drew inspiration from Trotsky, who allegedly held that writers and artists should avoid all political "commitment." The other journal, *Voprosy Istorii*, makes a fresh effort to exorcise Trotsky from the history of the Red Army and the civil war. This is not as easy a job as it used to be in Stalin's days. The "freedom" of historical falsification is now greatly restricted, and the archives have been thrown open to young historians, who have been startled to discover how large Trotsky looms in them as the founder and leader of the

This review was originally published in the New Statesman, *London, 24 August 1957.*

Red Army. *Voprosy Istorii* tries discreetly and rather feebly to soften the impact of this discovery.

These new attempts to lay Trotsky's ghost do not alter the fact—indeed they confirm it—that a new generation of the Soviet intelligentsia is grappling with the significance of Trotsky's struggle against Stalin and with its relevance to the problems of the post-Stalin era. The issue of Trotsky's rehabilitation lurks behind some of the current political conflicts as well. The downfall of Molotov and Kaganovich has certainly brought the rehabilitation nearer. To be sure, Khrushchev, who was a very zealous Stalinist for over twenty-five years, does not favor it; but he is no more likely to have the last say in this matter than Molotov and Kaganovich have had it.

What is involved here is not merely history or the rendering of posthumous justice to the reputation of a great revolutionary leader. If this were all, Trotsky would not occupy such a place in Soviet discussions seventeen years after his assassination and thirty years after his deportation from Moscow. The intelligentsia of Moscow, Warsaw, Prague, East Berlin, and perhaps even of Peking are wondering whether they can learn anything from Trotsky. Do his writings convey any message to communists who are freeing themselves from Stalinism and trying to shape an alternative to it?

Tito, Gomulka, Mao and Khrushchev have, each in his own way, provided some of the short-term practical answers to questions raised by de-Stalinization. But none of them has provided any serious theoretical generalization; none has offered a broader historical perspective, and none has even tried to explain the origins and the nature of Stalinism and to facilitate thereby the proper approach to its legacy. They have all been more lucky than Trotsky was in resisting Stalinism—they have resisted it during its decline. But, of all Stalin's opponents, Trotsky alone has produced a systematic and comprehensive critique.

In *The Revolution Betrayed* he offered the final version of that critique. He wrote the book in Norway in 1936, just before the great purges, and it has since become the bible of latter-day Trotskyism, quoted *ad nauseam*, as the final argument in any controversy, by the devotees of the various Trotskyist sects and chapels. However, the work also made its impression far beyond these circles. In a curious way it has been one of the most influential books of this century. Some of its ideas, torn out of context, have become widely popularized by a host of writers who have lived on crumbs (and not the best crumbs) from Trotsky's rich table. James Burnham, for instance, has based his *Managerial Revolution* on a few fragments of Trotsky's theory. *The Revolution Betrayed* echoes through much of Koestler's writing. Orwell was strongly impressed by it: the fragments of "The Book," which take up so many pages in *1984*, are a paraphrase of *The Revolution Betrayed*, just as Emanuel Goldstein, the author of "The Book" and Big Brother's enigmatic antagonist, is modeled on Trotsky. Finally, some of the intellectually ambitious propagandists of the Cold War have also drawn their arguments from this source.

Despite the adventitious use made of it, *The Revolution Betrayed* remains a classic of Marxist literature (and, unlike some of those classics, it can be easily read and absorbed by non-Marxist readers). There are admittedly various layers of thought in it: not all of them are of equal value and not all have stood the test of time equally well. But this is only natural. Trotsky's fertile mind grappled here with a vast, complex and novel problem. He threw out various, sometimes contradictory, hypotheses; and he sought to facilitate analysis by means of somewhat shaky historical analogies. He dealt with his subject matter in his various capacities: as a detached and rigorously objective sociologist and analyst; as a fighter and exiled leader of a suppressed opposition; and as a passionate pamphleteer and polemicist. The polemicist's contribution, his brilliant anti-Stalinist invective, forms the more ephemeral and exoteric part of the work, and it has, naturally, tended to overshadow Trotsky's deep and strictly analytical argument.

Nothing is easier than to compile from this book a list of errors and false prognostications. Trotsky argued gravely that the Stalinist bureaucracy strove to abolish public ownership and that its members might soon become the shareholding owners of the Soviet industry—he even saw in the "Stalin Constitution" of 1936 "the political premises" for such a change in property relations. He forecast that in the course of the Second World War the collective farms would dissolve, the Soviet monopoly of foreign trade would collapse, and Western (allied) capital would penetrate into Russia. He did not see how Stalin's Russia could emerge victorious, with its social structure intact, if the war was not brought to an end by proletarian revolutions *in the West;* and he was strangely confident that such revolutions would stop the Second World War much more decisively and much earlier than they stopped the First.

But there is perhaps more to be learned even from Trotsky's mistakes than one can learn from the "correct" platitudes of most political writers. Even his erroneous hypotheses and predictions contain important elements of truth and most often follow from premises which retain full validity. He is in this respect not unlike Marx: his thought is "algebraically" correct even when his "arithmetical" conclusions are wrong. He overrated the "bourgeois" element in the Stalinist bureaucracy, but he was absolutely justified in exposing it, and this at a time when so many "friends of the Soviet Union" were utterly blind to it. His specific forecasts about revolutionary developments in the course of the Second World War have been falsified by the events, largely because he viewed the Second World War too much in terms of the First; but his general insights into the mutual relationship between war and revolution were deep and still offer the clues (but not more than the clues) to an understanding of the revolutionary aftermath of the Second World War.

What gives *The Revolution Betrayed* its weight as a document of our time is the masterly critical panorama of Stalinist society during its early and middle periods which

Trotsky drew here—of Stalinist society in all its aspects, from the economic to the cultural. While the polemicist denounces the "betrayal" of the revolution and the "conspiracy" and the "plots" of the bureaucracy and above all of Stalin, the sociologist sees Stalinism and its growth as a historical process determined by objective circumstances, by the isolation of the Russian revolution and the appalling poverty and backwardness of the environment in which the first "workers' state" had set out to build socialism:

> The justification for the existence of a Soviet state as an apparatus of compulsion lies in the fact that the present transitional structure is still full of social contradictions, which in the sphere of *consumption*—most close and sensitively felt by all—are extremely tense. . . .
>
> The basis of bureaucratic rule is the poverty of society in objects of consumption, with the resulting struggle of each against all. When there are enough goods in a store the purchasers can come whenever they want to. When there are few goods the purchasers are compelled to queue up; when the queues are very long, it is necessary to appoint a policeman to keep order. Such is the starting point of the power of the Soviet bureaucracy. It "knows" who is to get something and who has to wait. . . . Thus out of a special necessity there has developed an organ which has far outgrown its socially necessary function, and become . . . the source of great danger. . . . The poverty and cultural backwardness of the masses have again become incarnate in the malignant figure of the ruler with a great club in his hand. . . .

Trotsky does not content himself with exposing inequality and bureaucratic domination against their peculiarly Russian background. From the experience of his time he draws a wider conclusion which may be read as a warning to communists and socialists everywhere: "The tendencies of bureaucratism, which strangles the workers' movement in capitalist countries, would everywhere show themselves even after a proletarian revolution," although they are most unlikely to assume the barbarous forms they had assumed in Russia. He held that this danger was all the greater because inequality was bound to persist "even in the most advanced countries, even in the United States" after a socialist upheaval, for even American capitalism had not developed the nation's economic resources sufficiently to prepare the ground for an egalitarian society. This statement contradicts facile assumptions to the contrary, which are widespread in Marxist literature and can be found in Trotsky's own earlier writings; and it may serve as a starting point for a new Marxist analysis of the state of Western capitalism and socialism in this century.

An article in a weekly review cannot do justice to the wealth of ideas that are found in this book, to the burning socialist faith that informs it, and to its imaginative force and literary élan. Some of Trotsky's conclusions are open to doubt. He certainly underrated, to some extent, the vitality that socialist institutions and traditions retained even under the Stalinist regime and, by implication, also the reformist potentialities inherent in the Soviet Union. He insisted that the conflict between bureaucracy and workers cannot be resolved in a reformist manner and that it necessitated a new proletarian revolution, although he himself had most vigorously combatted this view in the course of many years. Was he right in abandoning the reformist and adopting a "revolutionary" attitude towards the Stalinist regime? Only further developments within the Soviet Union can provide the answer to this question. But history is already proving him profoundly right in his inspired prophecy:

> . . . the actual establishment of a socialist society can and will be achieved, not by these humiliating measures of a backward capitalism, to which the Soviet government is resorting, but by methods more worthy of a liberated humanity—and above all not under the whip of

a bureaucracy. For this very whip is the most disgusting inheritance from the old world. It will have to be broken in pieces and burned at a public bonfire before you can speak of socialism without a blush of shame.

the february regime

The Kerensky Memoirs are an essential part of the historical documentation on the Russian Revolution; and their publication on the eve of the fiftieth anniversary of the fall of tsardom is to be welcomed. True, this volume is, as critics have pointed out, largely a rehash of the author's earlier *Prelude to Bolshevism* and *Crucifixion of Liberty*. But those books, published in 1919 and 1934 respectively, have long been out of print; and young readers have now their first opportunity to acquaint themselves with the self-portrait of the man whose name has been the symbol of the "February regime" of 1917 and with his account of "History's Turning Point." The fact that Mr. Kerensky, now in his middle eighties, does not try to startle us with new revelations, but repeats the version of events which he gave when his memory of them was fresh, speaks in his favor. And although he is not

This review of The Kerensky Memoirs, Russia and History's Turning Point, *by Alexander Kerensky (Cassell; London, 1966), was originally published in the* Times Literary Supplement, *London, June 1966.*

by any means an outstanding writer this is a readable book: it still has the breath of great events about it. It contains vivid scenes and character sketches, those for instance of the tsar and the tsarina, of ministers of the *ancien régime,* and of a few Conservative and Cadet leaders—though, characteristically, none of the men of the left ever comes to life. And although there is no lack here of heavy emotional overtones, the *Memoirs* are not quite as overloaded with polemical and stylistical excesses as was *The Crucifixion of Liberty* —whoever has done the pruning has rendered the author a good turn.

For all that, the present volume is not likely to enhance Mr. Kerensky's historical reputation. His name remains the epitome of utter failure in revolution. Of all the men whom the great wave of 1917 raised up, none had been less prepared for his role in the drama and none was more fortuitously involved in it. The early, strictly autobiographical chapters confirm Trotsky's verdict: "Kerensky was not a revolutionist; he merely hung around the revolution." A revealing incident shows the author at the opening of his legal career, just before the 1905 revolution: "To be called to the Bar one had to give the names of three references. . . . I put down a former Governor, a former Prosecutor . . . and . . . a member of the State Council. . . . But I had made a mistake . . . these highly placed references were unacceptable to the Board of Junior Barristers. . . . I was rejected on the grounds that my references were from higher bureaucratic circles." And this is how the author describes the mood in which he received the tsar's October Manifesto of 1905, with its spurious promise of freedom: "I spent the rest of that night in a state of elation. The age-long bitter struggle of the people for freedom . . . seemed to be over. . . . A wave of warmth and gratitude went through my whole being, and my childhood adoration for the Tsar revived." He was disconcerted by the fact that not only the workers' deputies of St. Petersburg but even Professor P. N. Milyukov, the Liberal leader, rejected the Manifesto with the words "Nothing has changed; the struggle continues." Kerensky was elated even by the so-called Bulygin Duma, the State Consultative Council, a parody of Parliament, which the whole opposition boycotted.

Yet before the year was out the young lawyer became disillusioned with the tsar and volunteered to participate in an attempt on his life. But "my requests had been turned down because I had no experience of a revolutionary and could not therefore be relied upon." The political volatility, the proneness to illusion and gesture, and the lack of political sense he exhibited in this prelude to his career were ominous. After a brief imprisonment in 1906, he kept aloof from politics for years, except that he acted as counsel of defense in political trials, and so as a lawyer he was in some touch with clandestine socialist circles. In 1912, almost fortuitously, he entered the Fourth Duma. "I had never given much thought to the future and I had had no political plans. My only desire, since the beginning of my political life, had been to serve my country. As a result I had been taken unawares when . . . asked . . . to consent to stand for election to the Fourth Duma as a *Trudovik* candidate." (The *Trudoviks* were semi-liberals and semi-populists.) It was not Mr. Kerensky's fault that the Fourth Duma was the least representative and the most discredited of the tsar's pseudo-Parliaments; but it was through its rusty door that he was to enter the stage of revolution.

As a historian, no less than as a politician, he rides incessantly on the high horse of moral principle in a flood of sentimental phrases, and hardly ever has the time to put two and two together. Relating the outbreak of the First World War, he proclaims categorically his "contention that the great war was absolutely contrary to the national interests and aims of Russia in 1914"; and he is unaware that in saying this he is politically knocking the ground from under his own feet. After all, the wicked Bolshevik defeatists said nothing else, only they acted on their conviction, whereas Mr. Kerensky speaks in the same breath of the nation's sacred patriotic duty to wage the war that was so "absolutely contrary" to its interests. "I felt," he confesses, "that the battle we had been waging against the remnants of absolutism could now be postponed." "On my way back to St. Petersburg I worked out a plan of action for the war, based on a reconciliation between the Tsar and the people," a plan of which the men of the Duma did not even want to hear. As late as in the days of the Rasputin affair, he still believed that "the best solution to the problem" would be that the tsar should save his throne by "sending the Empress away to the Crimea or to England." Who would have thought that this loyal though discontented subject of Nicholas II would turn so soon into the very embodiment of republican virtue?

The monarchy was already in ruins and the Petrograd Soviet was forming, yet Kerensky still tried to induce the men of the Duma to make some move. "From the very beginning," he remarks, "my relations with the leaders of the Soviet were strained," although those leaders were the Mensheviks and Social Revolutionaries who supported him. He considered that "the Duma was the only national center of power," the Duma whose rapid fading away in impotence and ignominy he himself describes. As, in one of the last days of February, masses of revolted soldiers and workers converged upon the building of the Duma, he suddenly felt in himself an upsurge of subversive energy similar to that which had led him once to volunteer for an attempt on the tsar's life: "Without stopping to put on a coat, I ran out through the main entrance to greet those for whom we had been waiting so long. I hurried through the center gate and shouted some words of welcome on behalf of the Duma. . . . I urged the soldiers to follow me into the Duma building in order to disarm the guard and defend the building in case of attack by troops loyal to the government." For a moment the young lawyer, all legalistic scruples gone, was carried by the whirlwind. He ordered the arrest of various tsarist dignitaries, among them of Shcheglovitov, former minister of justice and president of the imperial council. Prince Lvov offered him the portfolio of minister of justice in the first provisional government: "It was not until I reached home that the full impact of recent events hit me. For two or three hours I lay in a semi-delirious state, then suddenly the answer to my problem came to me in a flash: I must telephone my immediate acceptance of the government post. . . ." "Oddly enough, my decision . . . was strongly influenced by the thought of the prisoners in the Government Pavilion. If any Minister from the Progressive Bloc could succeed in protecting them from the fury of the mob and keep the revolution free from bloodshed, it was I." In a different context he states: "I had no use for people who could not genuinely accept the *fait accompli* of the revolution." He himself had certainly accepted what he thought was the *fait accompli*. It was his misfortune that he mistook the prologue of the revolution for its epilogue.

What then brought the young political dilettante so soon to the top, as minister of war and premier of the provisional government? His personal qualities? Yes, to some extent. The upheaval brought out in him unsuspected gifts, an ability for political maneuvering, oratorical talent, and a flair for "projecting his image." But behind these qualities there was neither genuine revolutionary conviction nor conventional realistic statesmanship. His declamatory speeches intoxicated the masses while they were in a holiday mood, rejoicing rather prematurely in their triumph and unaware of the grave issues posed by the fall of tsardom. Of that holiday mood Kerensky was the sonorous mouthpiece, pouring forth generalities and pious wishes which for a moment sounded meaningful, even sublime, and brought bliss to many. Yet it is impossible to quote a single memorable phrase of his, a phrase of the kind that springs from deep feeling or thought. His audiences mistook his self-intoxication with his own slogans and appeals for sincerity and revolutionary fervor. "From the moment of the collapse of the monarchy . . . ," he says, "I found myself in the center of events. I was, in fact, their focal point, the center of the vortex of human passions and conflictive ambitions which raged around me in the titanic struggle. . . ." On the face of things this is true; in a deeper sense it is an illusion. He was the "focal point" and "the center of the vortex" for as long only as the "passions and ambitions" were in a state of unstable equilibrium and relative rest. In all parties, on the left and the right, there were men of incomparably greater weight and stature: Kerensky loomed large while they were marking time. He moved with panache, before the blows came down, between anvil and hammer, kicking the anvil, shaking his fist at the hammer, and imagining himself to be in control.

When Mr. Kerensky became prime minister he took over a hopeless legacy. The summer offensive of the Russian army had ended in appalling disaster, and Petrograd had just lived through the convulsion of the "July Days." The Bolshevik Party was being denounced for demoralizing the troops and was driven underground. Lenin, branded as a traitor and a paid agent of the German General Staff, had gone into hiding. Trotsky and most Bolshevik leaders were imprisoned. Even now Mr. Kerensky echoes volubly the old anti-Bolshevik accusations, although he also states that "the main reason for the failure of the offensive . . . was that the Russian army was opposed by first-class German troops" and than two-thirds of the Russian infantry had been killed or wounded during preceding years. Not surprisingly, he relies heavily on the recently published German diplomatic archives for "incontrovertible evidence" that the German General Staff had indeed financed Lenin and the Bolsheviks, as he, Mr. Kerensky, had known all along.

This is hardly the place to go into that "new evidence"—the reviewer intends to do so in a special study. Here it will be enough to say that the German documents (handy though they came in, a few years ago, to propagandists of the Cold War) have not done anything at all to substantiate the accusation against the Bolsheviks. What the documents show is what had long been known anyhow, namely that the German government spent during the war much money on propaganda and espionage in Russia (though it appears that they spent there only one-tenth of their expenditure in other Allied countries); that, having been made aware by the notorious Parvus-Helphand of the importance of Lenin's party, they sought to establish contact with it; that Parvus, whom Lenin had denounced in 1915 as one who had "sunk to the gutter of German social imperialism" and who subsequently had no connection whatsoever with the Bolsheviks, bluffed the German diplomats and generals, in truly Falstaffian manner, about his influence with the Bolsheviks, promising to work miracles in Petrograd and pocketing meanwhile millions of marks for himself. But not a single piece of evidence has been found in the German archives to show that Lenin and his party ever entered into any *secret* contact with the Kaiser's government or accepted any money from it. (There is enough evidence from other sources to show that they never did anything of the sort.) Mr. Kerensky now produces various conflicting sets of figures about the German "secret funds for propaganda and special expeditions" with so triumphant a mien that one might think that he produces receipts from Bolshevik headquarters. If not as a historian and political leader, then at least as a lawyer, he might have spared us such hocus-pocus. He is understandably concerned with justifying his action in prosecuting the Bolshevik traitors in 1917. But what a peculiar lack of historical sense, if not of elementary respect for his own nation, he exhibits when he still maintains that all the upheaval that Russia has been undergoing for half a century now was set in motion by the German secret service and a few Russian criminals and spies.

Mr. Kerensky's next historic quarrel was with General Kornilov and the general's sponsors and adherents. His account of that conflict is very instructive indeed. If Lenin aroused in Mr. Kerensky the most intense animosity and suspicion from the outset, Kornilov inspired him with the utmost confidence. In the early days of the February regime he entrusted the general with responsibility for the tsar's detention; and no sooner had he himself become prime minister than he appointed him commander-in-chief of Russia's armed forces. Almost at once the general began to work for the overthrow of Mr. Kerensky's government and for the suppression of the Soviet and the parties of the left. Mr. Kerensky leaves us in no doubt that Kornilov, who looks here like a prototype of Spain's General Franco, was backed by many influential Russian bankers, industrialists and generals, and also by the Allied embassies in Petrograd. What Mr. Kerensky says about this agrees with what the Bolsheviks, who did not know the "inside story," were saying in 1917; and reading his account of the affair, one sees very well why even Mr. Kerensky's Menshevik and Social Revolutionary supporters suspected him of complicity with Kornilov in the early stages of the plot. The military coup was defeated without the firing of a shot, because Kornilov's soldiers refused to fight for him and because the workers rose en masse. The Provisional Government was saved, but only for a few weeks. As Mr. Kerensky rightly points out, Kornilov's defeat had set the stage for the Bolshevik insurrection.

About the October dénouement, the author has nothing of historical interest to say; he can only curse it. He concludes with several melancholy chapters describing his last months in Russia, spent in hiding; his escape on board a tiny British trawler; and his experiences in western Europe. Here and there in these pages there is a touch of tragic pathos, but under Mr. Kerensky's pen it resolves into melodrama. He describes, for instance, how in January 1915, he came from hiding to Petrograd, just at the moment when the Constituent Assembly was convened, and he volunteered to address the Assembly. His closest political friends, however, did not want him: "The situation in Petrograd has changed radically [they warned him]. If you appear at the Assembly it will be the end of all of us." The author has the honesty to relate this—or is it that in his self-righteousness he does not realize what devastating verdict on him these words implied? He hints that he intended to commit suicide while the Assembly was in session; but "I did not cross the Rubicon of death."

No less disheartening were his later meetings with Lloyd George and Clemenceau, who, having in the meantime put their stakes on Admiral Kolchak, Kornilov's successor, had no longer any use for the democratic ex-premier.

Behind this tale of woe there looms, of course, the fundamental question of whether a bourgeois democracy could have been established in the Russia of 1917 or of subsequent years. Mr. Kerensky is convinced that he would have established it, *if* only he had not received so many "stabs in the back" from Milyukov and Kornilov, from the industrialists and bankers, from Lenin and Trotsky, from the Mensheviks, from his closest political associates, and from the Allied embassies. But do not all these "stabs in the back" add up to the conclusion that a parliamentary democracy had no chance of survival in Russia's political and social climate? It took the nations of western Europe centuries, during which revolutionary convulsions alternated with long, slow, and organic growth, to develop their parliamentary democracies, of which outside the Anglo-Saxon countries few were really stable. It was the height of naiveté to imagine that Russia, having in the middle of a war emerged from centuries of autocracy, with a shattered semi-feudal structure, with a land-hungry peasantry, with an underdeveloped bourgeoisie, with the national minorities in uproar, and with a highly dynamic, Marxist-oriented, and ambitious working class, could be charmed into the mold of a constitutional monarchy or a liberal republic. No doubt, Russia is now sick with the terror and bureaucratic dictatorship of recent decades and appears to be laboriously groping towards some kind of freedom, perhaps towards a socialist democracy. Of that democracy, however, Mr. Kerensky is not likely to be the tutelary spirit.

georg lukács and "critical realism"

The following remarks on Georg Lukács's literary criticism have been occasioned by the reading of a recently published collection of *Essays on Thomas Mann*, which he wrote between the years 1909 and 1955, but mostly in the 1930s and 1940s. The book is fragmentary, and the assembled pieces do not add up to a coherent study. All the more remarkable is the consistency of Lukács's basic interpretation of Mann's work. In his earliest essay he thus summed up in a single conclusive sentence his impression of *Royal Highness*, Mann's novel which appeared shortly after *Buddenbrooks*: "There is in Mann's writing that now vanishing sense of bourgeois patrician dignity: the dignity which derives from the slow movement of solid wealth." The critic who penned these words was, of course, not yet a Marxist. But he set here the tone for many of his later comments. Taking up the

This review of Georg Lukács's Essays on Thomas Mann *(Grosset; New York, 1965) was originally broadcast on the Third Programme of the British Broadcasting Corporation in March 1968.*

theme between the two world wars, and then again in 1945, he emphasized "the bourgeois ideal as the guiding principle in Mann's life and work." This was, of course, meant as an objective judgment, as classification and assessment, not as denunciation. "Mann's stories," Lukács says, "never reflect the day-to-day moods of the German middle class," still less its reactionary moods; they mark, on the contrary, the "summit of bourgeois consciousness." Even when Mann is in opposition to the bourgeoisie, "he never parts company with it," and "his influence reposes on this firm social basis." ". . . he symbolizes all that is best in the German bourgeoisie." Finally, in 1955 Lukács reiterates: "Mann's originality—his buoyancy, serenity, and humor—springs from a true self-knowledge of the contemporary bourgeoisie."

Unfortunately, this "*true* self-knowledge" is a rather elusive, quasi-Hegelian concept: it denotes presumably the summit of consciousness to which the German bourgeoisie ought to have risen but did not rise; it expresses an ideal rather than a historic reality, but it presents the ideal as reality. (How often writers who think that they can, like Marx, "turn Hegel upside down" and set him on his feet end up by standing themselves on their heads!) In truth, Mann's attitude toward the German bourgeoisie was less idealistic than Lukács suggests. From *Death in Venice* and *Buddenbrooks* through *The Magic Mountain* to his last novels Mann dealt with the splendors and miseries, the predicaments and the decay of his social class in a spirit of tense love-hate and even of despair rather than of "buoyancy and serenity." And how indeed could he, while embodying the "conscience" and the "true self-knowledge" of bourgeois Germany be so "serene"?

However, we are dealing here with something like Lukács's intellectual love affair: he interprets every one of Mann's novels as a stage in the writer's heroic struggle for the soul of his nation or in his "search of bourgeois man" in Germany. ("He seeks the spirit of democracy in the mind of the German bourgeois, tracking down the newest hints and

signs in order to awaken and foster them in fictional form.")
True, Mann had his slips: during the First World War he
exhibited a vulgar militaristic chauvinism and a haughty hostility towards all that the German left and German democracy had stood for. In a passage not quite free from special
pleading, Lukács speaks of "Mann's paradoxical and near-
tragic situation," and adds: "even the greatest of men need
not feel ashamed of having made mistakes . . . especially as in
this case they were not subjective and personal, but arose out
of Mann's deep involvement with Germany. . . ." Then again,
in the early years of the Third Reich, certain ideological ambiguities in Mann's attitude aroused Lukács's apprehension:
he wondered whether Mann's "slow, organic growth" which
had already once, in 1914, "landed him in a dangerous situation" might not once again "threaten his development." Did
Lukács fear a temporary conciliation between Mann and the
Nazis? If so, the fear was groundless; but its mere possibility
points to the ideological complexities that were inherent in
Mann's outlook and his "deep involvement with Germany."

The sincerity and courage of Mann's opposition to the
Third Reich were beyond any doubt; and the significance of
his attitude was all the greater because of the inner resis-
tances he had to overcome. But the impulse that moved him
into opposition and exile was not just "progressive anti-
fascism" or the "search of the bourgeois man"—it was rather
the antagonism of the cultivated patrician bourgeois to the
savage plebeians, the *Kleinbürger* and *Lumpenproletarien*
who were running amok in the shadow of the swastika.
Because of its so strongly defined character, the writer's
antagonism to Nazism was "organic" and intense, but also
relatively narrow, although he sought to overcome its limitations.

Somehow Lukács does not come to grips with this problem, perhaps because he does not properly appraise the social
background of the Third Reich against which so much of
Mann's work has to be set. Generally speaking, Lukács's writing here falls well below his own standards in *The Historical*

Novel. There is far less insight here, less clarity and precision. Considering that most of these essays were written in Russia and Hungary at a time when literary criticism was reduced to the crudest Stalinist clichés, it is remarkable to what extent Lukács remained true to his discriminating tastes and his academic Hegelianism, with all its good and bad qualities. Even so, he belongs essentially to the Stalin era; and, despite the legend that presents him as the hero of an intellectual resistance to Stalinism, and despite his brushes with the Rakosy regime in his native country, he may be described as the only Stalinist literary critic of high stature. To be sure, his philosophical background and aesthetic fastidiousness did not allow him to become totally submerged in the orthodoxy. His case was nevertheless one of genuine surrender to Stalinism, a surrender which was difficult and painful, yet voluntary and therefore in a sense irrevocable.

This is not only a matter of Lukács's ritualistic participation in the "personality cult," of which he reproduces a few shocking examples even in this volume to which he wrote a preface in 1963. He says, for instance, of the traditions of German democracy and socialism that "since Marx and Engels they had been buried under reactionary falsification. One mark of the poverty of German history common to both bourgeoisie and working class is the fact that Marx and Engels have so far not entered into the national cultural heritage as Lenin and Stalin have in Russia." Historically this is not quite true: during the half century that lay between Marx's death and Hitler's rise to power, Marxism penetrated deeply into the consciousness of the German working class— at least as deeply as Methodism and Fabianism impressed themselves on British labor. With a stroke of his pen Lukács deletes from history that half century, and with it the work of Rosa Luxemburg, Karl Liebknecht, Franz Mehring, not to speak of Kautsky (whose better writings exercised a decisive influence on Lenin), Bebel, and others. True enough, after 1933, and then again after 1945, the Marxist tradition was discredited and destroyed in Germany by the efforts of

Nazism, social reformism, and, last but not least, Stalinism. Instead of acknowledging these facts, Lukács simply opposes to Germany's "historic poverty" the edifying Stalinist contribution to Russia's "national cultural heritage." In his foreword he does not even hesitate to state without qualification that "for over thirty years socialism has existed and grown strong in the Soviet Union."

Lukács's ideological dependence on Stalinism is deeper than even such declarations suggest. He has been one of the very few theoretically educated adherents of "socialist realism," perhaps the only important expounder of the "aesthetic ideal" of Zhdanovism. Analyzing Mann's *Doctor Faustus* (in a 1948 essay) he states: "By a remarkable coincidence (if coincidence that be) I had just finished reading *Doctor Faustus* when the Central Committee of the Communist Party of the Soviet Union published its decree on modern music. In Thomas Mann's novel this decree finds its fullest intellectual and artistic confirmation. . . ." The decree to which Lukács refers contained the Zhdanovist denunciation of the works of Shostakovich and Khachaturian, the ill-famed signal for a furious witch-hunt against the "decadents," "formalists," and "cosmopolitans" in music and the other arts. Lukács, of course, was not one of the vulgar witch-hunters; but he had zealously embraced the principle underlying the witch-hunt and elevated it to the level of philosophic-historical theory. He carried the campaign against "modernistic decadence" into the field of the "cultural heritage." Socialist realism having been proclaimed the aesthetic ideal of the postrevolutionary epoch, Lukács found its antecedents in the "critical realism" of the great bourgeois literature and arts of the prerevolutionary epoch. He undertook his elaborate classification and assessment of the cultural heritage in accordance with this principle: he identified critical realism with progress and rejected any discordant idea and style as reactionary. The exalted place he accords to Mann is that of "the last great representative of critical realism" who "has never been modern in the decadent sense."

How does Lukács define "critical realism"? Sometimes he interprets it so broadly that the concept becomes useless as a tool of criticism; at other times he interprets it so narrowly that he turns it into lifeless dogma. "Thomas Mann," he remarks, "is a realist whose respect, indeed reverence, for reality is of rare distinction. His detail, still more his plots, his intellectual designs may not stay on the surface of everyday life; his form is quite unnaturalistic. Yet the content of his work never finally leaves the real world." This is sheer tautology. Of nearly all the despicable "decadents," from Proust and Joyce to Sartre and even Beckett, it may be said that the "content of their work never *finally* leaves the real world." Mann himself gives Lukács some trouble, for his attitude towards the "decadent avant-garde" was ambivalent and he claimed affinity with Joyce and the "un-novelistic novel." At this point Lukács rushes to rescue Mann from Mann himself and explains in a few profoundly cloudy passages that Mann's rationality and objectivism set him apart from the literature of bourgeois decay. Lukács equates critical realism with rationalism, objectivism and social optimism; he subtly projects the "positive hero" of the Zhdanovist canon into the Western novel and drama. He fails to see that the pessimism and despair of the contemporary Western artist may be forms of protest against our social order and the disarray of our civilization, and that much of the irrationalism of modern writers and painters expresses a distrust of the banal and complacent "reason" of the bourgeois Establishment. Even the "decadents' sense of doom" reflects in some measure the destructive global stalemate between revolution and counter-revolution (or between degenerate possessing classes and politically paralyzed working classes), a stalemate affecting the whole spiritual climate of our time. How can Marxists expect art and literature to be able to break morally the historic deadlock that politics has so far failed to break practically?

The antithesis of self-confident rationalism and irrationalist pessimism is, of course, deeply rooted in bourgeois ideology. In Victorian England Macaulay and Carlyle embodied the contradiction. Marxism, at its best, has not identified itself with one of these elements and rejected the other, but has absorbed what was vital in each of them and transcended them both. Marx and Engels themselves had just a little more tenderness for Carlyle's "rebellion against reason," despite its dark implications, than they had for Macaulay's brilliantly superficial optimism. Lukács's predilections go the other way. He argues primarily from his German background and sees the ideological sources of Nazism in Schopenhauer's, Wagner's and Nietzsche's *Zerstörung der Vernunft*, even though he senses at times that he may be doing Nazism a quite undeserved honor by attributing to it such ancestry. Actually, Nazism, insofar as it appropriated any philosophical tradition of the "rebellion against reason," only parodied it in the most repulsive manner, just as, on a different level, it caught the anticapitalist emotions of the ruined middle classes of the 1930s only to exploit them and deceive them. It appropriated even the name and the symbols of socialism; it called itself *Arbeiterpartei* [worker's party]; and in this way it harnessed to its counterrevolutionary cause many immaturely revolutionary moods floating about in German society. Indeed, it derived an immense dynamic momentum from its identification with every kind of rebellion against the bankrupt "reason" of the capitalist establishment. It managed to do so because the parties of the working class failed politically and spiritually to make a common stand against it. In any case, the task of Marxists was not to invoke against Nazism the "reason," the "patrician dignity," and the respectable traditions of the bourgeoisie; still less was it to denounce all the immature and irrational forms of rebellion. Marxism could prevail, if at all, only by restating convincingly its own program and principles and by demonstrating their relevance to the terrible crisis of those years. Yet Lukács's literary critical work consisted precisely in invoking against Nazism the rationalism and the respectability of the bourgeois tradition. His approach reflects the failure of his party to see its task and even to grasp its error after the event.

The corollary to this is Lukács's essentially conservative aesthetics. "It is characteristic," says he, "of both Goethe and Mann that though they never ignore new literary trends, they greet them with reserve." This is certainly more characteristic of Lukács than of either Goethe or Mann. Goethe was himself a great innovator, and even in his old age he greeted, without reserve, Byron's poetry, the boldest innovation of European romanticism. As to Mann, we have seen how Lukács has been trying to explain away Mann's foible for Joyce. Lukács's own reserve towards "innovation" touches the absurd when he approaches modern psychology and voices his violent and ill-informed prejudice against Freud. Psychoanalysis is to him still one of the repugnant excesses of reactionary irrationalism. "Just as Nietzsche and Spengler [he states], so Freud and Heidegger . . . are . . . the veriest signposts of the intellectual disasters of the imperialist period. . . ." He even manages to put Freud and the Nazis into one and the same ideological bag. Here again he is in trouble with Mann, who was Freud's devoted admirer; but he tries to get out of the difficulty by dismissing Mann's famous *Festrede* on Freud as the aberration of an "idea-spinning essayist." Inevitably he treats all artistic repercussions of psychoanalysis as worthless and culturally harmful. Here the conservatism of the pre-Freudian academic philosopher blends with plain Zhdanovist incomprehension.

A further remark about the political background to this attitude will not be out of place here. In surrendering to Stalinism, Lukács did not adapt himself to all its aspects with equal ease. The crudities and cruelties of the "personality cult" must have made him shudder more than once. He was certainly disturbed by the ultraleft zigzags of Stalinism even while he was following them obediently. But he identified himself wholeheartedly with the "moderate" and rightist aspects of Stalinism, in particular with the Popular Fronts of the 1930s and their prolongations in the 1940s. It is no matter of chance that most of his literary critical *oeuvre* dates from these two periods. He elevated the Popular Front from the level of tactics to that of ideology: he projected its principle into philosophy, literary history and aesthetic criticism. It will be remembered that the Popular Front was Stalinism's reaction against its own ultraleft follies through which it had smoothed Hitler's road to power. Stalinism then sought to insure itself against the consequences of that disaster by means of an appeal to the "antifascist conscience" of the Western bourgeoisie, for the sake of which it abandoned, and indeed banned, all forms of revolutionary-proletarian and socialist-oriented action. Stalin resumed this line after Hitler's attack on the USSR and persisted in it in the early aftermath of the war, when he still hoped to keep up the Grand Alliance. In all these situations the Communist parties outside the USSR worked to overcome the bourgeoisie's distrust of Russia and fear of communism; and so they played down or even denied their revolutionary Marxist commitments and upheld (and where necessary helped to restore) the regimes (and ideologies) of bourgeois democracy. Since Nazism had aroused the lower middle classes against the traditional ruling groups, Stalinism aligned itself, wherever possible, with the latter and helped them to maintain their sway over the popular masses. For the intelligentsia which followed the Communist parties this entailed certain historical-philosophical reorientations and a break with many habits of thought. Leftish academicians, writers and artists were persuaded that they ought not to "reject" patriotic fetishes any longer, that they must not indulge in militant anticlericalism, and that they should not show too marked a preference for the revolutionary-plebeian, as opposed to the "aristocratic" strands in their cultural heritage. Communists learned to behave as good patriots, to "stretch out a hand" to their erstwhile clericalist enemies, and to treat with discreet or open flattery the conventional cultural values of the bourgeoisie.

Lukács's work is the great, refined masterpiece of that flattery. His writings on Mann are a *pendant* to the Stalinist "struggle for allies." It was Lukács's assignment, as it were, to establish a common ideological front with those "intellectual forces" of whom Mann could be regarded as spokesman—Mann, the only great, truly patrician and truly German anti-Nazi writer in exile, the only one whom the Wilhelmine and Weimar Establishments had accepted and honored for decades. The premise for such a common front was a "liberal" appraisal of Mann's work, an appraisal in which the edges of Marxist criticism were blunted.

This is not to suggest that Marxists should not have been or should not be concerned with the struggle for allies or that they should not be intensely preoccupied with the problem of the cultural heritage. The point is that Stalinism abused these concerns and preoccupations for its shallow and opportunistic tactical games. The Stalinized parties conducted their search for allies so unscrupulously and perversely that they lost themselves in the process; i.e., they lost sight of the interests and aspirations of the working classes. Their much advertised anxiety over the cultural heritage provided them with excuses for startling displays of philosophic and artistic philistinism. This was the context in which Lukács vented so freely his prejudice against "artistic innovation." This accounts, *inter alia*, for the fact that while he was eulogizing Mann's alleged "search of the bourgeois man" and artistic traditionalism, Lukács had nothing to say about Bertolt Brecht, the other great anti-Nazi writer who was, however, in a sense, Mann's antipode. Brecht's utter irreverence for the "bourgeois man," his provocatively plebeian sympathies, and his extreme artistic unconventionality—so many dialectical counterpoints to Mann's outlook—implicitly conflicted with the mood of the Popular Front and were alien to Lukács. His silence about Brecht is thus an unwitting commentary on his own shortcoming as a critic.

This is not to deny Lukács's better qualities, for even when he speaks from a notoriously Stalinist standpoint, he still does it with the erudite sophistication which is able to present the most ludicrous superstition and the most rigid dogma as a rational, or at least a debatable, idea. He moves with apparent freedom and ease and "dignity" within the confines of the most constricting orthodoxy; and so he even manages to loosen its constraints. Hence the fascination but also the deceptiveness of his argument and style, especially for some people of the New Left. Lukács's role in Budapest during the events of 1956 has done something to surround him with a halo; and people recall vaguely that even several decades earlier the Comintern had frowned on his *Geschichte und Klassenbewusstsein* [History and Class Consciousness]. In an upsurge of sympathy for him one is apt to forget his Stalinist record and the ambiguities of his behavior in the critical events of 1956. This is unfortunately one of those cases when a cultus is established without sufficient prior examination of the virtues, the martyrdom, and the miracles attributed to the venerable or blessed person. The record of this particular claimant deserves serious attention, perhaps even respect; but an *advocatus diaboli* has still to throw full light on its seamy side.

the poet and
the revolution

The news of Mayakovsky's suicide reached us, a small quasi-illegal group of left-wing writers in an Eastern European country, only a few weeks after we had had the poet as our guest in our midst. We were depressed and bewildered. . . . Suicide was anathema to our revolutionary code of behavior. The revolutionary's duty was to live in order to struggle. This seemed so plain and elementary a truth that Mayakovsky's sudden "withdrawal from the battlefield" was in our eyes almost a blasphemy. But it was more than that—it was a disturbing enigma. Here he had sat with us, bursting with energy, enthusiasm and sarcasm, only a few weeks ago. He drew before our eyes the grandiose prospects of that second year of the first Five Year Plan. He recited his latest verses on industrialization at the top of his overwhelming metallic voice; that voice without whose sound his poems may be read and perhaps understood, but not *heard* and felt. The ring of

This essay was originally published in Horizon, *July 1943, under the pseudonym "D. Martens."*

that unique voice was still in our ears. The *élan* of his gestures was still before our eyes. His untamable tall and massive figure still stood in front of us. We searched our memories and recalled the details of the days spent with him. Not a trace could we find of that hidden worm that must already have gnawed his heart while he was with us. Not even the slightest doubt seemed to have clouded his thoughts. Not once did moral weariness seem to have crept into his mind and mood. . . . And yet suicide *was* petty-bourgeois coward-ice. It was an act of capitulation which could spring only from faint-hearted and weak-kneed pessimism. It spelled unworthy dread of life. . . . But was Mayakovsky a coward? Was *he* poisoned with pessimism and fear?

—"Impossible."

But the "impossible" was a fact. The details of the poet's erotic life which had been given as the motives of his suicide appeared to us trivial and unconvincing. We had been trained to look to the social background hidden behind the personal motives of human deeds. Soviet historians of litera-ture used ironically to dismiss the accepted explanations of the deaths of the greatest poets of old Russia—Pushkin and Lermontov. The romantic personal motives, they said, had been nothing but the immediate reasons for their quasi-suicides. The deeper cause was the stifling atmosphere of the tsarist autocracy which had left no scope for the poets' urge and which had impelled them to seek an escape in adventures and duels. Both Pushkin and Lermontov were mercilessly drowned by the moral and political squalor of their epoch.

Somebody hinted at the analogy. Surely, Mayakovsky's sense of solidarity with the new revolutionary community must have been sapped or weakened if personal frustrations could have prevailed over it. And the disquieting question emerged: why did death through virtual or actual suicide rob Russia of her best poets after the revolution just as it had done before the revolution? Mayakovsky's was not the first suicide. A few years earlier Essenin had chosen the same path to nothingness. What was the fate that hung over both of them? The question mark was drawn; but none of us would answer it. None of us would let his doubts take on the definite shape of words. . . . It seemed so obviously nonsensical to draw a comparison between Stalin and Nicholas the First.

To formulate the question along that line was certainly rather too narrow. It was not only Mayakovsky's death—his life, too, was stamped with tragedy. Mayakovsky's poetry has remained as the unconscious testimony to a great and very painful *quid pro quo*, which occurred between the poet and the Revolution. The suicide was hardly more than an epilogue which threw the problem into sharper relief. The problem itself has by far surpassed the poet's personal fate. It bears on the role of the poet amid the convulsions and changes of our age. It is connected directly with what might be called the social homelessness of modern poetry.

It is futile to portray Mayakovsky as the orthodox, perfect Communist or—as his English translator puts it*—as "the poet who expressed in his work the vast gamut of the Socialist Revolution."

True, almost at the threshold of his poetical life Mayakovsky wrote:

> I,
> jeered at by tribal contemporaries,
> like a lanky
> discarded rhyme,
> see that which nobody sees,
> coming over the mountains of time.
>
> There where man's cut short of vision
> by the heads of the hungry that surge,
> in the thorny crown of revolution
> I see nineteen sixteen emerge.

* All the Mayakovsky verses in this article are quoted from *Mayakovsky and His Poetry,* compiled by Herbert Marshall (The Pilot Press).

Thus, the anticipation of the revolution colored Maya-kovsky's poetical vision at a very early stage. It would not do justice to his artistic sincerity to suggest that the "thorny crown of revolution" was merely a literary metaphor, and that it was used just in order to refresh the poetical vocabulary of Russian poetry which had then been made barren by the symbolists' detachment from life. No, the poet was out for something more than *épater les bourgeois*. In fact, the "thorny crown of revolution" was then unmistakably casting its shadow ahead. The Russian volcano was restive. The fumes after its recent grandiose eruption of 1905–1906 were not yet altogether dispersed. The great disturbances of 1912 and the St. Petersburg barricades of the 1914 summer were portending the brewing storm. In the second year of the war which tsardom precipitated, without being able to cope with the most elementary tasks of modern warfare, Russian life was anything but stable. The poet's sensitive intuition absorbed the atmosphere of growing uneasiness; and, because his was not a passive but a highly active intuition, he was able to translate the prevailing mood into words of dynamic expectation and hope. The poet's intuition certainly showed more political acumen than could be found in the views and calculations of the official legal politicians of that time; and this justified his claim to "see that which nobody sees coming over the mountains of time."

Yet, there were only very weak links between the poet's vision and that shape of a new Russia which was then being forged in the underground circles of the Bolshevik "professional revolutionaries." True, in his teens Mayakovsky came in contact with some of the clandestine revolutionary groups; and that contact could not have failed to leave some mark on the poet's outlook. But the contact was on the whole superficial and casual—one of the many "eccentric" experiences which served the unruly youth as raw material for his "poetical output." He could find very little inspiration in the stern rules of organization to which the professional revolutionary of the Bolshevik school had to submit. Nor could the interminable interfactional arguments on the future structure of Russian agriculture, the trends in international socialism and the political tactics of the Social-Democratic deputies to the Duma capture his imagination. To see the mole of revolution burrowing at the bottom of the social pyramid was surely for the young Mayakovsky an exciting and joyful experience. But he could have been only very remotely concerned with the specific program and the scheme of action of the revolutionary mole.

The poet's rebellion had its own motives as well as its own independent logic. Its immediate target was the accepted traditional code of literary style—the poetic *bon ton*. His "class foe" was not the landlord nor the capitalist, it was rather Konstantin Balmont, the exquisite symbolist, or Dymitry Mereshkovsky, the "decadent mystic." The sphere in which he strove to achieve a radical upheaval was the technique of verse-making and the vocabulary of the poet. His *Cloud in Trousers*, written on the eve of the First World War, was a bold challenge to nostalgic lyrics:

> Gentle souls!
> You fiddle sweet loves
> But the crude club their love on a drum.
>
> Do you know that
> Francois Villon
> when he finished writing
> did his job of plundering?
> And you,
> who quake at the sight of a penknife
> boast yourselves guardians of a splendid age.
>
> Gentlemen poets,
> have you not tired
> of pages,
> palaces,
> love
> and lilac blooms?

> If such as you
> are the creators
> then I spit upon all art.
> I'd rather open a shop,
> or go on the Stock Exchange . . .

The rebellious bohemian was insulting the "contempt-ible pack of the literary brethren," but, in spite of all appear-ances to the contrary, he remained of and in it. The literary bohemia had few reasons, if any, to addict itself to the de-fense of the rotting social system of tsardom. It lived uneasily on the outer fringe of that system. Nor did it feel any partic-ularly strong urge to leave the ivory towers of art and to plunge into the whirlpools of social strife. The refined sub-tlety of the symbolist and neoromanticist poetry reflected an attitude of individualist haughtiness and social equanimity. But the quietism of the literary Olympus could hardly satisfy the young political innovator. The peaks of recognized poetry repelled him by their majestic immobility. The style of Balmont, Sologub and Mereshkovsky was as finished and polished and smooth as the unruffled surface of a dead pond. The young Mayakovsky was desperately trying to trouble that surface by throwing hard stones of futurism into it. The literary Olympus frowned upon or ignored those attempts on its tranquillity. But on the other hand, did not each of its legitimate lodgers start climbing the pathless mountain in a similar manner? Standing at the bottom one used to swear that one would climb the slope not in order to enter the temple at the top, but in order to destroy it. In the process of climbing, weariness was overcoming the wanderer until, when the top was reached, the initial fury had petered out. And the temple itself looked much more attractive when seen from the top than looked at from the bottom. In the literary threats thrown out by the vigorous and young Russian futur-ist the historian of literature might easily detect some fea-tures familiar to almost any conflict between two literary generations and two artistic styles. The annals of art are full of similar episodes. There was, therefore, little connection between the poet's artistic ego, which sought to assert itself by breaking the conventional codes of the literary milieu, and the stern collectivist creed of Lenin's underground Marxian circles. The common feature was a negative one: hatred of an established hierarchy. But the struggle was being conducted on widely different planes. Had there been no revolution in Russia, the bohemian youth might in the course of time have finished his career as a recognized luminary of Russian poetry, just as his Italian confrère Marinetti, who also started by storming the fortresses of literary tradition, has ultimately won his place in the Parnassus of fascist Italy.

But the Russian revolution broke out before that act of literary reconciliation could materialize. Mayakovsky's poetical opposition had not yet been tamed by official recognition when it received new momentum from the tremendous social upheaval of 1917. The revolution appeared the most gigantic futurist spectacle that the poet could dream of. History itself was throwing overboard the old-fashioned mode of life—ergo the old-fashioned style of writing and painting and building. The new reality was crying out for new rhymes, new metaphors and new words. Who could provide them if not the author of the *Cloud in Trousers?* The quietist style of the traditionalist poet was suddenly reduced to a miserable relic of a doomed past; and the aggressive futurist metaphor found itself in harmony with the spirit of the time. Only yesterday it sounded an eccentric freak of poetic fancy—today the new reality imparted to it a compelling genuineness and a new weightiness:

> Does the eye of the eagle fade?
> Shall we stare back to the old?
> Proletarian finger
> grip tighter
> the throat of the world.

Words which in 1916 might have been regarded merely as an arbitrary violation of the conventional now had the backing of the social atmosphere of the country; and thus the alliance between futurism and Bolshevism became a fact. Mayakovsky was the ardent flagbearer of that alliance.

The heroic period of revolutionary strain and stress marked the climax of Mayakovsky's poetry. The alliance with Bolshevism elevated Russian futurism to intellectual heights it would never otherwise have reached. It opened before the poet vistas which would probably have remained sealed to him in a quieter era. The fate of human masses, the potentialities hidden in them, the grand trends of history, the grappling of opposed social orders, these were the problems which the revolution brought home to the rebel of the *bohème*. The ethos of the civil war, the unparalleled selflessness of the Red Guards, the upsurge of mighty "heavenstorming" hopes, the moral appeal inherent in the endeavor to put an end to the exploitation of man by man—all these could not fail to capture the poet's mind and heart. True, there was also the squalor of the revolutionary terror, the outbursts of age-long and hitherto suppressed hatreds, the merciless anger of rising slaves whom life had not trained to exercise mild justice and human pity. This was but the dark lining to hopeful events; and the poet welcomed the revolution for its good as well as for its evil—as one mighty whole of the proudest human endeavor. At the end of the sanguinary path, there loomed the realm of freedom, the "Mystery Bouffe" in which man had conquered the world of things to which he had before been subjected.

The bohemian did not dissolve in the roaring wave of the revolution. He retained his personality and remained true to his irrepressible individualism. He sang, of course, of the masses and despised the self-centered outlook of the prerevolutionary lyrics. But, in a sense, he remained even more self-centered than his older literary brethren. He was not concerned with the subtle shades and half-shades of private and intimate emotions. He beat the drum of the revolution instead. But in doing so he remained self-assertive to a rather unusual degree. The favorite pattern of the poetic drummer was to talk about *himself* and the army of the revolution; not about his love, his human joys and sorrows, but about his, the drummer's, contribution to the battle, "at the top of his voice"—as if he wanted to overshout the raging elements of history. Even when he tried to become one with the collectivist orchestration of the revolution he remained true to a deeply-seated individualism. This did not prevent Mayakovsky from becoming the poet of the revolution *par excellence*, but this was the germ of his tragedy. He would never be able to merge with it to the end. Some false tone in the drummer's poetry could hardly have escaped the revolutionary trained in the Marxist school. Lenin himself dismissed Mayakovsky with the somewhat passéist observation that Pushkin's verses had been much better. The *quid pro quo* between the poet and the revolution could not be easily disentangled.

When the storm of the civil war was at last over, the poet found himself in a blind alley. The heroic epic of 1917–21 gave place to the prose of the NEP. Lenin proclaimed the Bolshevik's duty "to learn from the bourgeois how to trade and to do business." The new prose of the revolution was outwardly gray and uninspiring. This was hardly the truth. The manner in which the revolutionaries of yesterday turned from destruction to construction, from the negative to the positive part of their task, was indeed one of the most dramatic chapters of the revolution. The writer with a more philosophical approach might have found in this the subject matter for the true masterpiece of fiction. The onlooker with the élan of a Balzac or a Tolstoy might have put the new characters in the grandiose setting of history. The brilliant drummer of the revolution was, however, helpless. His voice, which harmonized so well with the tumult of the civil war, was now strangely out of tune with the new phase. His inclination and liking for hyperbole contrasted uncannily with the changed style of Bolshevism. The literary critics wrote of the crisis in Mayakovsky's development. His aggressive egocentricism was obviously alien to the philosophy of dialectical materialism and his bustling metaphors carried little conviction in that quieter era. The poet responded violently and scathingly. He accused the critics of passéism and once again proclaimed futurism to be the style of the socialist society. But this did not help him much in overcoming the spiritual crisis in whose throes he found himself. The crisis was not invented by the critics. It sprang from the tension between the poet and the revolution.

The rebel was no longer able to revolt. Not because censorship or external pressure forbade him to do so; the inhibition was of an internal and psychological nature. He was unable to keep abreast with all the twists and turns of new Russia, but he was equally unable to detach himself from them. He could not revolt against the greatest revolt in human history.

It is interesting to follow the poet's attempts to adapt himself to the new conditions. He tried to strike a utilitarian and didactic note. He turned to satire. The new world was not yet altogether new and it definitely called for some satirical whipping. The audience of that time was extremely receptive to the topical pointed verse which ridiculed the vices of the new rulers. Mayakovsky proved himself a master at that genre, as the English reader can perhaps judge from his verse "In re conferences." But this definitely gave too little scope for his poetic temperament. In spite of the poet's claim to have inaugurated a new era of socially utilitarian poetry, his Muse was utterly un-utilitarian. Curiously enough, his best verses of that period were written on the journeys to capitalist Europe. There the Bastille stormer found his Bastilles still standing. He was again able to give vent to his combative temper and his poetic élan revived somewhat. In the atmosphere of the past, his futurist tirades and apostrophes were regaining their old defiant ring. It was in front of the Eiffel Tower, for instance, that he could again afford to indulge in the iconoclastic style:

> It's not for you—
> model genius of machines—

here
to pine away from Apollinairic verse
No place
for you—
this place of degradations
this Paris of prostitutes,
poets,
bourse.

The subtle escapism underlying such verses can hardly be missed. That the poet needed such escapes from the reality of the revolution was certainly no fault of the revolution; but it was the tragedy of the poet.

Years ago, it was fashionable in Russia to contrast Mayakovsky and Essenin. Indeed, the contrast between the two is in some respects very striking; but this merely stresses the ultimate analogy. Essenin was definitely "passéist" in the social as well as in the poetic sense. His poetry was full of despair and longing after the old and doomed Russian village. It was, of course, not the feudal village of the old Russian literature, it was the muzhik's melancholy which filled the cup of his poetry to the brim. And, like the muzhik of 1917–19, he too was shaken by and drawn into the vortex of the revolution.*

Hey, Russians!
Trappers of the universe,
Trapping the sky in your net,
Blow loud your trumpets.
A modern sower
Roams in the fields,
Casting new seed
Into the furrows.

---

* Essenin's verses are quoted from *Modern Poems from Russia*, translated by Gerard Shelley (Allen & Unwin; London, 1942).

But the muzhik was not the master of that revolution. After the storms of the civil war, he was again reduced to that state of political muteness, or semi-muteness, which had always been the lot of the peasantry. The shape of a new reality was destined to be forged in the town and to be imposed on the countryside. In the long run, the Russian peasantry could submit, only more or less reluctantly, to the schemes of collectivization and industrialization. The village was unable to produce its own independent revolution; it could only bow to a revolution from without. The sociologist may state the rule in detached, exact and cold terms. What the sociologists' formulas cannot express is the deep and endless sorrow of that Russian village which now belongs to the past, but which was still awaiting the *coup de grâce* in the twenties. Essenin's poetry was an infinitely beautiful elegy on the doom of that village whose Russian name (*derevnya*) is in its very sound associated with words like "wood" (*derevo*) and "yore" (*drevlye*). Here was the drunken and desperate poet whom the old wooden Russian village had sent to meet with a mournful swan-song the onslaught of the steel columns of tractors and harvester combines on its moldering palisades.

> I am the countryside's last poet,
> A bridge of planks with lowly songs.
> I stand at the farewell Mass of the birches
> With quivering leaves like incense clouds.
> My body like a waxen light
> Will burn away in golden flame,
> And like a wooden clock the moon
> Will grind out my last twelfth hour.
> An iron guest will soon appear
> Along the track of the azure steppes.
> His swarthy hand will gather the crops
> Spilt all around like the golden dawn.
> O lifeless cold and alien hands!
> My songs can never live with you.
> Only the ears of corn like steeds

Will mourn their tender master of old.
The wind will gather their plaintive neighs
And hold with them a memorial dance.
Soon . . . soon . . . the wooden clock
Will grind out my last twelfth hour.

"O lifeless cold and alien hands"—this was the greeting and the curse with which the poet met "the iron guest." In a sense, it is, therefore, true that Mayakovsky and Essenin were on the different sides of the barricade. They were certainly on the opposite sides of the poetical barricade. One was the drummer and the other the flautist. Both saw a world crumbling and old shapes pulled down by the avalanche of the revolution. Hence, their common disbelief in the solidity of any "realistic" shapes. But here the difference begins. It would perhaps be difficult to find a poetic contrast sharper than that between Mayakovsky's hyperbolism and Essenin's "Imagist" style. Essenin's verse is permeated with that image and color that were almost entirely lacking in Mayakovsky's rugged poetical *paysage*. It breathed the elemental lyricism of the shepherd forlorn amid the dawn of Russian urbanism.

To every cow on the sign of a butcher's shop
He doffs his hat from the distance,
And when he meets a cabman in the square,
Recalling the smell of his native fields,
He's ready to carry the tail of the horse
Like the train of a bridal gown.

Essenin's poems are now almost proscribed in Russia. This is surely one of those gross abuses in which postrevolutionary bureaucratic wantonness excels. In a historical perspective, cleared of the distortions of bureaucratic omnipotence and omniscience, Essenin will appear as the peak of contemporary Russian poetry. True, this is a highly passéist, one might say reactionary peak, but not more so than, for instance, Cervantes' *Don Quixote*, which nobody has yet dared to suppress on account of its underlying sorrow and sympathy for the early feudal world of knights-errant. The obtuse postrevolutionary cacique "in charge of literary affairs" has proved unable to sense the beauty of Russia's last peasant poet; he has not even been able to approach Essenin's poems with the detachment of a sociologist—which he purports to be—who may ponder with genuine curiosity over a most unusual and authentic document of the life of his generation. He has unscrupulously pigeonholed Essenin as the bard of the counterrevolutionary kulak. The next Russian generation will surely take to re-reading the numerous palimpsests of Russia's postrevolutionary era and, from under the clumsy daubs of the official scripture, it will rescue and recover—among many other names—the name and the memory of Essenin. True, it will find in Essenin's verse the beauty of decay and death rather than the grandeur of strife and endeavor—but it will be civilized and generous enough to allow the Muses the right to mourn their dead—a right which poetry has never ceased to claim—and to remove from the graves the policeman who now forbids access to them.

Essenin's capitulation to death was in a sense natural. Too deeply had he been rooted in the past and in a passing social environment (only poets and artists so deeply rooted in a social milieu can be emotionally so genuine and convincing) to be able to reconcile himself to the new age. Not so Maya-kovsky. He was in fact socially uprooted, and this ought to have made it easier for him to merge with the new reality of the revolution. Seemingly, he had very little, if anything, to suppress in his own mentality. In 1924, when Communist Moscow was burying Lenin's dead body in the mausoleum on the Red Square, he was still able to burst out:

> The fist of Europe
> is clenched
> in vain
> We'll crush them to dust.

But below the surface of the blustering rhetoric, there

was already an uneasy misgiving about the bureaucratic Frankenstein which had been emerging from the revolutionary chaos.

> I
> clean myself
> > by Lenin
> to cruise
> > still further
> > > in revolution's sea.
> Yet I fear
> > the lines I'm penning
> as a youngster
> > fears hypocrisy.
> That head is now laurel-wreath illumined
> I'm only anxious
> > it shouldn't shroud
> the genuine
> > wise
> > > human
> tremendous
> > Lenin
> > > brow.
> I fear
> > the mausoleum
> > > the official functions,
> established statute
> > servility
> may clog
> > with cloying unction
> Leninist
> > simplicity.

And further:

> We
> > bury
> > > now
> > > > the most earthly,

> of all
> who have lived
> on this earth of men.

This vision of the new orthodoxy—the State-Church—which was to overshadow the revolution and subdue it to lifeless uniformity and thoughtless discipline—was in his poem on Lenin perhaps the most genuine and sincere flash coming from the depth of the poet's experience and emotion. In its intuitive strength and historical sensitiveness, it might be compared with that image of the "thorny crown of revolution" which, almost a decade earlier, the poet had projected upon the screen of 1916. Then, he greeted his own vision and was ready to give himself up to it. Now, his vision was hunting him and he was trying to escape it and seeking to reassure himself. If need be, he would still be able to exorcise the ghost of the new orthodoxy with "curse-words" and blasphemies: and "they" would hardly be able to smother his cry and to drown him. But what if they would? What if the heavy, massive, relentless and blind Inquisition of the new Church proved—as it was bound to—the stronger side? It would, perhaps, mean reading too much into Mayakovsky's apostrophes to assume that the poet did ever put that question quite so clearly to himself. But there can be no doubt that he was acutely aware of the problem; and there can be no doubt, too, that his suicide gave, by implication, his reply.

The new Church was to gain an amazing hold both over the minds of its adherents and over those who rebelled against it. It was to leave no room for schisms, heresies and iconoclastic sects. Its spiritual strength was—in spite of its utter lack of spirit—to become so compelling because it had never definitely severed the links with its revolutionary origin. In this one respect, it still stands almost unique among the older churches. True, it has already been able to lure the conservative with its obvious denunciation of revolutionary leaders and to exact the most ghastly confessions from them. The rebels of Bolshevism found themselves in a blind alley in which to fight the new Church was psychologically almost as impossible for them as to serve it. This was the background of their spectacular mass suicide in the trials of 1936–38. Mayakovsky's suicide in 1930 may be regarded as the poet's lonely prelude to the drama. Certainly, the poet was made of different stuff. He had no programs and no slogans to propound. He would probably have been unable to reason over the conflict against which his life and poetry were about to founder. He simply sensed it with the infallible instinct of the rebel; and—without even trying to talk it out—he went under.

Thus, his death, like his life, was an unconscious testimony to the *quid pro quo* of the poet and the revolution and to the strange mixture of enthusiasm and frustration which filled him as he saw the land of his "Mystery Bouffe" coming so near, and yet being conquered by the priests of the new orthodoxy. In this last gesture, he nevertheless remained true to himself and to the *credo* of his youth. *Habent sua fata, poetae.* The other drummer of European futurism, Marinetti, has, in the meantime, been swallowed and absorbed by the tide of fascism. In the autumn of 1942, he landed as a major of the Italian army somewhere on the steppes between the Don and the Volga. There, he stared into the face of bleeding, embattled Russia. There he was—as he said in an interview with the *Journal de Genève*—awestruck by the vastness of the Russian distance and the incomprehensible spirit of the Russian people. His confessions from the Russian front did not contain any note even slightly reminiscent of the blustering optimism of his youthful manifestoes. On the contrary, their pessimism was as unintentional as genuine. Did this "crusader" in the uniform of an Italian major stop for a while to catch and recognize in the great Russian holocaust the rhythm of Mayakovsky's verse:

> There—
> beyond sorrow seas
> Sunlit lands uncharted.
> Beyond hunger,

beyond plague's dark peaks,
marching of millions imprint!
Let armies of hirelings ambush us,
streaming cold steel through every rift,
L'Entente can't conquer the Russias,
Left!
Left!
Left!